Open Book

The Inside Track to
Law School Success

OPEN BOOK

The Inside Track to
Law School Success

BARRY FRIEDMAN
Jacob D. Fuchsberg Professor of Law
New York University

JOHN C. P. GOLDBERG
Eli Goldston Professor of Law
Harvard Law School

To contact Customer Service, e-mail customer.service@wolterskluwer.com, call 1-800-234-1660, fax 1-800-901-9075, or mail correspondence to:

Wolters Kluwer
Attn: Order Department
PO Box 990
Frederick, MD 21705

Printed in the United States of America.

4 5 6 7 8 9 0

ISBN 978-1-4548-7356-3

Library of Congress Cataloging-in-Publication Data

Names: Friedman, Barry, 1958- author. | Goldberg, John C. P., 1961- author.
Title: Open book : inside track to law school success /
    Barry Friedman, Jacob D. Fuchsberg Professor of Law, New York University;
    John C.P. Goldberg, Eli Goldston Professor of Law, Harvard Law School.
Description: 2nd edition. | New York : Wolters Kluwer, 2016. | Includes
    index.
Identifiers: LCCN 2016000698 | ISBN 9781454873563
Subjects: LCSH: Law examinations—United States. | Law students—
    United States—Handbooks, manuals, etc.
Classification: LCC KF283 .F75 2016 | DDC 340.076—dc23
LC record available at http://lccn.loc.gov/2016000698

About Wolters Kluwer Legal & Regulatory US

Wolters Kluwer Legal & Regulatory US delivers expert content and solutions in the areas of law, corporate compliance, health compliance, reimbursement, and legal education. Its practical solutions help customers successfully navigate the demands of a changing environment to drive their daily activities, enhance decision quality and inspire confident outcomes.

Serving customers worldwide, its legal and regulatory portfolio includes products under the Aspen Publishers, CCH Incorporated, Kluwer Law International, ftwilliam.com and MediRegs names. They are regarded as exceptional and trusted resources for general legal and practice-specific knowledge, compliance and risk management, dynamic workflow solutions, and expert commentary.

To our students, for everything they have taught us

TABLE OF CONTENTS

ACKNOWLEDGMENTS

Acknowledgments to the Second Edition

We stand by the Acknowledgments in our First Edition, which are reprinted below. To those, we add a few further notes of gratitude.

First and foremost, we thank the many students who have read Open Book, and have written in, or called, or stopped into our offices, to tell us how helpful it was, and—more importantly—to offer ideas and suggestions for improvements. Particular thanks to Beth Gettinger, and to Caleb Barker and Nathan Palmer, for their very detailed and thoughtful feedback. We have done our best to incorporate those suggestions in this new edition.

We also have enjoyed getting to partner with our longtime friends and colleagues Tracey George and Suzanna Sherry, authors of *What Every Student Really Needs to Know: An Introduction to the Study of Law.* Our two books offer complementary information, advice and perspective that should help every law student get the most out of school, and to be successful. We are delighted to collaborate on this "joint venture."

Our new team at Wolters Kluwer has been good to us. Thanks especially to Nicole Pinard and Casey Pickering for their oversight of the revision. But for their industry and willingness to iron out all the wrinkles, this Second Edition may not have come into being. Thanks also to Angela Dooley for her excellent redesign of the book. The fabulous Claire Suni somehow found time amidst her busy law practice to provide wonderful new illustrations for this edition. And Lesley Schoenfeld again helped us out by arranging for our use of the image of Christopher Columbus Langdell, which is courtesy of Harvard Law School Library's Historical & Special Collections.

As was true for the last edition, we thank our schools and our deans (Martha Minow and Trevor Morrison) for their relentless support. We are very lucky to be in places that allow us to pursue whatever ideas we have, whacky or wise, allowing time to be the judge.

We would be remiss—and remiss we would never want to be—if we did not yet again thank our families. Our spouses continue to contribute advice and support, moral and otherwise, beyond anything to which we are entitled. And our children do the same while also providing us with irreplaceable moments of chaos and joy.

We'd say more, but as we said in the prior edition . . . shouldn't you be studying?

Barry and John
The Open Book Guys

Acknowledgments to the First Edition

The initial plan was to write a study aid. Two things conspired to change that. We are longtime friends and colleagues who share a love of teaching, and have talked a lot about it. The more we worked on the book, the more we realized that a book about exams has to be a book about law school, and also a book that relates law school to the practice of law. Second, the amazing folks at Aspen jumped on board in ways we never could have imagined. They have helped us produce something far bigger and better than we hoped, and along the way we incurred many debts and so we have many people to thank.

This book never would have been written but for Chris Bradley suggesting it, and offering his insights.

The folks at Aspen have been terrific. First and foremost is Carol McGeehan; but for her energy, determination, and enthusiasm, we'd not have arrived here. Thanks, Carol! Kris Clerkin stepped in at a critical moment and gave the green light. Carmen Corral-Reid, Aaron Reid, Sarah Hains, and Wendy Hickey carefully and creatively shepherded a simple manuscript into a book and beyond. Teresa Horton (copyediting) and Christie Rears (production) have been a pleasure to work with. Special thanks to the chief tender of the flock, Christine Hannan, who is constantly there for us.

Our design team brought the book to places we never imagined. Sarah Hains's judgment and willingness to experiment was invaluable. Karen Quigley, who did the design itself, is our hero. She knew what was in our heads even when we didn't. Then there is the incomparable Claire Suni, the world's best, most dedicated, and funniest 1L illustrator. We wish we could doodle a thank-you that would convey all the hilarity and tenderness of your pen. Kristen Slater deserves thanks for so many things, not the least of which is her creativity in getting our logo just right. Also, a shout-out to Erin Fiore for wise and caring counsel along the way. Lesley Schoenfeld arranged for our use of the image of Oliver W. Holmes, Jr., which is courtesy of Harvard Law School Library's Historical & Special Collections.

Many people read and commented on the manuscript and ideas. With fear of forgetting someone, we thank Anita Bernstein, Curtis Bridgeman, Sam Buell, Jonathan Cardi, Maria Glover, Rachel Goldberg, Helen He, Troy McKenzie, Sara Lewin Meyers, Martha Minow, Daria Rothmayr, and Cathie Struve. And thanks to the many anonymous reviewers—students, legal writing professors, academic support personnel, and fellow law profs—who offered their valuable insights into how we could improve the book.

The web project is coming along thanks to Aaron Reid's willingness to make almost anything work. Great appreciation to Matt Shahabian for the prototype for student resources, and to Nick Axelrod for help with final, critical details.

Our agents Christy Fletcher and Rebecca Gradinger at Fletcher and Company worked out of the usual box, and figured out how to make this work. Rebecca, who was once a 1L herself, has been a great contributor to the book, and advocate for it. Our deans, Martha Minow and Ricky Revesz, seem to support whatever whacky ideas we have.

And last—but most important—our families. Our kids put up with us when we should have been with them. Our wives contributed in innumerable ways. Julie Faber gets the nod for coming up with "Open Book," and for free legal advice. Jill Anton had much to say on the creative front. But mostly you did what you always do: supported us and encouraged us. For that, our profound gratitude and love.

We'd say more, but . . . shouldn't you be studying?

Barry Friedman
John Goldberg
The Open Book Guys

PREFACE

Are you starting law school this fall, and a little anxious about how that is going to go? Or maybe you are several weeks in and wondering what you are supposed to be learning and why no one has told you much about exams. Perhaps you have already been through a semester of law school and feel frustrated because your exam performance was not what you'd expected, given your hard work and what you thought was a sound understanding of the material.

Not to worry, help is on the way! This is a straightforward book with one goal: to help you do better in law school. Enabling you to excel on exams — that is the unwavering goal of this book. But we also believe we can help make you a better law student. And a better lawyer too. All this, because — and this is a key theme of the book you are about to read — we strongly believe that law school classes, law school exams, and good lawyering are all related. If you do the things we suggest, you will get more out of your classes — or, rather, the *right* things out of them — you will be happier with your performance on exams, and you will probably do a better job representing your clients, whomever they turn out to be.

We wrote this book because we recognize that most law schools and law professors don't spend much time discussing the logic of classes or exam taking, and certainly not in any systematic way. They don't explain how it all fits together. This book fills that gap.

We don't think it is maliciousness on the part of law schools or law professors that no one prepares you very well for taking exams. Professors teach what they teach, and believe that taking their exam follows naturally from the classroom experience, like night follows day. Besides, most professors did really well on law school exams. Like anyone who is good at something, they often assume that others can do it as easily as they can. Your professors might not be able to explain what made them good at it, even if pressed. They know a good exam from a bad one; they just haven't given a huge amount of thought to how to improve exam performance.

A book about classes and exams will never be a page-turner, but we hope you find ours readable, informative, and even at times engaging. We want to make clear up front that we don't offer any exotic formulas or techniques, nor do we claim to have discovered some nifty new method or gimmick. We don't think there is any magic to taking exams. To the contrary, we think the law school exam process is straightforward and, in its own way, logical. Our goal is to explain to you *how* things work, and *why* they work this way. We're confident that once you better understand how law school exams work, and how they relate to the process of going to law school and to what you learn in class, you'll do a better job on them.

We've thought a lot about exams. One of us, Friedman, started tutoring students on exam taking when he was a 3L. He has been teaching for over thirty years; for much of that time he has been giving a talk on exam taking. One day, after hearing the talk, a student came up to him and asked, "Why don't you write that down? No one ever tells us all of that." Friedman thought about it for a while and decided it was a good idea. Goldberg has spent a lot of time thinking and writing about legal reasoning. Friedman is a public law guy—meaning he works on the law that governs relations between people and their governments; Goldberg does mostly private law, the rules governing interactions between and among persons and private entities (such as business firms). Between us we have taught almost every course in the typical 1L curriculum, and a fair number of upper-level courses as well.

It's a little embarrassing to say, but we love the law. We love talking about it, writing about it, and teaching others about it. Even a chunk of our scholarship is about the methodology of law.[1] (Not that we recommend reading it; you have better things to do right now.) We've also both spent several years as a vice or associate dean, listening to and addressing student frustrations with law school and the exam process.

Like we said, we don't promise you anything exotic. Exam taking is not overly complicated, which is why this is a relatively short book. But we don't want to undersell what is in here: the book describes what we believe are a super-essential set of skills. Still, we think it contains what you need to prepare for, understand, and take law school exams, and to get the most out of law school as you anticipate taking them.

---

1. Barry Friedman, *Taking Law Seriously*, 4 Perspectives on Politics 261 (2006); John C. P. Goldberg, *Review: The Life of the Law*, 51 Stan. L. Rev. 1419 (1998).

GUIDE TO THE BOOK

(Don't skip this!)

We intentionally wrote the first edition of this book backwards. It started with a discussion of how exams work and how to take them, and only later talked about the classes that precede exams. We adopted the backwards format for two reasons. First, we assumed most students would be reading Open Book after they'd been in law school for a while. In fact, we recommended that it be read on that schedule. Second, we felt we should address directly and immediately students' exam-related concerns, then work back to the beginning of the law school experience.

For this edition, we've changed our tune, and it is important to explain why. The main reason for the change is simple. We heard from law students that, even after a few weeks of school, they felt too busy to give Open Book their full attention. They also told us in no uncertain terms that, as helpful as the book was to them, it would have been more helpful if they had read it earlier — maybe even before they started law school. And they suggested for that reason that we both add some material and reorganize the book so that it proceeds forwards rather than backwards, from classes to exams.

Like all good lawyers, we are open to being persuaded by a strong argument. (As you'll soon see, law school is about learning to make arguments, law school exams are about making good arguments, and this book repeatedly discusses this critical aspect of law school.) Our students made good arguments, and this Second Edition of Open Book reflects our acceptance of them, both in substance and structure.

One thing hasn't changed: Chapter 1 still contains our central, overarching point. If you want to do well on law school exams, you need to understand how exams, classes and the practice of law are related to one another. Students often complain that law school exams don't test what lawyers do. We completely disagree. (And though you don't have to agree with us, if you want to do well in law school we suggest you try to swallow that disagreement and give us a fair hearing.) Exams are all about skills that lawyers use every day.

What we do understand, however, is that students often see a disconnect between class and exams. Thanks to a lot of student feedback, we now better grasp the basis for this complaint. We offer a lot more help on this problem than we did in the First Edition.

Indeed, Part I of the book—Chapters 2 through 6—is all about relating law and law school classes to exams. In consecutive chapters it explains: (a) how the institutions of lawmaking work; (b) how basic legal reasoning works; (c) how to brief cases in a way that sharpens your analytical skills; and (d) how to attend classes in a way that allows you to make the most of them both in the moment and as you prepare for your exams. Particularly if you've not yet begun law school, we believe you will find this to be an invaluable primer.

Next, Part II of the book—Chapters 7 through 12—is about the logic of the classic law school essay exam that features fact patterns and calls for issue spotting and analysis. This part of the book explains how to take the legal reasoning skills discussed in Part I and translate them into success on exams. Here we introduce you to a framework of analysis called "IRAC," and to our "Pinball Theory of Exam Taking." Together, they give you the tools that you will need to perform really well on your exams. Then, in four meticulous chapters dealing with issue spotting and issue sorting, identifying rules, applying rules, and drawing conclusions, we drill down to explain in more detail how to rack up points on your exams.

Part III is about managing the transition from classes to exams. In Chapter 13 we discuss course outlining. Chapter 14 teaches you a skill that we think is critical to writing a good exam: the exotic, esoteric (not!) job of making lists. Chapter 15 talks about exam formats other than traditional "issue spotting" exams. Chapter 16 highlights the importance of practice exams and gives you tips on how to make the most of them. Finally, Chapter 17 describes how to recover when things (sometimes things out of your control) go wrong.

We close with an Afterword that we admit is a bit schmaltzy. Sorry, that's just who we are. And whatever else you can say about us, we've seen a lot—we feel like we're entitled to hand out a little gratuitous advice on how to "live" law school.

OPEN BOOK DIGITAL

Besides reading what follows, we urge you to check out the materials that are available on **Open Book Digital**. (*For instructions on how to gain access to Open Book Digital, check out page xxvii of this book.*) **Open Book Digital** has a treasure trove of helpful stuff for law students, and you get it all free of charge when you buy this book. Among the many things you'll find there — checklists to help you manage your time, answers to questions posed in the book, tips on briefing cases and outlining courses, and much more — there is one thing that we think is truly unique. We've gotten law professor-colleagues from around the country not only to provide you with exams they have actually given to their students, but also to annotate them for you, showing what they expected from their students, as well as annotated examples of stronger and weaker exam answers. Students are always telling us they want more feedback. We don't think, short of working with each of you individually, that it gets any better than this. You can get a glance at the sort of materials you'll find at **Open Book Digital** by turning to the Appendix located in the back of this book.

THE LAW SCHOOL — AND OPEN BOOK — SCHEDULE

Law school has its own rhythm, particularly the first semester of the first year. At the outset, you might feel like you are being thrown into the deep end of a swimming pool. You are asked to read vast amounts of dense material, and your classes might seem like they are designed primarily to add to the confusion rather than to clarify. A month into school, you might pause and wonder how you will keep track of all that you are learning. Also, you might hear people talk about exams, but the talk is vague — and vaguely ominous. Two months into school — assuming you are on a semester system, as most law students are — more work comes flooding in, and (we don't love it, but we acknowledge it) anxieties are mounting. With a few weeks left in the semester, crunch time arrives. Everyone is now frantically preparing for exams: meeting in study groups, preparing and reviewing outlines, and taking practice tests. Just as suddenly, it's all over and you are exhausted.

Our first piece of advice? ***Grab a calendar***. Now! A good practicing lawyer works with a calendar close at hand because life in the law is largely about schedules, meetings, phone calls, and deadlines. Rather than wandering about with only a vague idea of what is coming down the road, get a clear sense of where you are in an unfolding process, and when you expect to arrive at certain destinations. So find your calendar, and (assuming it is available as you read this book) get a hold of your school's academic calendar as well. There is a good chance your exams have already been scheduled. If so, note those dates on your calendar and count backward to where you are today.

You'll want to adjust this advice to your school's own schedule, but here are some tips about what to put on your calendar.[2]

1. Put all your exam dates on the calendar. Notice how long you have between each of them. Most likely there is not enough

---

2. The following proposed study schedule is designed for students enrolled in semester-long courses that run for twelve to fourteen weeks. If your school operates on a trimester system, then you will obviously have to condense the time frame for the various steps that we describe. If you are taking year-long courses, you might be required to sit for at least some exams at the end of the first semester, in which case the schedule outlined here is applicable. If, however, exams are at the end of the full school year, you should still follow the schedule, except perhaps hold off taking practice exams until you near the end of the spring semester.

time to start studying for each exam as the prior one ends. See? Here's an important lesson you get just from looking at the calendar. You are going to have do some pre-studying before you get to focusing on any given exam.

2. Note "practice exams" for each subject 2–3 days before the exam. As we explain in Chapter 16, practice exams are in our view one of the most valuable things you can do in preparing to take an exam. But you don't want to take them too early (before you know the substance).

3. About six to eight weeks into school, write "START OUT-LINING" in large capital letters on your calendar. (Goldberg always tells his students that Halloween is a scary day not only because of the freaky costumes, but because it marks the day you really need to start taking exam-preparation seriously.) As we explain in Chapter 13, we believe you should prepare your own outlines for each course. This is not a deviation from time spent studying; it is the most valuable studying time you will spend. Some people think you should start out-lining earlier. We are all for a healthy difference of opinion (as we are going to say over and over, law is about making arguments), but we want to make one critical point: you can't outline any part of any course until you have covered enough material that you get some distance from it and can take more of a bird's-eye view.

4. That's enough for now, but be warned: once school starts, a lot more will go on this calendar, from student events to deadlines in your 1L legal writing class. It will all feel a bit overwhelming at times. Don't let it overwhelm you; Keep Calm and Stick to Your Schedule.

5. One final calendar pitch. In invisible letters every day from the first day of classes, write "Brief cases." We believe you have to brief each of your cases. We don't buy into all the shortcuts and study aids that will do this for you. We're annoyingly insistent on this point, and we think good habits make for great exams, so do this from the start. You'll get a lot more out of class that way.

THE PRIME DIRECTIVE: WHAT THE PROFESSOR SAYS GOES

Before we dive into substance, we have one last but critically important thing to say. Following the original *Star Trek* TV series, we will call it "The Prime Directive." (For more about the show and the idea, go to **Open Book Digital**.) Here it is:

What the Professor Says, Goes

We've done our best to write a book that contains good sense, clear guidance, and even some occasional humor. But here's the thing. We aren't going to grade your exam, your professor is. And there will be some things she wants done a certain way. If that is so, then no matter what we say, do it her way. She has her own reasons, and even if she doesn't explain them, she is not going to reward you for doing things differently.

For example, we suggest that it probably won't be worth your while to use precious in-class exam time to ensure that your answers are highly polished. But suppose you are sitting in a review session for a particular class and your professor says, "I will deduct points for poorly organized answers, incomplete sentences, and grammatical and spelling mistakes." You would be foolish to ignore these specific instructions, no matter what we have told you. The same goes for instructions that appear on the exam itself—even more so.

Some professors are more communicative about what they want in exam answers, others more tight-lipped. But it usually doesn't hurt to ask them about their expectations. Note that once you've read this book, you will not only have a better understanding of what law school exams typically are about. *You will also be in a better position to figure out the kinds of answers a particular professor might be looking for. In turn, that will permit you to ask him or her some fairly concrete questions about his or her methods of evaluation, or at least try to divine those from the focus of classroom discussion, as well as old exams and model answers.* Is Professor P someone who is likely to want "kitchen-sink" answers that err on the side of raising every possible issue? Does he seem particularly interested in emphasizing the law's open-ended quality and the space it allows for creative arguments? Or is he more on the buttoned-down side, wanting you to hone in precisely on particular doctrinal puzzles? As you read the book and come to better appreciate the "hows" and "whys" of exams, *use that knowledge* to form judgments about what particular professors are likely to want from you.

You might complain that this piece of advice — pay close attention to what your professor expects — is so obvious as to not be worth mentioning. If so, your premise is right, but your conclusion is wrong. Year after year, we have students who lose points because they write answers that are not responsive even to clear statements of what we are looking for when we read exam answers. There's no reason for this to happen. Just remember the Prime Directive.

• • •

Okay, now you're ready. Remember, this is all supposed to be exciting. Challenging, yes, but exciting, too. Challenges are a good thing as long as you are prepared for them. You came to law school to learn to be a lawyer, and as we're about to explain you'll start thinking like one very quickly. Good luck, and enjoy yourself!

HOW TO ACCESS YOUR *OPEN BOOK DIGITAL* MATERIALS

We've got a lot more material to help you with law school and exams, but it made this book too long, and some of it works better if you view it in a web browser. So we've created **Open Book Digital**.

In **Open Book Digital**, you will find examples of student notes and outlines. We have checklists to get ready for exams. You'll also find answers to the exam questions in the book. Most importantly you will find practice exams and answers that have been annotated by professors with helpful exam-taking tips. Want to see a sample of what is included? Check out the Appendix in the back of the book (page 227), where we've placed a taste of what you will find in **Open Book Digital**.

In order to get all this good stuff, check out the card that was included with your book, which explains how to gain access to **Open Book Digital**. We encourage you to access these materials now, before you start reading, in case you want to look when we reference them throughout the text.

Chapter 1

THE WHAT AND WHY OF EXAMS

☑ Why law school exams look the way they do.

☑ How exams test for skills that are essential to law practice.

☑ What it means to "think like a lawyer"—because that is what exams are testing.

T his is a book about doing well in law school. In particular, our aim is to help you to do the best that you can do on your exams. For that reason, we are going to jump right in and start talking about them.

"But wait," you may be thinking (depending on when you are reading this book), "I don't know much about law or law school classes yet. How can I start learning about exams?" Good question! Immediately after this chapter, we are going to drop back and teach you some basics about law and law school. By way of overview, though, we want you to start thinking about your short-term and longer-term goals. The short-term goal is, of course, to do your very best on your exams. The longer-term goal is to harness your talents as a trained lawyer to do work that you find rewarding. It turns out that these two goals are related.

Law students dislike law school exams, and it is not hard to understand why. They are stressful. They come after weeks of classes in which vast amounts of material are covered and little feedback is provided. There is enormous time pressure, especially for in-class exams. Professors rarely are clear on exactly what they are looking for. And a lot seems to turn on exams; for many courses this is the primary determinant of the grade, and everyone will tell you that grades matter.[1] Even students who do well often are surprised, wondering what separated them from their peers. Students see exams as some sort of torture that professors delight in inflicting on them. Worse yet, law students often complain that exams don't test what real lawyers do. Were that true, it is difficult to imagine a more damning condemnation of the entire process.

Well, we want to start by letting you in on a little secret. Law professors dislike exams, too. They agonize over writing them. And no part of the job is more distasteful than grading them. Reading one answer after another to the same question is mind-numbing. Law professors envy colleagues in other departments who rely heavily on teaching assistants to grade exams. They fantasize about giving pure multiple-choice exams graded by a computer. (Some do; we discuss these sorts of exams in Chapter 15.)

We're not trying to evoke pity. Law professors have terrific jobs. Our point is that if there weren't something valuable about the traditional format of law school essay exams, law professors would be the first to abandon them.

Here's the thing: law professors believe that they *are* testing for a skill critical to being a good lawyer. In fact, they believe that understanding—*really* understanding—the skill that is at the heart of the practice of law is essential to doing well on exams. Your professors might even tell you that this skill is the main thing that law school is designed to teach. And we agree with all this. We are pretty certain that what law schools teach, what exams test, and what lawyers do all fit together. It would be surprising, would it not, if things were otherwise?

Still, we understand that the connection between taking exams and the practice of law can seem pretty elusive. The point of this chapter is to make explicit why law school exams look the way they do, and the

---

1. For what it is worth, even though we are selling a book about exams, we think all the talk of the importance of grades should be taken with a grain of salt. Grades are important, particularly in tough times, when hiring slows. Yet we know plenty of people who have not done as well as they would have liked in law school and have gone on to enormously satisfying careers. For more on the subject of perspective, see the Afterword.

way that those exams relate to what it is lawyers do. Then, the next part of the book will explain how classes fit into the picture.

THE JOB OF A LAWYER

Obviously there are important things lawyers do that exams don't test. Lawyers talk a lot on the phone, but law school exams do not measure phone skills. Successful lawyers have to juggle their cases and calendars, and learn how to delegate work to others. Exams don't test these things either. Exams don't reward the ability to interview a client, let alone find one. Deposition-taking and deal-making skills also go unexamined. Many very successful lawyers were not great law students, which is to say they did not do terrifically well on their exams. We're sure there are some poor lawyers who did well on exams.

And yet the criticism that exams don't test what lawyers really do misses the core of what exams are supposed to test, and what most lawyers are actually called on to do.

Imagine that you are a lawyer. (You will be one soon enough!) There are all kinds of practice settings, a point we return to in a moment. For now, suppose you are a lawyer in a small, local firm that takes business as it comes. A person—a client—walks into the office. She isn't a lawyer. She's just a person with a problem. She tells you a story. Or perhaps she tells the story to a senior attorney, who then relates it to you. The neighbor's dog bit her son, who is seriously injured. Or the bookkeeper stole all the money from her small business. Or her new business partner promised to cover certain expenses if she contributed to get the business going, and then the partner reneged.

Note what your client does not do. She does *not* walk in the door and say, "I have a Contracts problem. There's clearly going to be an issue whether my agreement with my partner was supported by adequate consideration. I think, however, that I can take advantage of the doctrine of promissory estoppel as defined by Section 90 of the Second Restatement of Contracts. What do you think?"

Most people who seek out lawyers have no clue about this sort of thing. They are laypeople, with their stories and their circumstances. They need a lawyer's help to decode their story and translate it into law. The person who walks in the door has a problem but she has no idea what the law has to say about it. *That is your job.*

Now, take a look at a law school exam. We've got plenty of them at
Open Book Digital. Don't expect to be able to answer anything. Just
read over a question or two, to get a sense of what an essay question
looks and "feels" like. What do you see? Exactly! The questions are
stories—"fact patterns," in law school lingo—that look just like the
sort of thing a client might come tell her lawyer. They are stories
about something that has gone wrong in the world, be it a horrible
accident, or a set of odd circumstances involving criminal activity,
or a deal gone sour. At the end of the story, the exam-taker is usually
asked to take on a role, be it an attorney, or judge, or law clerk to a
judge. And from the perspective of that role, the exam-taker (you) is
asked to analyze the fact pattern, giving just the sort of advice a lawyer
might give a client.

We hope we are convincing you early: law school exams test
what lawyers do, which is to give advice to clients about legal
problems.

WHAT LAWYERS HEAR.

ADVISING CLIENTS

As you might guess, some stories that clients tell their lawyers are relatively easy to analyze; others are more difficult. Once in a while you will hear a story that rather obviously does not give rise to a legal claim. "That's too bad," you'll say sympathetically, "but there is nothing I can do to help you." By the same token, you will occasionally encounter a client who has so plainly been wronged (at least if you have been told the facts correctly) that you cannot wait to jump into action.

In many cases, however, it will not be obvious — and certainly not immediately — whether the case is a winner or a loser. Real-life events and transactions are complicated. The law is similarly complicated. Maybe it is uncertain. Or maybe the law is clear, but what is uncertain is how precisely it applies to your client's case. It's a puzzler, and it will require some research, thinking, and creativity to help your client out.

This is a good moment to drag onstage Oliver Wendell Holmes, Jr. Holmes was a Supreme Court Justice at the turn of the twentieth century, but he was much more than that. He remains to this day one of our most acclaimed lawyers and legal scholars.[2] In 1897, he gave a remarkable speech to law students, later published as an essay titled The Path of the Law.[3] (The essay is right there at **Open Book Digital**; you might give it a read at some point.) One aim of the speech was to administer a modest shock to a group of "green" students as they prepared to emerge from the cloistered classroom; a shock that would help them appreciate how law looks to an actual practitioner.

---

2. Like the law itself, Holmes was complicated. An abolitionist in his youth, he fought bravely in the Civil War, in which he was thrice wounded. While still a young practicing lawyer, he wrote an important scholarly book — *The Common Law* (1881) — that, along with other writings, has long been praised for introducing "pragmatism" into academic analyses of law. Holmes later served as a Justice on the Massachusetts Supreme Judicial Court and the U.S. Supreme Court, earning the reputation of a "progressive" primarily because of his unwillingness to invoke the U.S. Constitution to strike down reform legislation. Ironically, Holmes was by this time a committed Social Darwinist who had little sympathy for the progressive reforms he voted to uphold.

3. 10 Harv. L. Rev. 478 (1897).

What Holmes told the students was that if they were going to be good lawyers, they had to imagine that they were representing the "Bad Man." What distinguishes the Bad Man from others, Holmes explained, is that he—unlike most of us—is completely indifferent to whether a given course of action is morally right or wrong. He just wants to do what he wants to do, and he wants to do it without getting arrested, sued, fined, or imprisoned. (Just imagine hearing this speech at your law school!) In short, what the Bad Man wants from his lawyer is an expert assessment of his odds for avoiding or facing legal trouble if he acts this way, or that way, or some other way.

Oliver Wendell Holmes, Jr.

Holmes's point was not to praise amoral client behavior or immoral lawyering. Rather, he used the Bad Man as a device to get his audience to see that the practice of law can profitably be thought of as an exercise in *prediction*. What counts as "knowledge" of the law, he insisted, is the ability to predict whether a certain course of conduct will result in the person who engages in that conduct being subjected to a court-ordered sanction or penalty. At times lawyers will be able to make precise and highly confident predictions. More commonly, however, because of law's complexity and ambiguities, they will only be in a position to make provisional and qualified predictions. In short, the Bad Man's lawyer will typically tell his client that if he (the Bad Man) does *x* or *y*, there is a 30 percent or 50 percent or 75 percent chance that he will go to jail, or be subject to an injunction, or pay a fine or money damages.

There's a way in which Holmes's stylized picture of legal advice is too passive — good lawyers do more than merely report a set of odds that their clients are facing. They also advise their clients, and argue on behalf of their clients, in order to improve those odds. Nonetheless, the basic point is sound. It is extremely helpful to think about practicing law in terms of making provisional predictions about how judges — in light of the case law and statutory law that they are required to apply — will respond to various *arguments* about certain *sets of facts*.

So, how does one make these predictions? Well, *that* is what law school is all about. It is not simply about learning or memorizing black-letter law. It is about developing "judgment," an informed feel for how judges and other "deciders" are going to resolve legal claims.

The analogy holds true no matter what the practice setting. Most of you won't sit in a storefront waiting for a client to come in with a story. Some of you might, in small towns or in Legal Aid settings. Others will work in law firms, or for corporations, or in public interest litigation groups. Others will be transactional lawyers, assisting with deals to sell property, buy companies, or convert rivers into hydroelectric energy. You'll become tax lawyers and criminal prosecutors. You'll work for a government agency. It doesn't matter what you end up doing. In the course of your day, whether you are the most junior associate at a law firm, or counsel to the President of the United States, you are going to hear stories and be asked you to offer *legal advice;* that is, your assessment of the best arguments, and whether they are likely to prevail.

We hope you can now see how law school exams connect to this core aspect of law practice. Day in and day out, lawyers listen to their clients' stories. They then apply their knowledge of the law, and develop arguments to assist their clients. Finally, they offer an informed prediction about whether those arguments are likely to prevail. That is exactly what you will do on law school essay exams. And it is what law school is going to prepare you to do.

LEARNING TO THINK LIKE A LAWYER

To be clear, law school will teach you more than how to make good predictions of legal consequences. Indeed, it is going to teach you precisely what you thought it would: the law. You will learn rules: lots and lots of rules. But learning the rules is the easy part of law school. If that is all there was to it, we'd give you a book of rules and have you memorize it. (Bar exams are a bit like this.)

The hard part of law school is learning how to make effective legal arguments on your client's behalf, and how to predict whether those legal arguments will succeed or fail. And it is this ability to make legal arguments, and to separate good ones from bad ones, that law school exams are all about.

In short, the one central, yet elusive, skill that law school exams test is whether you are able to "think like a lawyer." This is a phrase you are going to hear until you are sick to death of it. But there is a reason it gets repeated. It nicely captures the heart of what law professors are trying to teach, what they will test on law school exams, and what they believe is the core skill for a practicing lawyer.

Let's start with the basic idea. Thinking like a lawyer refers to the ability to give a client legal advice. It means being able to digest a set of facts (the client's "story"), to identify the legal problems or issues posed by those facts, to apply governing legal principles to those facts, and to come to a conclusion about the possible consequences for the client under the law given those facts.

But as you now know—because that is what Holmes was explaining—in real life (and thus on law school exams), legal issues usually do not admit of definitive answers. Instead, there are *provisional, probabilistic* answers. And because the answers are not clear and pat, the most essential skill to being a lawyer is learning to make *arguments* about what those answers should be — to identify what might persuade a judge or other decisionmaker. What matters most for lawyers, and for exams, is the ability to make cogent arguments about how legal rules apply or should apply to a certain set of facts. As we said, law school classes aim to convey all sorts of information about the legal system, the law itself, and the ways lawyers practice law. But if there is one skill your professors universally hope to teach you, it is to make legal arguments based on a set of facts, and to get a sense of what makes for a weak or strong legal argument.

We're going to say this again, because it is the most important point. And yet, for some reason law students resist hearing it. *Law and law school are not about reciting legal rules or spouting information; they are about reasoning cogently and making careful and convincing arguments, on the basis of legal materials, for particular conclusions.* In this respect, legal education is somewhat unique, and probably unlike much of the learning you have done in the past.

So now you know: Being able to sift through and identify salient facts, and make the best arguments for your client, and to assess with some accuracy their chance of success, is what people mean when they speak of "thinking like a lawyer." And guess what? Doing this well isn't so easy. If making good arguments was a snap, law school would be unnecessary, and lawyers could not claim the professional status that they do.

LINKING LAW SCHOOL AND WHAT LAWYERS DO

Law students often are frustrated by what they see as coyness on the part of their professors. Questions are met only with other questions. Every issue discussed in class has another side to it. Nothing ever seems to be wholly settled or indisputable. New law students in particular are understandably hungry for simple rules and conclusive answers. Still, they rarely get them. This is what makes law school maddening and law exams frightening.

By now you should see why professors do this. They are not sadists. They do it because that's precisely how it is in the real world of law practice. The law is constantly in flux. Today's settled doctrines—like "promissory estoppel" in Contracts and "comparative fault" in Torts— didn't always exist. The law has evolved because smart lawyers helped judges to see the need to deviate from existing doctrine to help shape rules that met (in Holmes's words) "the felt necessities of the times." Should representing the Bad Man seem dismal to the altruistic among you, there is hope in the fact that even he might have the equities with him, even when the law is against him. In any event, a good lawyer must make cogent legal arguments on behalf of her client, which in turn requires an ability to distinguish arguments that are strong from arguments that are weak.

Students constantly want their professors to tell them what the answer is. Not only is that impossible — because many legal questions have no clear answer — but it would be doing you a disservice. The real world is just not that pat.

To do well on exams, and in the real world, you have to embrace a certain degree of uncertainty. Law is in equal parts knowledge and ongoing analysis. Good lawyers, no matter what the practice setting, spend their days making and analyzing arguments. Good lawyers know the difference between an argument that is likely to be a winner and one that will fail. Great lawyers recognize how to take an argument that seems weak and make it as strong as it can be. Star lawyers think of an argument no one ever has, or push an argument that most others thought couldn't possibly prevail, and in doing so change the path of the law.

Consider this story: When one of us (Friedman) was a 1L, he went to see a professor to ask some questions about the course. The professor asked, "So, how's it going?" Friedman remarked on the noticeable anxiety around the law school about exams. Friedman was anxious too, but he was feeling ready. Given how stressed out everyone else was, though, Friedman was worried he was missing something. The professor responded, "All I can tell you is that most of the people coming to my office still think there are answers to their questions."

What Friedman's professor was trying to underscore is that law students often misunderstand what they are supposed to be learning. Even after a year of being told the contrary, they still think that their job is to find "the" answer to a legal puzzle, when in fact there is no single answer. Rather, it is their job is to use legal concepts and categories to break down these puzzles into an orderly sequence of questions, to identify plausible answers to those questions, and to work through the strengths and weaknesses of the arguments for those answers.

If you think about it for a moment, you already knew all of this, although it is easy enough to forget while contemplating exams. You watch television, you go to the movies, you read books — lawyers and legal disputes are frequently the subject matter of good dramas.

Law is about making arguments

(Again, check out **Open Book Digital**.) Why? Because we have an "adversarial" legal system: There are always two sides (or more) to a dispute. Legal disputes are entertaining precisely because the sides are in tension, each making arguments about why their side should win. That's why there are many more shows about lawyers than, say, computer programmers. So if you find the "arguments-not-answers" idea perplexing, think about that adversarial process, and realize it is all about each side making the best arguments it can.

Indeed, what primarily sets judges apart from other lawyers is that it is their job is to pronounce the winner and loser. (If you think about it, *that* must be a stressful job.) Judges aren't necessarily smarter than the rest of us, or in possession of greater wisdom. But they *have* to decide, no matter whether a case is easy or difficult. They impose clarity on uncertainty.

Yet, to prove our point, judges often disagree. Judges in different times and places reach different answers. Judges on the same court frequently dissent. Speaking of the U.S. Supreme Court, Justice

Robert Jackson memorably wrote in the case of *Brown v. Allen*, "We are not final because we are infallible, but we are infallible only because we are final."[4] When the Supreme Court resolves a legal question, the resolution is final in that there is no higher tribunal — although it is always acceptable for lawyers to try to get the Supreme Court to change its mind.

PREVIEW: WHAT MAKES FOR A GOOD EXAM ANSWER

Anyone can argue. (Ask your parents about what you were like as a little kid.) What makes lawyers different is that they make *legal* arguments. In analyzing a client's story, they know which facts are relevant to the law. They know enough to figure out the legal issues that are posed. They know the law, and what they don't know, they know how to research.

Sometimes it helps to break this process down into a series of steps. In Part II of this book we are going to do exactly that. (As we explained in the preface, Part I is about how to hit the ground running in law school so that you are ready to roll when it comes time to take exams.) For now, though, just imagine you are a lawyer who takes all sorts of clients. So, you need to know all kinds of law. As it happens, all the law in the country is sitting spelled out in minute detail in an elaborate file system in your office. A prospective client comes in and tells a story.

The first step is to assimilate the facts of that story and know what file drawer and folder to look in for the relevant law itself. Is it a contracts issue, a torts issue, an issue of corporate or constitutional law, or all of these? If it is a contracts issue, is it one about formation, or a question of how to make sense of a condition in a contract? The second step is understanding and interpreting the legal rule(s) that fit(s) your case. What is the governing rule? Is there more than one that might apply? The third step involves making arguments why, under the relevant rule(s), your client should win. The final step is in giving the client an assessment, or prediction, of how likely it is she will win (and what it will cost to get there).

---

4. 344 U.S. 443, 537 (Jackson, J., concurring).

What are the ISSUES in Client's case?
What RULES govern their resolution?
What are the ARGUMENTS for and against Client's
    position?
What CONCLUSION can you reach as to the probability
    Client will prevail?

These four things — things that lawyers do every day — are precisely what you are going to be asked to do on exams. Based on the "fact pattern" — the client's story — you are going to: (a) figure out the legal issues it raises; (b) identify the relevant rule(s) or standard(s); (c) make arguments about how the legal issues should get resolved in light of those rules and standards; and (d) assess which arguments are best, in the form of a prediction about the ultimate outcome.

This process is so familiar to taking exams and being a lawyer, that there is an acronym for it: IRAC. Throughout law school — and throughout this book — you will repeatedly hear about IRAC (or some other version of it; everyone has his or her twist). As it happens, taking an exam is in some ways a lot easier than being a lawyer. On an exam you won't have to figure out if the story you were told is a contracts problem or a property problem, let alone some of each. You will know going into the exam that it is about contracts or property. And you don't even have to figure out the rules, because you'll have spent a semester learning them, and no one will expect you to know rules you did not learn. But you *will* have to recognize the issues as they present themselves, and you *will* have to make the best arguments.

In fairness, there are ways that taking an exam is more difficult than the practice of law too. You don't get to ask the client follow-up questions. You don't have time to research your answer. And real lawyers don't need to routinely write up assessments of a complex problem in a matter of hours, although sometimes — particularly as new associates at firms or law clerks to judges — they do. Nonetheless, the general structure of the task is very much the same.

We've spent our careers grading law school exams and helping students learn to take exams. If we've learned anything it is this: Many students, perhaps most of them, *can* learn to do better. We're going to explain how to do this. But as you learn these specific techniques, always keep in mind the central point of this chapter.

What you are doing on law school exams is what lawyers do, which is analyzing legal rules and making legal arguments.

The Bottom Line

☑ Taking exams, like advising clients, is about making arguments based on a set of facts and legal rules.

☑ Exam questions invite you to analyze and argue: Answers that merely recite rules and assert definitive conclusions are missing the point (and losing points).

☑ In law, conclusions usually take the form of predictions about the likelihood a given position or argument will prevail.

PART I

LAW SCHOOL 101: HOW CLASSES CONNECT TO EXAMS

Chapter 2

THE MISSING LINK

☑ Why law school classes can seem disconnected from exams.

☑ Classes require you to analyze judicial opinions; exams require you to analyze fact patterns.

☑ What you need to know for a strong start in law school.

In Chapter 1 we mentioned that law students sometimes complain that exams seem like random exercises that do not test what lawyers actually do. We also explained why this complaint is off the mark. We confess, though, that we've long puzzled over the source of the complaint. Most 1Ls don't really know much about the practice of law. So why do many of them have strong views about the supposed "artificiality" of exams?

It took us awhile — and a lot of conversations with law students — but we think we now understand the source of the confusion. And this realization has helped guide this edition.

What really throws off law students, we have come to believe, is not a gap between exams and practice, but a gap between exams and *classes*. Law school is an intense, immersive experience. You will spend hour upon hour in the classroom and preparing for the classroom. As you do — and with a little help from us — you will quickly get a sense of the skills you must master and display for class. It turns out, however, that these skills, though ultimately connected to the skills that must be displayed on exams, are quite distinct. *In short, while classes prepare you for exams, they do so indirectly.* Exams require you to take what you have learned and apply it in a new and different way. It is thus understandable that students experience a disconnect between exams and everything that comes before them, and hence regard exams as "artificial."

Now this is a problem we can get our heads around! It is also one we can help you deal with. So, having said a few general words about exams in Chapter 1, we're now going to go back to the beginning—of the semester—to talk about classes. The goal of this part of the book is to allow you to see, from the outset, how the skills you will be learning in class relate to what you will be asked to do on exams. To complete this task fully, you'll have to read Part II as well—that's where we talk about exams. Part I is mostly about how to be the sort of student who will get the most out of law school, in order to do well on exams. But we want to begin—you should begin—by getting some insight into why classes look different than the exams you will take.

HOW CLASS IS *NOT* LIKE EXAMS (OR PRACTICING LAW)

We saw in Chapter 1 how exams are usually fact patterns, mirroring the sorts of stories that clients tell their lawyers. The job of the lawyer, as with the exam taker, is to take that story and translate it into a set of legal issues, then analyze the issues, by recognizing and making good legal arguments.

Here's the odd thing. When it comes time for class, and preparing for class, you probably will not be given fact patterns, nor asked to analyze them. Instead, most law school classes are taught via what's called the "case method." According to this method, law professors require their students to read edited judicial opinions (the "cases"), and to come to class prepared to explain the disputes that gave rise to those opinions, the content of those opinions, and the reasoning deployed by the judges who wrote them. This method of discussing cases has a relationship to what lawyers and exam takers do: It is meant to develop the set of necessary skills, as we'll explain. But this is a very different kind of exercise than the exercise of analyzing a fact pattern or advising a client.

These days, more law professors are employing alternative teaching methods, including problem-based methods. When they do, it's often for the reason we've just been discussing. Solving problems is closer to what lawyers do than slogging through scores of judicial opinions. But most of the books you will use in law school are designed around the case method, and the problem-based approach is not the norm, particularly in core 1L classes such as civil procedure, contracts, criminal law, property and torts.

So there you have it. We law professors usually teach one way (by having you read cases), yet test another way (by having you analyze fact patterns). While this might seem crazy, there is a method to our madness. In fact, "method" is exactly what there is. That's why the way that law professors teach is referred to as the "case method" or the "Socratic method." Its development at the turn of the twentieth century still is heralded as a great advance in legal education. Prior to that time, law students learned by being lectured to about legal rules, and by sitting in court and listening to lawyers argue. (Yawn.) But, in 1870, Harvard Law School appointed a new dean with the formidable name of Christopher Columbus Langdell. (How about that facial hair!)

Christopher Columbus Langdell

Langdell, a contracts scholar, was firmly convinced that his subject, and pretty much every legal subject, would be best taught by having students read a bunch of judicial decisions in which judges applied and developed legal rules in the context of deciding particular disputes. Only by seeing law in its concrete application, and only by appreciating how later decisions built on, or departed from, earlier ones, would students come to understand the rules and principles around which each field of law is organized. Landgell's inspiration came from the natural sciences. His idea was that extensive, meticulous review of judicial decisions would permit a rational and useful classification of law's general rules or principles, much like extensive, meticulous observation permitted the biologists of his time to organize the natural world by reference to kingdoms, phyla, classes, families, and so forth.

Even though most legal scholars don't accept Langdell's biological analogy (law is not a natural science!), they continue to embrace his teaching method. In fact, the case method remains central to law school education for reasons already emphasized in Chapter 1: the case method is designed to show you how law is as much (or more) about arguments than answers, and to teach you how to make the sorts of good (and bad) arguments that lawyers make.

Through the case method, students are exposed to scores of judicial decisions. In the process, they learn the applicable legal rules. As importantly, they see *examples* of judges and lawyers reasoning through legal issues, making the sorts of arguments that lawyers make, day in and day out, in negotiations, in briefs, and in the give and take of the courtroom. (Indeed, debates in court over the law and its application to a case are called "oral *arguments*.") Each judicial decision represents the triumph of one side's arguments over the other. A good professor, by asking the right questions, can elicit the competing arguments from students, and help them — through these discussions — get a feel for what makes for a good legal argument or a poor one.

Make no mistake, the case method is intended to prepare you — and will prepare you — to be a lawyer and, before then, an exam taker. Nonetheless, your professors' use of this method means that daily discussions in class are going to look and feel quite different from the practice of law and the taking of exams. Probably the single most important skill, and most difficult-to-master skill, in taking an exam — and in practicing law — is spotting the critical legal issues within a set of facts. (As you'll see, much of our exam-taking advice concerns how to spot issues.) Yet, analyzing the cases that you read in class does not require this skill. Why not? Because judicial opinions usually state the issue(s) raised by the case right up front, saving you the need of figuring that out for yourself. Then the balance of the opinion is given to analyzing it to reach a conclusion.

LEARNING ABOUT LEARNING THE LAW

Ever since we realized that students are understandably confused about the mismatch between classes and exams, we've been focused on how we might do a better job of connecting the two. As we acknowledged at the outset, most professors don't spend much time preparing you to take exams. We have real sympathy for the generations of students who are perplexed about the exam-taking process; we wrote this book to fill the gap.

What we came to recognize is that it was not enough simply to jump in and explain to law students how to take exams. Instead, what is needed is to work up to that point, beginning with how law school itself works. That is what this Part will do.

Especially because many of you are just beginning (or are about to begin) law school, we start with some background information that will help you read cases and understand class discussions. Some readers will already know some of this stuff. Others won't. The point is to enable you to walk into your first class with enough information about the structure of our legal system, and about the methods and terminology used by lawyers, that you'll be well-prepared to answer the professor's questions, and participate in and understand class discussion. The next chapter offers a brief primer on the lawmaking institutions in the American legal system. Chapter 4 then reviews a basic form of legal reasoning that lawyers use, and that you will see in the cases you read for class; namely, reasoning from precedent. In Chapter 5, we're going to show you how to take this information and this technique, and put it to work in class. We'll close out the Part in Chapter 6, with some tips on how to get the most out of class.

(If when you're done with these chapters, you are thirsting for more information on the structure of our legal system and different modes of legal analysis, we encourage you again to take a look at the excellent companion book to ours, written by Professors George and Sherry, titled *What Every Law Student Really Needs to Know*. Their book goes into greater depth on these topics than we can here.)

It is our hope that this grounding in what classes are trying to accomplish will make the next Part, on how law school exams work, all the more lucid. This Part is, we have come to understand, the Missing Link.

The Bottom Line

☑ Classes prepare you for exams, but only indirectly.

☑ Reading judicial opinions introduces you to rules and to legal reasoning, but not to *issue spotting*—that's a skill you'll have to master in other ways (we'll tell you all about those).

☑ Understanding the logic of the case method will help you understand how to get the most out of class.

☑ Preparation is as important for classes as it is for exams.

Chapter 3

A SYSTEM OF RULES

☑ Laws are rules issued or recognized by governmental institutions.

☑ The sources of law.

☑ The hierarchical structure of our legal system.

O ur mantra—repeated ad nauseum throughout this book—is that legal analysis is about making arguments, not reciting rules. We need to make clear, however, why we are so keen to emphasize this point. It is *not* because we doubt the existence of legal rules, or the importance of learning them. Rather, it is to correct a common misimpression that students have about what the law is, and what their professors expect of them.

There *are* rules, you will learn them, and you most definitely need to know them. But the rules are just the beginning, and your professors are going to assume that, by the time exams roll around, you have the rules down pat. It is learning to make them work on behalf of your client that is the important skill.

For example, you'll learn a basic rule of contract formation, which states that (ordinarily) an agreement is not legally binding unless there has been an "offer" and "acceptance." Acceptance of an offer occurs when the offeree (the person to whom an offer is made) agrees to the precise terms of the offer. If Lisle says to Frannie, "I'll give you half of my can of soda for a buck," and Frannie responds, "Will you take 90 cents?" there is no contract. Indeed, Frannie has now become the offeror, by suggesting a new and different deal.

Suppose instead that when Lisle said, "I'll give you half of my can of soda for a buck," Frannie replies, "That seems high," but then holds out her empty cup in a gesture that seems to indicate she is expecting Lisle to pour some of her drink into it. Now do we have offer and acceptance? Imagine that Lisle fills the cup with half the can of soda, but after drinking it Frannie refuses to pay. Assuming (unrealistically) that contract law would apply to this micro-level transaction, would Lisle have a valid breach-of-contract claim against Frannie?

You're new to this, but we're betting you can already make an argument in each direction. On Frannie's behalf, you'd say she did not accept the offer: To the contrary, she suggested it was not a fair deal. But, Lisle will respond, how else can holding out the cup have been interpreted? And besides, Frannie drank the darn thing — it's not fair to gulp and not pay! (As it turns out, this last argument invites consideration of a separate branch of law known as "restitution.") These are the sorts of arguments you will be learning to make, and will need to make on exams and on behalf of clients.

Before you can begin to make *legal* arguments, however, you have to learn about the law. To learn the law, in turn, you need to understand the basic institutions of the American legal system. That is the function of this chapter. It will introduce you to a few of the most basic features of that system. If you have not yet begun law school, or have just started, you will want to read the chapter carefully. On the other hand, if you are several months into law school, this may seem old hat. But perhaps even for you we can clarify some things that may be confusing — in part because, as we are about to explain, your professors may not take the time to teach you this stuff.

Much of what you need to know to be comfortable discussing and analyzing law involves getting a handle on a few distinctions. The funny thing about these distinctions is that although they are incredibly important, no one is going to sit you down at the beginning of law school and set them out for you. This is a body of assumed knowledge that, regrettably (but understandably), professors never take the time to teach. Instead they assume that you will learn by osmosis. As you'll see, it transcends any given course, so perhaps that is why they don't teach it. Maybe they just assume someone else is telling you!

Some of what you are about to read comes straight out of your middle-school social studies class. That should be reassuring, not only because it is familiar, but because it would be alarming to come to law school and learn that the structure of American government is not as you'd learned it all your life. On the other hand, in the legal world, things quickly get complex. Not to worry; in no time flat this will be as familiar and natural as breathing.

WHAT MAKES A RULE A *LEGAL* RULE?

The first distinction is between public and private law. Public law refers to the rules that govern the interactions between citizens and their government. This includes constitutional law, regulatory and administrative law, and substantial parts of criminal law. Private law, on the other hand, is the rules that regulate the interactions among private parties, like you and your grocer, or your business partner, or the driver of the car that just rear-ended you.

Much of the first year of law school is devoted to private law. For example, you'll take Contracts, which sets out the rules that enable parties to make and enforce agreements among themselves. You'll also take Torts. Tort law specifies what counts (in the eyes of the law) as one person wrongfully injuring another, and the remedies that are available to those who are wrongfully injured. In later years you'll probably take Corporations, which is about — well — exactly what you'd expect it to be about.

The distinction between public and private law is important, but can also be highly misleading. Private law may be concerned with interactions between persons and private entities, but it is still law. And all law inevitably has a public dimension to it. To count as "law," in the sense that lawyers use the term, a set of rules must be promulgated or recognized by a certain kind of institution; namely, an institution of government. That is what we want you to understand: Law emanates from institutions of government authorized to make law. For this reason, there are lots of rules that are not, strictly speaking, *legal* rules. And that is why we are going to teach you about the institutions of government that make law in this chapter.

To see this point, suppose there are a bunch of friends who, once a month, get together in a public park to play games or just hang out. The group might have various rules. Likely none of these rules are written down anywhere. That's okay. A rule is just a norm of how one is required or permitted to behave in a certain setting. It doesn't need to be written down to be a rule.

For example, the group might have a rule that specifies which of its members is required to bring snacks for which of its get-togethers. Suppose that, on a given occasion, the member who is on "snack duty" fails to deliver. His friends will be irritated, and not just because they are without snacks. They will be irritated with him because he failed to do something that, according to the rule, he was obligated to do. In response, they are likely to express their displeasure, and perhaps will demand that he undertake some remedial action. ("Hey, come on! It was your turn to bring snacks. Go get some.") The imagined snack rule is very much a rule. But it is not a *legal* rule. It is instead a social rule.

In a similar vein, imagine a private tennis club that has a rule specifying that any player using the club's courts must wear shoes with "non-marking" soles. Like the snack rule, this shoe rule is not a legal rule — a lawyer might say that it "lacks the force of law." However, the shoe rule operates in close proximity to certain legal rules, and under the right circumstances can be converted to a rule that courts and other officials might recognize and enforce.

For example, the club probably has membership contracts with each of its members. Suppose that there is a clause in each of these contracts that empowers the club to cancel the membership of any member who repeatedly violates the club's rules, including the shoe rule. If the membership contract, including the membership rule, is made according to the *legal* rules that specify how to make enforceable agreements, the membership rule will be enforceable in court. Thus, if a member whose membership was terminated in accordance with the membership agreement sues to be reinstated, the club should win the suit. Likewise if an ex-member tries to use the club's courts, he will be considered a trespasser, and will be subject to removal and perhaps arrest.

What makes a rule a legal rule? It turns out that philosophers have debated this question for centuries. For now it is enough to say that *rules are legal rules when they are promulgated or recognized by governmental institutions such as courts, legislatures, and agencies.* When a court issues a decision stating that, in the absence of offer and acceptance, there is no contract, it is stating and applying a legal rule. So too when it rules that a contract has been formed through a bargained-for exchange (say, the exchange of money for a club membership). Likewise, when a legislature or agency enacts a statute or regulation prohibiting the emission of certain pollutants into the air, it is creating a legal rule.

This is why we need to talk about the institutions of government, and their authority: It is the authorized actions of these public institutions that make the law.

IT STARTS WITH THE CONSTITUTIONS (PLURAL)

One of the great innovations that came out of the American Revolution was the idea of a written Constitution. Our forbearers on the other side of the Atlantic had well-established constitutional traditions. But the rules embedded in these traditions were unwritten; they amounted to a set of shared understandings and commitments that (purportedly) stretched back to "time immemorial" and governed the relationships among the Crown, Parliament and the people. In part because the English colonists who founded this country felt that the unwritten English constitution had failed adequately to protect their rights, they decided to write down the rules governing these relationships, an idea that has stuck the world over.

The U.S. Constitution, initially ratified in 1789, is the source of law that authorizes the branches of the federal government to engage in lawmaking of their own. As you no doubt know, it does this in an affirmative and a negative way. On the one hand, it grants law-making authority. For example, Congress is given specific "enumerated" powers. On the other hand, it imposes limits on that authority, many of which are found in the Constitution's first ten amendments — the Bill of Rights — that came into force in 1791. For example, there is the First Amendment's dictate that "Congress shall make no law . . . abridging the freedom of speech."

Note that both in the title of this section and the text that follows we have referred to "constitutions" (plural). The reason for this is central to an understanding of the legal system in the United States. We have a *federal* system of government. It divides power among the national government and the fifty state governments. If you are a U.S. citizen, you are a citizen of the United States, but also a citizen of Arkansas, Utah, California, Texas, or some other state, district, or territory.

One of the great challenges for any student of American law and government is to understand the division of powers between national and state governments. And in truth, matters are more complicated still, for—as you well know—there are countless smaller units of government: counties, cities, school boards, water districts, and the like. Sometimes the American system of government is described as a layer cake of authority, with one government piled atop the other. More accurate, though, may be another metaphor. It is a marble cake, meaning the batter (authority) from each layer gets mixed up with the others. Fortunately for you, all governance below the state level is thought to flow from the state governments, so typically we talk of just two levels.

This brings us back to constitutions, plural. When lawyers and citizens talk about "the Constitution," they are almost always talking about the United States Constitution, which, as we noted above, originally came into force in 1789, and which has been amended twenty-seven times since. (We'll need to revise that last figure when the Constitution is amended again, but the national Constitution is not amended often, in part because the process for doing so was designed to make amendment difficult.) The Constitution organizes the national government—often referred to as the "federal government"—and sets limits on federal, state, and local governments. In law school, you will spend a lot of time on the national Constitution, and not just in constitutional law courses. Indeed, you'll quickly learn that the Constitution's guarantee of "due process of law" has important implications for other courses, such as Civil Procedure—the rules that determine when and how one person can sue another.

Each state also has its own written constitution. These constitutions empower the institutions of state government, and set additional limits on those powers, sometimes beyond the limits set by the federal Constitution. Importantly, when there are conflicts between the terms of the federal Constitution and a state constitution, the federal Constitution prevails. For vast areas of government regulation, there are no such conflicts—federal and state authority comfortably co-exist. But from time to time they clash, and when they do it is the federal rules that carry the day.

At least in principle, one of the major differences between the federal government and the state governments is that the federal government is endowed with a limited set of 'enumerated' powers. It can only do things that the federal Constitution authorizes it to do.

For example, the Constitution specifically grants Congress the power to enact laws regulating activities that affect "interstate commerce." It follows that Congress has no authority (under the Commerce Clause) to regulate activities that do not affect interstate commerce. Over time, courts and commentators have maintained different views about which activities do or do not affect interstate commerce, but wherever that line is drawn it sets a limit.

State governments, on the other hand, are said to possess all the power necessary to govern. Sometimes you will see the regulatory or governing power of the states referred to as the "police power." This is indeed confusing, conjuring up as it does the image of men and women in blue uniforms with badges. But the police power has little to do with the police; it is just an ancient way of referring to the power to pass and enforce laws to govern society.

Although the federal government is said to enjoy only enumerated powers, and not a general police power, it is important not to overstate this contrast. Its limited powers notwithstanding, the federal government has, since the 1930s, played an increasingly large role in regulating the day-to-day lives of citizens. Likewise, even though state governments are said to enjoy a general police power that the federal government lacks, there are significant limits on state governmental power set both by state constitutions and the federal constitution as well. A state government cannot, for example, enact a law that discriminates in certain ways against out-of-staters, or infringes on the free speech rights protected by the First Amendment to the federal Constitution.

THE THREE (FOUR? MANY?) BRANCHES

Now it is time to start talking about the institutions that the state and national constitutions authorize to serve as sources of legal rules. We can begin with what may be the first thing you learned about the American political system; namely, that our governments, state and federal, have three branches: the legislative, the executive, and the judicial. Undoubtedly you were taught that the legislative branch makes laws, the executive branch enforces them, and the judicial branch interprets and applies them. You were also taught about separation of powers, which ensures that each branch should do its job and not the job of others.

Under this simple model, there are two major sources of law, both of which will feature prominently in your early legal education. There are *statutes* — rules adopted by Congress or a state legislature, and signed by the chief executive, be it the President or a state governor. And there are *judicial decisions* — decisions issued by federal and state judges resolving particular disputes and, in the process, identifying or making legal rules.

Statutes are everywhere. They define crimes ranging from tax evasion to murder. They regulate commerce and protect the environment. Some address minutiae, others tackle massive social problems. A well-known example of the latter is the much-debated Patient Protection and Affordable Care Act (ACA) — better known as "Obamacare." It was enacted by Congress and signed into law by President Obama in 2010. The ACA is an enormously complex law dealing with the delivery of health care, but within it are many clear and important legal rules. For example, it contains a legal rule that requires insurance companies to sell health insurance to persons with pre-existing medical conditions.

Judicial decisions also come in many shapes and sizes. The most visible of these are the decisions issued by the U.S. Supreme Court interpreting the provisions of the United States Constitution. To pick another familiar and controversial example, in a case called *Obergefell v. Hodges*, the Court in 2015 concluded that the Equal Protection Clause of the Fourteenth Amendment to the U.S. Constitution includes a rule guaranteeing same-sex couples the right to be married on the same terms as heterosexual couples.

So far we have not gone much past basic civics. But of course, our systems of government are quite a bit more complex than the simple three-branch picture suggests. By the turn of the twentieth century, life was becoming too busy and complicated to be governed exclusively by legislation or judge-made law. In particular, with the coming of the industrial revolution — which changed late nineteenth and early twentieth century society every bit as much as the digital revolution is changing ours — legislative bodies simply could not keep up. As a result, today there is a "fourth" branch of government: the branch that is comprised of *administrative agencies*. Administrative agencies are governmental bodies usually assigned responsibility for a particular subject matter. For example, they include federal entities such as the Environmental Protection Agency (EPA) and state entities including Departments of

Motor Vehicles. Insofar as people come into contact with government in their day-to-day lives, they usually do so through agencies.

Although in a formal sense administrative agencies are typically housed in the Executive Branch, they are often called the fourth branch because they combine the powers of the other branches. This was a key innovation associated with the rise of the administrative state in the early twentieth century. For law to work well it had to work more quickly, and that could be accomplished if the three functions of government — legislative, executive (law enforcement), and judicial — were housed under the same roof.

Take the Securities Exchange Commission (SEC), an agency of the federal government that regulates financial markets. The SEC owes its existence to congressional legislation — specifically, post-Great Depression statutes that created the agency and conferred on it broad authority and broad responsibility to maintain the integrity of financial markets. Under the delegated authority contained in this broad mandate, the SEC enacts specific regulations that, in many respects, resemble pieces of legislation. For example, it has rules that regulate the conduct of stockbrokers. It then enforces those regulations by investigating alleged violators. And it reaches "quasi"-judicial decisions about whether the agency's rules have been broken. The latter are rendered by so-called "administrative law judges" (ALJs) — agency employees acting in a quasi-judicial capacity who determine, in the first instance, whether violations of SEC regulations have occurred and who are empowered to suspend or revoke licenses and to impose fines.

You may well be wondering: whatever happened to separation of powers? It's a fair question with a complicated answer. You will examine it when you take Administrative Law or Constitutional Law. For now, though, it is enough to say that we maintain some degree of separation of powers by requiring agency actions to be authorized before the fact by legislation, and to be subject, after the fact, to certain forms of judicial review. Thus, people who disagree with agency rules or ALJ decisions often can challenge those actions in federal court, including on the ground that the agency or its employees exceeded the scope of their delegated authority. Here you can begin to see how even the modern administrative state maintains at least a semblance of the three-branch model.

What matters for you, the law student, is that now you need to keep in mind three (or more) sources or types of law: legislative enactments (statutes); rules promulgated by agencies (typically called "regulations"), and judicial decisions. And, in truth, there are countless variants on these. For example, the Internal Revenue Service (IRS) — yes, the nice folks in the federal government who collect taxes — issues something called "revenue rulings," which are basically legal memoranda giving the IRS's view of the very complicated tax code that it administers. These too are "law."

All this may sound a bit abstract, so **Open Book Digital** provides you with an example of each of these: a statute, a regulation, and a judicial decision. Go ahead, take a look. Don't get lost in reading and interpreting them; just get a sense of how they differ from one another. What you will realize right away is that statutes and regulations look somewhat similar to one another, and judicial decisions are very different. The former are relatively formal statements of legal rules, almost like computer code. Judicial decisions, on the other hand, read like stories, describing a set of facts (like in our fact patterns) and discussing the resolution of legal issues raised by the facts.

The administrative state is so vast and important today that, rather than addressing agencies and the rules governing their activities exclusively through upper level courses such as Administrative Law, many schools include a course on it in their 1L curricula, often combining it with materials on statutory interpretation. And everyone agrees it is very important for law students to spend time learning how to read statutes and administrative rules. Still, one thing you will definitely notice about your law school classes is that you will be spending most of your time reading judicial decisions. Indeed, perhaps ironically, given the perceived need to teach you more about legislation and regulation, you will frequently be introduced to statutes and regulations by being assigned to read judicial opinions that discuss them! The next set of distinctions may help explain why this is the case.

OUR LAW IS COMMON; FOR OTHERS, THE LAW IS CIVIL

You will be hearing or seeing lots of references to "common law." Occasionally, these references will contrast common law with something called "civil law." This distinction — between common law and civil law — is hard to get a handle on, so we'll make it super simple. As you'll see, all that matters for you right now is the "common law" part of it. We have a common law system in this country, which means judicial decisions play an extremely important role. That's in part why you'll spend a good chunk of your 1L year reading judicial decisions.

The legal systems of "civil law" countries—including most of those on the continent of Europe, and countries that were colonies of these countries—are built around comprehensive legal codes that look like statutes. By contrast, legal systems in "common law" countries, which tend to be those that were colonies of Great Britain, lack comprehensive codes, and give judges a more prominent place in shaping the system's rules.[5]

For example, if you are a lawyer advising a client on when she might get in trouble for committing a tort under German law, you probably would begin with §823(1) of the German Civil Code. (It states, roughly, that anyone who injures another intentionally or negligently must compensate the victim for her losses.) Meanwhile, if you were a lawyer advising a client on when she might get into trouble for committing a tort in New York, you would read prominent decisions of the New York Court of Appeals (the state's high court), in which the court was asked to rule on the validity of a particular litigant's tort claims. In Germany, the tort law is grounded in the Civil Code. In New York, tort law is grounded in judicial decisions—there is no code provision or statute for the courts to interpret.

The historical reasons for the differences between civil and common law systems are complex and not particularly relevant here. And the stark contrast that we have initially drawn is simplistic. In reality, codes require and rely on interpretation by courts and academic commentators, and common law systems contain comprehensive statutory schemes to address many aspects of modern life. Still, the two systems do generate genuine differences. Even when

---

5. Just to make your life more confusing, there is another important distinction that is drawn using the phrase "civil law." This distinction—between "civil" and "criminal" law—has nothing to do with the distinction between civil and common law: both common law systems and civil law systems contain criminal law and civil law. Roughly speaking, what makes criminal law distinct from civil law is that the former marks off conduct for public condemnation and punishment. (Some law that falls on the civil side of the criminal-civil divide—most notably tort law—resembles criminal law in that it identifies conduct that is wrongful. However, for the most part, it does not do so in an effort to condemn and punish publicly that conduct.)

they are speaking the same language, it is not always easy for "civilians" to understand the "common law mind," and vice versa.

What matters for you right now is that American legal education, because it is rooted in a common law system, gives pride of place to judges' written decisions—called "opinions." Some feel that this dominance is a bit out of kilter in the modern era, in which legislation and agency regulations tend to dominate the legal landscape. They argue that law school should from the get-go give more attention to statutes and regulations. There's some force to these complaints; balance is usually a good thing.

Yet even where statutes and regulations are concerned, the decisions of judges are often the last word in the United States. Suppose there is a statute (there is) that makes it a crime to "use" or "carry" a gun "in relation to" the commission of a drug offense. And suppose that someone who doesn't have money to pay for drugs makes a deal to barter his gun for some drugs. Has the statute been violated? (You might as well get started—go ahead and try to argue both sides of this issue.) In fact, there turn out to be a number of judicial decisions addressing this exact question. The courts that have made these decisions rely heavily on the wording of the statute, which is codified in Section 924 of Volume 18 of the United States Code. But they also rely on the judicial analysis of that text found in prior court decisions. And they might interpret the statute against the backdrop of certain general principles articulated in prior judicial decisions, such as the principle that ambiguous criminal statutes should be interpreted narrowly.

As we discuss in more detail in Chapter 4, in the United States and all other common law systems, judicial decisions are *precedents* that bind or at least guide later courts deciding the same issue. They are the most common source of authority in resolving a legal dispute—they are in many ways the building blocks of our law. In cases that do not involve statutes—including many cases that involve the application of contract, property, and tort law—there is nothing else to look at other than judicial decisions. But even where there is a regulation, statute or constitutional provision at issue, once a court has interpreted its language, the judicial decision becomes as important, if not more important, than the words of the statute or regulation itself. This is why you are going to spend most of your law school career reading judicial decisions, and much of your legal career—especially if you become a litigator—arguing about them.

A HIERARCHY OF LAWS

With all this in mind, we can now get to the punchline of this chapter, which is not only to teach you the distinctions we have encountered above, but to get you to appreciate that the law within our legal system is arranged hierarchically. Not only is law a system of rules to govern society, there is also a body of law about law!

The Hierarchy of Three-Branch Law

In our system, the federal Constitution is the biggest law on the block. What it says, goes. End of story, full stop.

Among other things, the federal Constitution says that no one under the age of 35 may serve as President of the United States. One could argue that, back in 1789, the framers chose "35" based on shorter average life expectancies, so that today "35" should be understood to mean "45." (We'd put that in the category of legal arguments that are unlikely to persuade.) Whatever "35" means, it is the rule. Congress could enact a statute tomorrow, signed by the current President, which purports to lower the eligibility age to 25. But if that law were challenged in court, it almost certainly would be declared unconstitutional. Statutes that violate the federal Constitution are null and void. So too are state constitutional provisions, agency regulations, and judicial decisions. Of course, much of the federal Constitution is written in generalities, so it is often unclear whether a statute or regulation or judicial decision is constitutional. This gives judges — and law professors and law students — a lot to talk about.

Statutes come next in the hierarchy. In areas where they govern, federal statutes reign supreme (right below the Constitution), although sometimes in our federal system there will be a question whether the federal government has the authority to legislate on a given topic. Regulations tend to occupy about the same place as legislation, at least when they are clearly applicable — or "on point" as lawyers say.

At the bottom of the hierarchy reside judicial decisions. In short, if a legislature wants to change the rules that courts have adopted for a particular area of law, they usually can, though there may be some restrictions in how they go about doing so. For example, if a state legislature doesn't like the rules of contract formation that have been developed by its courts, it can adopt by statute a different set of rules that supersede the judge-made rules. (As you will learn in your Contracts course, state legislatures have in fact done something like this by enacting through legislation the provisions of a model law called the Uniform Commercial Code.)

Before you feel too bad for courts, however, remember that they are often called upon to interpret ambiguous provisions in constitutions, statutes, and regulations. As a result, they end up having a lot of say about how those kinds of law are actually applied. Congress can enact a statute criminalizing the "use" of a gun in relation to the commission of a crime involving the distribution or possession of drugs, but courts will have to figure out, in concrete cases, what that language actually means. True, if a court interprets a statute or regulation in a way that a legislature or agency does not approve, it may be open to the legislature or agency to rewrite the statute or regulation. But legislatures and agencies have limited resources (both with respect to time and political will), so there is no guarantee that they will be able to undo particular judicial interpretations.

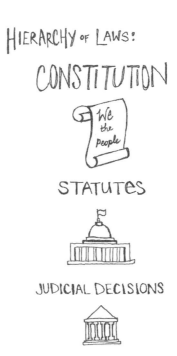

Moreover, the federal courts, and particularly the U.S. Supreme Court, have claimed for themselves the authority to finally resolve disputes over the meaning of the federal Constitution. While (as Friedman has written about) this claim is contentious — the Constitution itself does not explicitly confer final interpretive authority on the Court, the Congress, the President, or anyone else — in practice, it has meant that judicial interpretations of the Constitution, rather than the Constitution as written, dominate constitutional argument and analysis. If you want to know what the Fourteenth Amendment's guarantee of the "equal protection of the laws" really means, you have to read a slew of Supreme Court decisions interpreting that guarantee.

The upshot of all this is that courts are in practice a lot more powerful and important than their place on the organizational chart may suggest. Indeed, some complain that we live in an era of judicial supremacy.

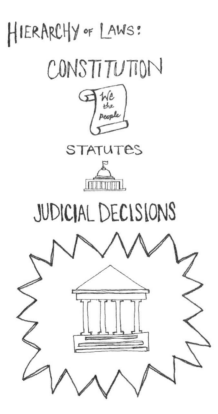

The Judicial Hierarchy

The judiciaries of both the national and state governments have their own hierarchies, as you know because you are familiar with the Supreme Court.

Let's start with the state courts, because those are the ones whose decisions you will tend to be reading in the early days of law school. It is typically (but not universally) true that state court systems have three tiers. At the bottom level are trial courts, or courts of first instance. These are the courts that you see in TV dramas, where evidence is taken and juries vote to acquit or convict (in criminal cases), or to award damages or not (in civil cases). Shockingly, TV doesn't quite give you an accurate picture of litigation. Criminal prosecutions and civil suits rarely result in a jury trial. The vast bulk of cases are resolved without a trial. In criminal cases this happens through "plea bargains;" in civil cases through "settlements." (Were this not the case, our entire legal system would likely come to a crashing halt; on the other hand, watching plea bargains get accepted by a court does not make for very good television.)

At the next level within state court systems are the so-called intermediate appellate courts, often called courts of appeals. As their name suggests, they hear appeals from trial court decisions brought by a party who is unhappy about the outcome of the trial court and believes that outcome was the result of a misapplication of relevant legal rules. Whereas in trial courts the primary focus is on resolving factual disputes (did the plaintiff really accept the defendant's offer? did the defendant intentionally push the plaintiff?), appellate courts almost always defer to the factual findings made in the trial court, and instead focus on questions of law.

For example, suppose a patient sues her doctor for medical malpractice (which is a tort). If the case goes to trial, the focus will be on what the doctor did or didn't do, and the causes and extent of the patient's injuries. If the patient prevails, and the defendant doctor appeals — at which point he is deemed the "appellant" and the patient the "appellee" — the doctor's lawyer is unlikely to get the result reversed by arguing that the jury's findings of fact were mistaken. Instead she will need to convince the appellate court that the trial court misapplied a rule of law. The doctor's lawyer might argue, for example, that the trial court incorrectly described the legal definition of malpractice to the jury, thus allowing the jury to find malpractice where there was none.

Finally, atop the state courts' judicial hierarchy is a high appellate court. Thus, just as there is a Supreme Court of the United States—SCOTUS, or #SCOTUS for those of you that frequent Twitter—there is also a Supreme Court of Michigan, or Indiana. (However, as we said above, New York's highest court is the New York Court of Appeals, and its trial courts are collectively referred to as the Supreme Court of New York. Sometimes it seems things are named just to make law students miserable.) State high courts have the final word when it comes to interpreting state laws.

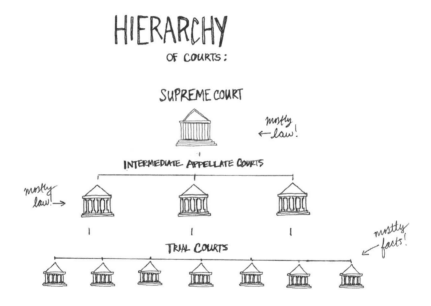

Like state court systems, the federal court system has three levels. First, there are the district courts, which are the federal trial courts. Then there are the Circuit Courts of Appeal, which are the intermediate appellate courts. Finally, there is the U.S. Supreme Court. The Supreme Court is the boss when it comes to interpreting federal law. Its views on the United States Constitution, federal statutes, federal regulations, and federal court decisions are the last word (among courts) on these matters.

The relationship between the federal courts and the state courts is quite complex—you will talk about it some in Civil Procedure, and in upper-level courses, especially a course that is called "Federal Courts." For now we will simply treat the federal courts as a separate court system within our overall system of government. Still, it is important to recognize that although the U.S. Supreme Court is often described as the highest court in the land, that phrase must be qualified in one important respect. When it comes to questions of state law, the Supreme Court does *not* have final say (unless the issue is whether the state law contradicts or interferes with federal law). Rather, that honor goes to the high court of each state. This is a particularly important qualification for new law students to observe, because a lot of the law you will be learning in the first year is state law. If the California Supreme Court interprets a statute enacted by the California legislature in a particular way, and if that interpretation does not raise any problems of federal law, then the U.S. Supreme Court has nothing to say about it.

The Crucial Importance of Hierarchy

Here's just a bit more nomenclature, so we can make a final point and round out this chapter. In the federal court system, the country is divided, geographically, into twelve circuits, named aptly the First Circuit, Second Circuit and so on . . . except for the District of Columbia Circuit. (The D.C. Circuit handles a large number of appeals from federal administrative agencies, which for the most part are based in the nation's capital.) Each Circuit has a set of trial courts ("District Courts") and a set of appellate courts ("Courts of Appeal") that convene ("sit") in courthouses located within the geographic area of the circuit. For example, the district courts and the Court of Appeals for the Eleventh Circuit sit in courthouses located in Florida, Georgia, and Alabama. If there is a legal issue that a federal Court of Appeals has resolved, but the Supreme Court has not—and there are many of these!—the Court of Appeals' resolution of that issue is binding on all the district courts *in that circuit*, but not the district courts in other circuits.

Geographic Boundaries
of United States Courts of Appeals and United States District Courts

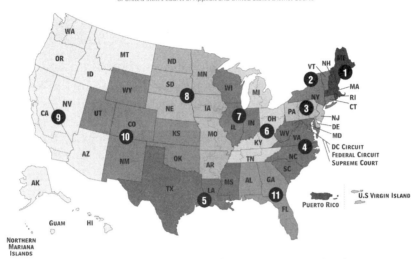

www.uscourts.gov/file/document/us-federal-courts-circuit-map

Here's the stunning denouement to all this: In the authority of the law, hierarchy matters. Sometimes it is everything.

Remember our case about "using" guns to commit a drug offense? In a case called *United States v. Phelps*, the Ninth Circuit (which encompasses California, Alaska, Arizona and Hawaii) decided ("held") that trading a MAC-10 automatic weapon in exchange for the drug ephedrine did not violate the statute. In part, it reasoned that there was no intention on the part of the defendant being prosecuted to use the gun as an "offensive weapon" in relation to a drug crime. But in a case decided by the Eleventh Circuit, *United States v. Smith*, the court held just the opposite, in a case also involving the trade of a MAC-10 for a drug (in that case, cocaine). In the Eleventh Circuit's view, the use of the gun was an "integral part of" the drug transaction.

Now suppose — in the aftermath of those decisions, and before the Supreme Court decided the matter definitively — that you were representing the United States government in federal District Court (the trial court) in a criminal case that arose in California and involved a gun-for-drugs trade. You would be stuck with the decision in *Phelps*. There is nothing you can do about it. In the language of the law, "*Phelps* governs" any other case in the circuit at the trial level. The hierarchy of the pyramid rules.

Now, when you get up to the appellate court, the Ninth Circuit, you could suggest it reconsider *Phelps* in light of *United States v. Smith*. (*Smith* came after *Phelps*, and had explicitly rejected the court's reasoning in *Phelps*). The judges of the Court of Appeals on the Ninth Circuit—for reasons we are about to explain in the next chapter—will have the option of adhering to their decision in *Phelps* or changing their minds in light of *Smith*.

And if you were representing one of the parties in the case that eventually made it to the Supreme Court—the *Smith* case as it happened in real life—you could refer to both lower court cases, and make arguments about the reasoning in each. The Supreme Court, being atop the pile, is not bound by any lower court decision when it comes to interpreting federal law.

• • •

That was a big gulp. Hopefully you followed it all—if not you might give it a quick re-read, or refer back to parts of it as you read for your classes. But the main point for now is that there is hierarchy to the law: withn the federal system or a given state system, constitution trumps statute and statute trumps court decision, and the decisions of courts higher in the judicial hierarchy trump the decisions of lower courts. So long as you get that, you'll be fine to keep reading.

You are now in a position to see how legal argument works, and to try your hand at reading and analyzing a real judicial opinion. That then will lead us into our discussion of law school and how to relate the classroom to the exams you will take.

The Bottom Line

☑ Law is rules enacted or recognized by governmental institutions.

☑ Federal and state governments are hierarchically organized, as are the federal and state judicial systems.

☑ Recognizing the legal system's hierarchies is necessary to understand legal reasoning.

Chapter 4

LEGAL REASONING, THE COMMON LAW WAY

☑ Precedents: how judicial opinions state legal rules.

☑ The "vertical" and "horizontal" dimensions of precedent.

☑ Following, overruling, and distinguishing precedents.

☑ Distinguishing rules from other parts of a judicial opinion.

I n Chapter 3, we reviewed some of the basic features of the American legal system. We did so because those features are, in a sense, always present in any discussion of law. Sometimes they are in the foreground—for example, when, in a Constitutional Law class, you discuss whether Congress or the President has the authority to undertake a certain action. More often, they are lurking in the background, which is why your professors may not spend a lot of time talking about them, and indeed may simply assume that you understand them. But, as you are about to see, understanding the idea of hierarchy is essential to understanding how law works, and how legal arguments are fashioned.

Our next topic—common law reasoning—has a similar set of attributes. At times, there will be cases or topics that directly raise the question of what is involved in this sort of reasoning. But in other instances, that sort of question will be lurking beneath the surface of a discussion about some other topic. If the hierarchy we described in the last chapter is the skeletal structure of the law, common law reasoning is its tissue. So, once again, we're going to try to shed some light on the topic. In this way, you can be better prepared for assigned readings and class discussions. And you can start to see how law school classes relate to the exams you will take.

PRECEDENTS AND *STARE DECISIS*

As we noted in Chapter 3, Anglo-American legal systems are "common law" systems. They are not organized around comprehensive written codes, but instead rely on judges to articulate the law in the course of deciding particular disputes. In the United States, there remain important bodies of law that have been defined largely (or even solely) by judges. This is especially true of the law you will learn at the outset of law school, such as torts, contracts, and property. If you are trying to figure out the rule that will determine whether a contract has been formed, or a tort has been committed, or which of two claimants is the rightful owner of a piece of land, odds are that you will find the answer, or at least the materials for making a good argument about the answer, in judicial decisions.

At this point, you might fairly ask: How does a court decision — which, after all, resolves a particular dispute between particular parties — tell us anything about the rules that will resolve other parties' disputes? In what sense do cases "make law"?

The answer to this last question has two parts. First, in our system, when courts resolve disputes between parties — particularly appellate courts — they usually do so by issuing written decisions. Second, in those written decisions ("opinions"), courts will, explicitly or implicitly, state rules of law that then govern later disputes. Understanding how this is so, and about how to make arguments regarding these rules, is the heart of what this Chapter is about.

A First Case: *Baker v. Farmer*

Let's travel back in time to 1875. Imagine there is a baker, conveniently named Baker. Baker has brought a lawsuit against a farmer, conveniently named Farmer. The suit, which claims that Farmer breached a contract between them, was filed in a trial court in the state of Illinois. (We're making up this case, but it's not a far-fetched example.) Specifically, the suit alleges that Farmer failed to honor an agreement between them, according to which Farmer was to supply Baker with a certain amount of wheat. The suit further alleges that, as a result of Farmer's failure to deliver, Baker was forced to buy wheat from another seller at a higher price. Thus, Baker is suing to recover the difference between the higher-priced wheat he bought and the lower price wheat that Farmer had agreed to provide.[6]

Farmer's lawyer—who is obviously hoping to convince the court that Baker's suit is without merit—makes the following argument to the trial judge: "Your honor, we are not conceding that there was any agreement here. But, for purposes of argument, suppose there was one. Even so, there is no written documentation of this alleged agreement. Respectfully, I submit that courts, including this court, should not enforce unwritten agreements. I therefore move that Baker's lawsuit be dismissed."[7]

The trial judge, convinced by this argument, dismisses the suit, leaving Baker with no remedy. Baker, through his lawyer, decides to appeal. His appeal is heard initially by a panel of three judges on the Illinois Court of Appeals—the state's intermediate appellate court. To these judges, Baker's lawyer argues that the trial court made a mistake of law in dismissing his lawsuit. Under Illinois law, the lawyer argues, at least some agreements, including the simple agreement to supply wheat in this case, don't need to be in writing to be enforceable. Requiring every business agreement to be in writing would be unworkable, he says, given the business realities of the time. Unmoved, the appellate court unanimously upholds ("affirms") the trial court's ruling.

Baker has one last shot—an appeal to the Illinois Supreme Court, which has the final say on matters of Illinois law. Happily for Baker, in this forum his lawyer's argument wins the day. Indeed, each of the seven Justices on the Supreme Court concludes that the lawyer's argument is compelling. One of them, Justice Major, issues a written

---

6. Because the following examples are set in the nineteenth century, we're going to use masculine pronouns.

7. In law, a "motion" is a request made by a lawyer to a judge. Roughly speaking, when a lawyer representing a defendant makes a motion to dismiss ("moves" to dismiss), the lawyer is requesting that the trial judge throw out the plaintiff's lawsuit on the ground that it has no basis in prevailing law.

opinion on behalf of his fellow judges, which is published in full just below. (Justice Major was known for his brevity.)

Before you get to the opinion's substance, note that we "cite" this case as *Baker v. Farmer*, 79 Ill. 798 (1875). Baker is the original plaintiff, and in the Supreme Court is the appellant; Farmer is the original defendant and is the appellee. The case was decided in 1875. And it is published at page 798 of Volume 79 of the "Illinois Reports" — a collection of Illinois Supreme Court opinions published by the state.[8]

BAKER (PLAINTIFF/APPELLANT) v. FARMER (DEFENDANT/APPELLEE)
79 ILL. 798 (1875)

Major, J. The appellant Baker, a resident of Jasper County, sued the appelle Farmer, also a resident of said county, alleging damages from Farmer's failure to deliver wheat under an oral agreement between them. In the trial court, Farmer successfully moved for dismissal on the ground that, even if there were such an agreement, the suit must fail because the courts of this state cannot take cognizance of an agreement unless it is in writing. The Court of Appeals affirmed.

We reverse. The trial court committed an error of law in granting Farmer's motion. As long as there is reliable evidence from the parties or other sources as to the existence and terms of an agreement, a writing is not necessary.

Baker's suit shall proceed to trial to determine if in fact there was an agreement and, if so, its precise terms.

So ordered.

---

8. In American state and federal courts, appellate court decisions are conveyed in opinions authored by a single judge (here, Judge Major) on behalf of the other judges of the court. If there is a disagreement among the judges, the decision of the court is typically conveyed in a single opinion written on behalf of a majority of the judges of the court. Those judges who disagree with the majority of their colleagues often will write separate opinions — called "concurrences" or "dissents" — which explain why they disagree with the majority. In other jurisdictions, including those in the United Kingdom, it is more typical for each member of an appellate court to write a separate opinion.

What has happened here? Well, in one sense, the Illinois Supreme Court simply resolved a dispute between Farmer and Baker. (Notice that, in fact, the Court did not finally resolve the dispute, but instead sent the case back for resolution in the trial court. This is often what happens to cases on appeal.) Yet the Court also did something broader. For in explaining *why* it was reinstating Baker's suit, it articulated a legal rule — specifically, a rule of Illinois contract law. Before you read the next sentence, take a moment and see if you can state the rule.

Here's one way (but not the only way) to describe the rule: *an agreement need not be in writing in order to be a legally enforceable contract.*

With a statement of the rule in front of us, we can ask the next critical question: Why (or when) should a court faced with a subsequent dispute take any notice of the rule stated by the Illinois Supreme Court in *Baker v. Farmer*? The decision sets out a rule that resolves the specific case that came to the Court, but when — if ever — does it govern other disputes? To ask the same question a different way, what makes a decision like that in the *Baker* case a *precedent* — a decision to be observed and followed by other courts? The answer to these questions is absolutely essential to understanding how law works.

A typical answer to these questions might well end up invoking the Latin phrase "*stare decisis*," which translates as "let the decision stand." By itself, the phrase doesn't tell you much, but we can help explain it. To do so, it will be useful to separate two aspects of the *stare decisis* principle — its "vertical" aspect, and its "horizontal" aspect. Both, it turns out, are an outgrowth of the hierarchical structure of court systems. This is why our discussion of hierarchy in the previous chapter was so important.

The *vertical* component of *stare decisis* is quite simple. It tells us that courts occupying a lower place within the hierarchy of their court system must adhere to the rules set out by courts higher in the hierarchy. Once the Illinois Supreme Court decides a case, trial and intermediate appellate courts must follow it.

A moment's reflection will reveal the logic behind the vertical aspect of *stare decisis*. Most jurisdictions have many trial and intermediate appellate judges. If each court in each case were free to make a new set of rules, there would likely be a lot of variation, which would make the law highly unpredictable. It would also create a serious risk that the legal system would run afoul of a basic principle of justice;

namely, that similar cases should be treated in similar ways. Imagine two suits brought by two different bakers against two different farmers, each involving the same oral promise to deliver wheat. Without *stare decisis*, it might easily be the case that one baker would win his suit and the other would lose, even though their situations were identical. That sort of thing would bring the justice system into disrepute. It is a fundamental precept of law that, as much as possible, "like cases are treated alike."

Of course, as you already know from our discussion of *Phelps* and *Smith* in the last chapter, the principle of "treating like cases alike" operates *within* a given judicial system. When it comes to contracts for wheat and other goods, there may be a different rule in Indiana, or Georgia, than there is in Illinois, just as the Ninth Circuit and the Eleventh Circuit had different rules relating to guns being traded for drugs. When it comes to national, or United States, law, the Supreme Court can harmonize it across all jurisdictions. But there is no über state court. One important upshot of American "federalism" is that each state can have its own rules for matters governed exclusively by state law.

So, that's the "vertical" dimension of *stare decisis*. Once a court higher in the hierarchy adopts a rule, that rule governs any lower court litigation *in that jurisdiction* until such time as the higher court (or a legislative body) changes the rule.

A Second Case: *Buyer v. Owner*

Now let's consider the "horizontal dimension" of *stare decisis*. To do so, it will help to imagine a second breach-of-contract lawsuit. This one, filed in an Illinois trial court in the year 1885, was brought by a disappointed property buyer (named Buyer). Buyer claims to have had an oral agreement with the owner of a piece of land (named Owner). According to the alleged agreement, Buyer, who was planning to build his dream house on the land, was to purchase the land from Owner at a certain price. When Owner later refused to accept payment from Buyer, Buyer sued.

Suppose that the lawyer for Owner argues to the trial judge presiding over Buyer's breach-of-contract lawsuit that the suit should be dismissed because there was no written agreement. With *Baker v. Farmer* having been decided by the Illinois Supreme Court only ten years earlier, the trial judge denies the defendant's motion. In turn, based on the evidence presented, the jury finds that there was in fact an oral agreement. The trial judge thus orders Owner to sell the land to Buyer at the agreed-upon price. On appeal, the Court of Appeals affirms.

Having lost at the trial court and intermediate appellate court, Owner and his lawyer discuss whether it will be worthwhile to appeal to the Illinois Supreme Court. Owner worries that it will be a waste of time and money. "Won't the Supreme Court simply uphold the lower courts' rulings on the basis of *Baker v. Farmer*?" he asks. "Maybe not," responds his lawyer. "The Supreme Court's earlier decisions do not bind it in quite the same way that they bind lower courts." "Besides," the lawyer notes, "the membership of the Supreme Court has changed since 1875—three Justices, including Justice Major, have since retired and been replaced by different judges."

Owner's lawyer is on to something here. Precisely because it is the court of last resort on questions of state law, the Illinois Supreme Court—and every state high court—reserves the right to revisit its decisions about state law. It can, in the jargon, *overrule* its prior ruling. This is why your casebooks for classes like Contracts, Property and Torts, are likely to be filled with opinions issued by state high courts: they're the courts that are most open to rethinking or modifying existing rules.

And yet, if, in advising his client, Owner's lawyer offered *only* the quoted remarks above, he would have been seriously overstating the prospects for a successful appeal to the Illinois Supreme Court. While the Court is not 'vertically' bound to follow its own decisions, it would be a mistake to jump to the opposite conclusion that the Court's prior decisions carry no weight—that the judges are entirely at liberty to depart from prior decisions whenever they feel like doing so.

This is the *horizontal* dimension to *stare decisis*. The high court within a judicial system—whether a state supreme court or the U.S. Supreme Court—must treat *its own* prior decisions as precedents. Again, high courts have the power to overrule their own precedents. But most judges take *stare decisis* seriously, which means that, ordinarily, the prospects of getting a court to revisit its earlier decision, particularly a recent decision, are quite poor. If a good deal of time has passed, and the old rule has proven problematic, and the court has several new members, then there might be reason to suppose that there is a willingness on the part of a court to reconsider an issue that it has already decided. Overruling of precedents, though, does not happen often.

So does it follow from *stare decisis*'s horizontal dimension that an appeal by Owner to the Illinois Supreme Court is doomed to fail? Well, this is exactly the sort of question that a good lawyer will need to figure out so that she can properly advise her client on whether to appeal.

However—and this is *hugely* important—it turns out that the situation facing Owner and his lawyer as they contemplate an appeal to the Illinois Supreme Court is more subtle than we have thus far been suggesting. (We wanted to keep things simple at first.) It is more subtle because it is often the case that a litigant who hopes to avoid being subjected to a legal rule contained in a prior decision might be able to achieve that goal *without* having to convince a court to take the drastic step of overruling the prior decision. Instead, she can argue that the prior decision, while perfectly valid, simply does not apply to the litigant's case. The court's precedent, the litigant will argue, is *distinguishable*: her case is different.

Whether a precedent is distinguishable is pretty much the heart and soul of common law reasoning, both in court and in the classroom. This is what you are going to be doing in class, on exams, and as a practicing lawyer. (See? It all starts to come together.) It is to that topic we now turn.

DISTINGUISHING PRECEDENTS: ANALOGICAL REASONING

Until just now, we were supposing that the only argument that Owner's lawyer might make to the Illinois Supreme Court is to ask it to ignore or overrule *Baker v. Farmer*. But it is a rare case indeed in which an appellate lawyer finds herself in such a stark position. More commonly, she will be prepared to concede the validity of prior decisions that seem to run against her client's position, but argue that those decisions don't control the outcome of the client's case—*because her client's case is different in some essential way.*

Let's return to the imagined case of *Buyer v. Owner*. In that case, Owner's lawyer could concede that the trial court was bound to follow *Baker v. Famer,* yet still argue that *Baker*'s rule only makes sense *for some kinds of agreements and not others*. For example, he could argue that *Baker*'s rule, while perfectly sound when applied to oral agreements for the purchase of commodities such as wheat, should not apply to agreements for the sale of land. Hence, the absence of a written agreement, though not fatal to Baker's claim, should be fatal to Buyer's suit.

Law being an adversarial business, one can fully expect that any attempt by Owner's lawyer to distinguish *Baker* would be met by counter-arguments from Buyer's lawyer. (Just as making arguments is essential, a key to being a good lawyer and a good law student is to anticipate the arguments that will be made in opposition to one's own.) One such counter-argument might run as follows:

> Consider carefully Justice Major's *Baker* opinion. It does not even hint at a distinction among different types of contracts. Here is its key passage: "As long as there is reliable evidence from the parties or other sources as to the existence and terms of an agreement, a writing is not necessary." Given this language, any effort to "limit" *Baker* would in reality amount to an overruling of *Baker*, because *Baker* stands for the rule that *no* agreement needs to be in writing in order to be enforceable.

But here's the thing. Owner's lawyer would have a pretty good response to Buyer's counter-argument that the rule in *Baker v. Farmer* applies to *Buyer v. Owner*. (Welcome to law school!) Owner's lawyer's counter-counter-argument might go something like this:

> *Baker* was the first case in which the Illinois Supreme Court dealt with the question of whether an agreement has to be in writing to be enforceable. Even though the *Baker* Court understood that its rule would have application to *some* other cases, it seems unlikely that the Court affirmatively decided that the same rule should apply for *all* agreements. After all, those other agreements weren't even discussed by the Justices, and may not even have been anticipated by them. Whether consciously or subconsciously, the Illinois Supreme Court justices left open the question of whether *some* kinds of agreements might require a different rule than the rule adopted in *Baker*.

Now suppose Owner's lawyer has the better of this argument—in other words, that *Baker* is best understood as having left room for the *possibility* that some kinds of agreements need to be in writing to be enforceable. Has Owner's lawyer, by winning this argument, won the day for his client? Not yet. Instead, he has to go further and explain two crucial things: first, why, in the abstract, certain agreements might need to be in writing; and second, why the *agreement in his client's case* is of a sort that should only be enforced when written. To say the same thing, he has to identify a salient difference or *disanalogy* between the oral agreement between Owner and Buyer and the oral agreement between Baker and Farmer.

In an effort to distinguish the rule in *Baker v. Farmer* from his client's case, the lawyer for Owner could point to several differences. For example, the oral agreement between Owner and Buyer was made in a different calendar year than the agreement between Baker and Farmer. Do you think that difference justifies the application of a different rule in Buyer's case? Hardly, right? Already, you are beginning to see the difference between good and bad arguments. A good argument has to turn on a distinction that the law *should* take into account. Nothing about the calendar year ought to bear on the form that contracts can take. (Or nothing we can think of—were you able to do better than we did?)

Another distinction, alluded to above, might matter more. In *Baker*, the subject of the agreement was a quantity of wheat—a commodity. In Buyer's case, the subject of the agreement was a piece of land. Does this difference render Buyer's case *disanalogous* to Baker's case? Well, that's the $64,000 question, as they used to say when we were kids. (Adjusting for inflation, today it's the $400,000 question.) This is the question you are expected to ask yourself as you read cases, and expected to come to class prepared to discuss.

Land and commodities share certain attributes. Both are tangible. Both can be bought and sold. The question is, what makes them different in a way that would warrant a different legal rule governing contracts for the sale of commodities and contracts for the sale of land? Go ahead, take another moment, and see if you can identify differences of this sort . . .

We don't purport to have the 'right' answer to this question. Remember, as we stressed in Chapter 1, law is mostly about making good arguments. But we can offer some answers that are at least plausible. Commodities tend to be highly fungible. (If you don't know what "fungible" means, look it up! You'll see it a lot, and, more generally, you need to get in the habit of looking up words that you don't know.) A baker can probably find a number of farmers who will sell him wheat that is suitable for his purposes. This is less true for land, particularly land being used for a residence. People in the market for a residence tend to have very specific desires in terms of location, price, and other features, and it is hardly unusual for them to take months or years to find something suitable. Simply put, one piece of land—unlike one batch of wheat—is not like another one. Relatedly, a purchase of land by an individual for purposes of building a home is for many people an unusually significant and personal transaction. Not so for the purchase of commodities for commercial use.

Maybe you accept that these are genuine differences between purchases of land and purchases of wheat. Maybe you don't. But that is the whole point here. Those are the very sorts of questions the justices of the Illinois Supreme Court will have to grapple with—and the sorts of issues you will consider—as a law student, exam taker, and lawyer.

We're not done yet though: the analytic task at hand is still not quite complete. Even if you accept that wheat and land are different, you still must explain why their differences generate reasons that favor a requirement of written agreements for transactions involving the sale of land, but not for transactions involving the sale of commodities. Remember, the goal for Owner's lawyer is to convince the appellate court that, even though no writing was required in *Baker*, there should be a writing required here.

Let's try this argument on for size. Because land sales are high-stakes, and often have a personal dimension, such that disappointed buyers won't easily be able to find alternatives if a deal falls through, it is important for the law to give the parties incentives to be as clear as possible about whether they have reached an agreement to sell land. This is why there should be a rule of law stating that contracts for the sale of land should be in writing. And this is why such a rule would not contradict the rule in *Baker*—that rule was designed for a different kind of transaction.

Are you buying this argument? If not, that's fine. We are not trying to convince you that we are right. We are aiming for something more modest, which is to show you how to argue from precedent. The same will often be true in class: whether or not your professor has strong views on the right answer, she is more concerned to get you to make a good argument.

As you can probably guess at this point, we could go on—and on, and on, and on—from here. And in your classes, you sometimes will. Suppose the Court of Appeals, and the Illinois Supreme Court, were to accept the argument that agreements for the sale of land *are* different from agreements for the sale of commodities, and hence to rule in *Buyer v. Owner* that a writing *is* required for the former to be enforceable. Now comes the next suit, involving an oral agreement to sell land not for personal use, but instead for commercial use. The purchaser of the land is hoping to enforce it. Can you think of an argument that would win the day for this purchaser while adhering to both the *Baker* and the *Buyer* decisions? In other words, can you distinguish your case from those two?

Welcome to the art of reasoning from precedents.

BINDING AND PERSUASIVE AUTHORITY, HOLDING AND DICTUM, PRECEDENT AND POLICY

We'll close this chapter with a few last words on reasoning from precedents.

As we told you previously, the rule of *stare decisis* applies only within a court system. The Illinois Supreme Court's decision in *Baker v. Farmer* is binding on Illinois lower courts and (to some extent) on the Illinois Supreme Court itself. But it is not binding on *another state's courts* when they are applying that state's law. Still, it might be *persuasive* in other courts. Although a court in Indiana or Georgia could not cite *Baker* for having authoritatively announced a rule of Indiana or Georgia law, they could still rely on it (and cite it) as a thoughtful treatment of the issue of when to enforce unwritten agreements.

But even where there is an authority relationship between two courts, there is another condition that must be met before *stare decisis* applies. The rule in the prior decision—the rule that would bind the subsequent court decision—must have been *necessary* to the outcome of that decision. In other words, *stare decisis* only applies to rules that were central or integral to the prior decision, as opposed to rules that received a casual mention, but really were extraneous. The latter rules are called "*dicta*," whereas the former—the rules that were necessary to the resolution of the prior case—are called "*holdings*." Holdings are binding; *dicta* are not.

We can go back to the imagined case of *Buyer v. Owner* to capture the difference between holding and dictum. Recall that, there, the owner of a piece of land refused to abide by an oral agreement to sell the land and was sued by the disappointed buyer. Suppose that the Illinois Supreme Court issued a unanimous decision that contained the following passage:

We are convinced by Owner's argument that agreements for the sale of land are distinct from agreements for the sale of commodities. Land transactions tend to be high-stakes, and it is often not easy for purchasers of land to find adequate substitutes. Thus, oral agreements for the sale of land are not enforceable. Accordingly, Buyer's suit, based as it is on an oral agreement, must be dismissed.[9]

We note that the same considerations that warrant the requirement of a writing for land sales also favor a distinct remedy for cases, unlike this one, in which a written agreement for the sale of land is breached. Rather than awarding monetary damages to the disappointed purchaser, trial courts should order the breaching owner to sell the land to the buyer at the agreed-upon price.

The holding of this decision — its binding part — is that agreements for the sale of land must be in writing to be enforceable. (Of course, as we saw, this is an initial statement of the holding, it might later be qualified to apply, say, only to agreements for the sale of *residential* property.) The dictum in this decision, helpfully set off in a separate paragraph, is the discussion of the remedy to which disappointed land buyers are entitled. It is dictum because the Court had no

---

9. An interesting and at times controversial feature of common law is that judicial decisions will often have a "retroactive" aspect. Suppose it was the case that, when Owner and Buyer entered into their oral agreement, there was a general assumption that, in light of *Baker v. Farmer*, oral agreements would be enforceable. Is it fair to Owner for the Illinois Supreme Court to announce a new rule requiring written agreements for land transactions, and then apply it to Buyer, even though Buyer had little if any reason to expect that that rule would govern his transaction with Owner? On the other hand, would it be unfair to Owner to announce the rule requiring a written agreement, but not give Owner the benefit of that rule?

occasion to apply its rule about the proper remedy in *Buyer v. Owner*. Because there was no written agreement in that case, Buyer was not entitled to *any* remedy.

In this example, dictum and holding are quite clearly identifiable. In other situations, however, the line will be blurrier. Indeed, judges on the same court will sometimes disagree among themselves as to whether a particular rule from a prior decision is holding or dictum. (Once again: law is all about arguments!)

It is worth recalling yet again that, even when *stare decisis* clearly does apply, there is still plenty of room for argument. As we saw in the example of *Buyer v. Owner*, there will be arguments about whether an admittedly binding precedent actually resolves the particular issue that a court is now facing. Holdings, in other words, rarely "speak" unequivocally. Lawyers and judges spend a lot of their time thinking and arguing about how properly to characterize the holdings of prior decisions. You will too.

Also, as we emphasized above, even when there really is no basis for a distinguishing a precedent — even when a prior holding clearly governs the resolution of a later dispute — it remains open to the party adversely affected by the precedent to argue that the precedent should be overruled. Because our system takes *stare decisis* seriously, a lawyer who finds herself in the position of having to make this sort of argument is probably facing an uphill battle, especially when arguing in a lower court that a high court precedent should be overruled. (In all likelihood, the judge(s) in the lower court will tell the party seeking to overrule a higher-court precedent that it is not the lower court's place to do such a thing, and to take the case up the hierarchical hill.)

But law changes and precedents are sometimes overruled. Perhaps most commonly they are overruled slowly, by a series of decisions that so heavily qualify the rule as to 'gut' it. A famous example of this comes from torts. In the 1840s, English courts held that a product manufacturer could not be sued by a person injured by a carelessly manufactured product unless the person who was suing had purchased the product directly from the manufacturer, rather than through an intermediary such as a dealer or retailer. While purporting to observe this precedent, the New York Court of Appeals later identified an exception for "inherently dangerous" products, such as poisons accidentally mislabeled as medicines. After about 70 years, the list of inherently dangerous products had grown so long — extending to bottles of carbonated water and coffee urns — that there was almost nothing left of the original rule.[10]

On rare occasions, courts will quickly and dramatically reverse course. A famous example of this comes from federal constitutional law. In a 1940 decision, the Supreme Court ruled that public schools could compel students to salute the American flag and recite the Pledge of Allegiance. Three years later, the Court overruled its own decision, holding that compulsory exercises of this sort violate the First Amendment's guarantee of Free Speech.[11]

As you will see once classes get underway, when it comes to arguing about holdings — whether the argument is about how they should be interpreted, or why they should or should not be overruled — lawyers are open to making various different kinds of arguments. Lawyers are paid to be advocates, and when it comes to advocacy, any good faith argument that has a chance of prevailing is usually worth making. This is why lawyers aim to come to court with a handful of different arguments at the ready.

Let's return again to *Buyer v. Owner.* Were he to appear before the Illinois Supreme Court, the lawyer representing Owner would want to give the Court various reasons why *Baker v. Farmer* should not apply to the agreements to sell land, or, in the alternative, why it should overrule *Baker.* Some of these reasons might focus more on precedents — perhaps he might argue that a reading of *Baker* that limits its rule to agreements to sell commodities renders it most consistent with decisions by the Court on other aspects of contract law or property law. Other reasons will be more policy-oriented, explaining why a limited reading of *Baker* will best facilitate future transactions concerning land. This mix of precedent- and policy-based argument will become very familiar to you as you attend classes, and will be expected of you when you take exams.

On the other hand, as we also saw above, some arguments remain out of bounds. Owner cannot argue that he should win because his name is Owner, or because he is richer than Buyer. A lot of law school

---

10. *See MacPherson v. Buick,* 111 N.E. 1050 (N.Y. 1916) (discussing the development of New York law on this issue).

11. *West Virginia Board of Education v. Barnette,* 319 U.S. 624 (1943) (overruling *Minersville School Dist. v. Gobitis,* 310 U.S. 586 (1940)).

is learning what sorts of arguments are good legal arguments. Teaching that skill is a lot of what class is about.

The Bottom Line

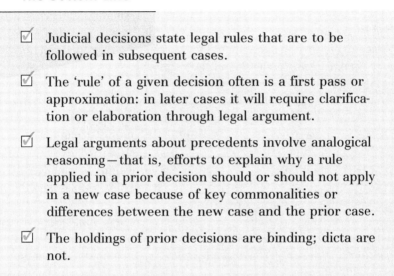

☑ Judicial decisions state legal rules that are to be followed in subsequent cases.

☑ The 'rule' of a given decision often is a first pass or approximation: in later cases it will require clarification or elaboration through legal argument.

☑ Legal arguments about precedents involve analogical reasoning—that is, efforts to explain why a rule applied in a prior decision should or should not apply in a new case because of key commonalities or differences between the new case and the prior case.

☑ The holdings of prior decisions are binding; dicta are not.

Chapter 5

CONNECTING CLASS AND EXAMS

☑ What to expect from classes.

☑ What to focus on in a case: facts, procedure, issues, rules, rationales.

☑ Why professors love hypothetical questions (and why you should too).

☑ What is "IRAC"? (And why is the "I" in IRAC missing from class?)

Now it's time to deliver on our promise to connect what goes on in class with what will happen on exams. You've learned about the basics of the system of lawmaking institutions, and in particular you've focused on the hierarchical structures of our legal system. You've also learned the basics of legal reasoning, and how that hierarchy governs a system of *stare decisis*. Most important, you've seen how arguments get made about decisions and whether one decision governs the resolution of a subsequent case. As we've told you all along, these arguments are the very essence of what law school exams test, and what good lawyers know how to do.

In this chapter we're going to discuss the way class teaches you about making good legal arguments. We're also going to return to our point about the ways in which class nonetheless differs from exams. Between the two, we hope you can see how classes prepare you for exams even though the methodology of class is quite distinct. (In the next chapter, right before we shift our focus to exams themselves, we're going to make some suggestions for how to get the most out of class).

Before we move on, one side note. Remember how we said that some people believe law schools cheat legislation and statutory interpretation in favor of common law judicial reasoning and cases? We agree. And yet, as you've seen, we've mostly dealt with cases. We're sticking with that theme so as not to distract you from the main argument here. But learning about statutory interpretation is important. So, we've posted a bonus chapter on **Open Book Digital.** In that chapter we do two things. We show you the basics of statutory interpretation, using the *Smith* drugs-for-guns case we've discussed previously. And we structured the chapter to resemble in some ways the opening discussion of a case in a real 1L class, so you can get a feel for how that discussion might go. Either before or after reading this chapter, you may want to go on **Open Book Digital** and read the bonus chapter. We think it will help when it comes time for classes.

WELCOME TO CLASS

Every professor teaches in his or her own way. Some use the Socratic method—lots of questions and few answers—while others lecture. Some "cold call" on students, meaning you never know when you'll be called upon to respond to questions. Some have students on a "panel" who know that they are "up" that day; and so on. Yet, no matter which methodology your professor employs, most still use the case method, and most classes follow a certain pattern. Probably, then, things will go like this . . . .

Class starts with announcements, pleasantries, and a summary of what happened the day before. Or not. Maybe the professor just jumps in. And then the drill begins.

The professor announces the assigned case. (Here, we're going to use *Baker v. Farmer,* the short case we discussed last chapter.) And then she asks a set of questions that will be very common from class to class, especially in the early days.

Quite likely, the professor will ask you to describe—crisply and accurately—the events that gave rise to the litigation. What the professor wants to know are the key *facts* of the case. How is it that these parties ended up in court? What was the basis of their dispute?[12]

This part of the discussion should not be taken lightly. One of the most important things about law school is learning what within a case is important and what is not. The fact that the contract between Baker and Farmer was not written down is crucial. The fact that Baker and Farmer both resided in Jasper County probably is not. Also, note that some judicial opinions *omit* key facts. This means that, as you read opinions, you should be thinking about not only what you do know about the case, but also what you *don't know, but should know.*

After a discussion of the facts you may get some questions about the ***procedural posture*** of the litigation. How did this case get to *this* court? As you know, *Baker* came up through the Illinois appellate courts. The trial judge dismissed the case for want of a written contract. These things, too, are very important. As you will learn in Civil Procedure, the fact that the case was dismissed on this ground means that: (a) there never was a determination of whether there actually was an agreement; and (b) for purposes of resolving the question of law — whether a writing is necessary — all of the facts are assumed to be true as the plaintiff, here Baker, alleged them in his complaint.

After these essential matters are dealt with, the professor will ask: "What's the **issue** in the case?" Here she wants you to describe — again, accurately and concisely — the question(s) of law that the court aimed to resolve with its decision. Each case has its own issue or issues. In *Baker v. Farmer*, for example, one could frame the issue as follows: "whether a contract must be in writing to be enforceable." (In *Smith*, the bonus cases posted on **Open Book Digital**, the issue was whether bartering a gun for drugs counts as "use" of a gun "in relation to" a drug trafficking offense.)

The nifty thing about judicial opinions — what makes them great for training neophyte lawyers in legal analysis — is that students usually don't have to work too hard to identify, at least in a rough way, the issue(s) raised by a given case. This is because opinions will usually do

---

12. In the first days of law school, before you get to the facts, you might spend time on preliminary issues, some of which we have covered in prior chapters. For example, you might be asked to identify the plaintiff and defendant, or appellant and appellee, or you might be asked to explain the information that is provided in the case caption.

it for them. True, a given opinion might not contain a sentence that reads: "The issue in this case is _____." Moreover, at times it can be maddeningly difficult to describe issues with precision. (Was the issue in *Baker* whether *all* contracts must be in writing, or whether *some* contracts must be in writing?) Still, these caveats aside, it is *much* easier to identify issues in opinions than in fact patterns. As we will discuss in a moment, this is one of the key differences between classes and exams.

After the class is clear on the issue(s), the professor moves to the substance of the case: "What did the court *hold*?" Here she wants to know the *rule* that the court used to dispose of the case. Technically, each case is simply a resolution of the parties' dispute: the plaintiff or the defendant wins. But as we saw in *Baker v. Farmer*, the court also will have stated a rule that, when applied to the facts of the case, generates a victory for the prevailing party and a loss for the losing party. (Again, that is to be distinguished from any *dicta* in the case.) One interpretation of the rule in *Baker v. Farmer*—the one you would almost certainly give if you'd read no other cases—is that a contract does not have to be in writing to be enforceable.

Finally—at least for this still preliminary part of class (and why it is preliminary you will see in a moment)—you might get some questions that ask you to discuss *why* the court adopted the rule that it adopted. In other words, you will be asked to discuss the *justification* or rationale for the court's holding. Perhaps this will involve reviewing what the court actually says on this question. Often, however, it will involve a more speculative or open-ended inquiry into *possible* justifications for the holding, including justifications not explicitly stated in the opinion. One could plausibly justify *Baker*'s holding, for example, on the ground that, at least in 1875, a hard-and-fast requirement of a writing to render any agreement enforceable would be impractical—it would introduce too much uncertainty in an era in which a lot of business was conducted on a relatively informal basis.

When you read an assigned opinion, you will sometimes think that the court did a lousy job of justifying its holding. (Perhaps you thought that about the imagined opinion in *Baker*.) It's perfectly fine to have that reaction. Some judicial decisions are badly reasoned, and your professor might occasionally assign you such an opinion just so that you can see what it looks like. But be careful! Before you trash a court's decision you should, in your own mind, make the best case that you can for it. And you should also come to class prepared to give reasons in support of your critical reaction. Simply asserting that "I don't like this decision," or "this doesn't seem fair" won't cut it.

EXPLORING RULES THROUGH HYPOTHETICALS: WHAT YOU'RE HERE TO LEARN

Thus far we have envisioned your professor walking you through a judicial opinion in a somewhat self-contained manner. In other words, the focus of the envisioned discussion has been on the text of an assigned judicial opinion. But at some point in the discussion, usually when you get to the holding of case and its justifications, you and your fellow students will be hit with the dreaded *hypotheticals*. The professor will ask, "Okay, I think we understand how the court reasoned through the case. But what if we change some of the facts? Would the holding still apply? Or, "What if the issue had been presented in a different procedural posture?" Or, "What, if anything, do changes in social and political circumstances tell us about the soundness of the court's holding?"

We saw just how this might go when we discussed *Baker v. Farmer* and *Owner v. Buyer*. Although we presented Owner's case as a 'real' case, we could just as easily have introduced it as a hypothetical. (And, in fact, at the end of Chapter 4 we did give you a hypothetical — namely, a case involving an agreement to sell land for commercial rather than personal use.)

This aspect of class frustrates many students, especially in the early days of law school. For one thing, your professor might ask hypotheticals that seem odd, if not bizarre. (It wouldn't surprise us if you were to encounter some hypothetical questions featuring alien life forms.) For another thing, the professor often won't give definitive answers to the hypotheticals that she raises — or sometimes any answer at all. (A 'hard-core' Socratic professor might ask only questions.) It might seem as if you are being teased or toyed with, and it may be hard to see the point to these exercises.

Given the mystifying aspect of what is going on, your inclination may be to scribble or type as fast as you can, simply trying to get it all down. Unless you are different than most students we encounter, for the first few weeks of law school this is no easy task. You won't understand many of the key terms in the cases, and the professor will be speaking a language you only partially understand. It is like learning how to construct or disassemble an automobile, which would be challenging enough, except the directions are being provided in a foreign language that you barely know. Worse yet, it will feel like there are all sorts of parts and implications of the case that others somehow had seen, but you hadn't. Then, to make matters completely impossible, the professor may not be answering any questions; she seems only to be asking them. Nothing fits together in an evident way, nothing seems clear or certain, there is just a lot of nodding and "what iffing" going on.

Getting dizzy? That's okay. Let's pause and take a breath. Remember what we have been saying from the outset. Law school is not merely about learning rules. It is about learning how to think and argue like a lawyer. *That* is what the questions, the challenges, and the weird hypotheticals are all about. Don't make the mistake of treating these as distractions that are getting in the way of you learning "what you need to know." They *are* what you need to know.

Hypotheticals and their discussion teach you two crucial things. First, they force you to realize that legal rules cannot simply be plucked from a rule book. When you initially read *Baker v. Farmer*, you understandably might have taken it to stand for the rule that *no* agreement needs to be in writing to be enforceable. But then we pushed you to consider additional cases where there were at least plausible arguments for the proposition that *some* agreements do need to be in writing to be enforceable, even if not the agreement in *Baker* itself. However, if some agreements are enforceable without a writing and others are not, which are which? These are the rules you are so hungry to learn when you come to law school. But, as we hope you now see, they may not be presented in a list, one after another. Rather, they are the conclusions you draw only by working through cases and hypotheticals.

The second function of hypotheticals is even more important. Wrestling with hypotheticals teaches you how to make legal arguments, and how to tell good arguments from bad ones. In the case method, the contours and justifications for a rule are explored by making arguments. And as those arguments are made and accepted or rejected (by the professor, by the class, or even just in your own mind), you begin to see what makes an argument strong or weak.

Again, to see this, you need only consider our old friend *Baker v. Farmer.* It is only by reasoning through the imagined "next case" — the case involving an agreement for the sale of land for personal use, or land for commercial use, or for shares of corporate stock, or for something else — that you develop the ability to defend and critique legal rules.

Given the central importance of hypotheticals, you might want to think about how you participate in class. We'll say something about that in the next chapter. First, though, we want to delve a bit more deeply into what is going on in class.

FINDING THE MISSING LINK

We promised we would connect law school classes to exams and to practicing law. If you have been following closely, you will see that we already have. But there's a lot to be said for making explicit what is implicit, so here goes.

Think back to Chapter 1. That is where you learned that in law there are as many arguments as answers. Argument is the name of the game. Arguments are what lawyers make to further their clients' interests. They insist that under the law (the rules) and their client's situation (the facts), the client should prevail.

What you are learning through the case method is how to make good arguments and recognize and avoid bad arguments. Yes, you are here to learn the rules themselves. But as we've said repeatedly, to state basic legal rules (at least roughly) is relatively easy. To *understand* them at the level at which you can bring them to bear for your clients is difficult. Through the process of thinking through hypotheticals, class is where you learn to think like a lawyer in just the way we described in Chapter 1.

As we've said again and again, countless law students get confused and think they are just in class to learn black-letter law. The reason we keep saying it over and over (and over) is precisely because — despite many people telling them this — law students have trouble hearing it. They are desperate to avoid this conclusion. They hold out the hope that all they need to learn are a simple set of rules that are amenable to clear application. But that is not how things are. The main point of the

1L year is to learn the methodology of law: how law works, how to make arguments like lawyers, how to know a good argument from a bad one.

It's more difficult than you might imagine teaching apprentice lawyers which arguments are good, which are bad, and how to tell them apart. This is because the differences are subtle and at times hard to articulate. It is a question of developing *judgment*. To help you do this, what your professors do—and perhaps all they can do—is put you through your paces, and then gently (or not so gently) reinforce or criticize what students say in response. Professors ask questions; students make arguments. The only way you can learn to tell good arguments from bad arguments is from observing the cumulative responses of your professors, and your classmates, to many, many arguments. Or, if the professor is one who only lectures, from listening to what that professor highlights or ignores in the reading, and what arguments he or she makes. That is how you come to understand the structure of legal argument in this specific subject, and more generally.

This point about learning to make arguments through the question-and-answer of the case method yields an interesting point about the rigor of law school. If you've watched a movie like *The Paper Chase*, or heard stories about the 1L year, law professors might seem to be terrifying creatures. The truth is that over time we've become (on average) less so. Law professors of old prided themselves on intimidating their students; today, many of us understand that it is easier to listen, and learn, if one is a bit more relaxed.

And yet, because there is something ineffable about learning what good and bad arguments consist of, we teach the way we do so you can see in action what we can't fully describe. For this reason, very sharp indications of approval and disapproval to answers proffered by students have their value. They make clear the lines between a good and bad argument. To the extent we've softened our responses to students to make them more comfortable—and we'll concede we have—we may not be fully doing the process justice.

All of which is to say: leave your ego behind in class. You're trying to learn by listening to and engaging with the sorts of arguments that work best in the law. This means labeling arguments—*not* students—as better or worse. It is about the argument, not the student, and it is best not to lose sight of that. Indeed, be grateful to your fellow students who are game to have their arguments shot down: they are helping to teach you.

Having explained why and how classes teach you the central skill for law school exams and for being a good lawyer, we want to revisit the puzzle of why exams seem so different and disconnected from classes. We mentioned it to you earlier, briefly, and we've alluded to it throughout. But we're pretty confident that you are now ready to take this on board fully. It's what we realized as we talked with students about their confusion concerning exams. And it highlights what is so important to learn in Part II of this book.

Although law school classes are a terrific vehicle for learning to make arguments, they are not a good venue for learning the most basic and important skill for taking exams: *issue spotting*.

As we told you at the conclusion of Chapter 1, there are four steps to giving legal advice, whether on an exam or as a practicing lawyer. We'll repeat them here: (a) identifying the issue; (b) stating the rule(s) that may apply to that issue; (c) making arguments as to whether and how the rule(s) might apply to the issue; and (d) drawing a conclusion.

These four steps provide the basis for the all-important acronym: IRAC. We are going to begin Part II by discussing this acronym in greater depth. For now we hope you can see clearly that law school classes do a great job of teaching three quarters of the formula: "RAC" without the "I." You learn legal rules, you learn to make arguments about how to interpret and stretch them, and in assessing good and bad arguments, you can evaluate the probabilistic conclusions we discussed in Chapter 1.

Where the case method does a disservice, though, is in spotting issues and prioritizing among them (the latter being what we will later call "issue-sorting"). *This is because judicial decisions typically will frame one issue or a couple of issues for you.* It may be tough specifying those issues precisely, but they are right there, front and center, in the case. What you don't get in class is a fact pattern, in which no one even begins to identify the issues for you. On exams, typically, it is for you to spot and sort the issues.

We get that this drives law students nuts. No worries: we devote a lot of time in both Parts II and III to compensating for it. But we have one more topic to cover before then — the topic of how to get the most out of your classes.

The Bottom Line

☑ Class discussions will focus mainly on the *issue(s)* raised by a judicial opinion, the *rule(s)* adopted to resolve the issue(s), and the *reasoning* behind the rule(s).

☑ Hypotheticals test the limits of rules and their underlying rationales.

☑ Discussions of hypotheticals help you learn you how to make arguments.

☑ Issue-spotting is less emphasized in class, but is at the center of exams.

Chapter 6

GETTING THE MOST OUT OF CLASS

☑ Why the case method?

☑ Briefing cases.

☑ How to participate.

Before turning to an in-depth discussion of how exams work, we want to end this Part by talking a bit about how to go to class. At this point in your educational career, you might think that this is a bit like being offered advice on how to chew gum. But you should resist that impulse: law school classes are different.

We should also warn you that, on this topic — and a few others, such as briefing cases, or outlining for exams — we can get a little preachy. What can we say? We have strong feelings about the right and wrong way to do these things. Or, more accurately, we have strong feelings about *doing* them.

Undoubtedly you'll start law school with the best of intentions: "I'll be a great participant in class; I'll brief all my cases; I'll outline all my classes." (If you don't know what all of this means yet, they're just a way of saying that you are committed to doing your best.) That's the spirit! But here's the thing. Law school is hard work, and most of us get a little lazy at times. Then we run into people who feed our lazier sides by telling us "don't worry about it, there are these great shortcuts."

Shortcuts are things that take you from A (where you are) to B (where you want to go), in a faster or easier fashion, without losing anything important along the way. When it comes to doing well in law school, or on law school exams, or as a practicing lawyer, the shortcuts people will sell you just aren't real. They are a way for other people to feel good about justifying the work they did not do, by telling you that you don't need to do it either.

You'll have to make your own decisions, but we want to set out our view of how things will go well for you. You are probably spending a lot of money to be in law school. We want you to make the most of it, and get the most out of it. Even if it means doing a bit of extra work. Here, we'll explain how—and explode some of those myths you'll hear.

GO TO CLASS

Perhaps you have heard of "the Phantom." During the first semester, he never went to class, and never was seen in the library. He just showed up for exams and nailed them. The thought of the Phantom might have you feeling awed and annoyed. Imagine how he makes us feel! We professors like to believe we add some value.

Here's the good news: The Phantom is an urban legend. Throughout law school, but especially in the first year, what happens in class matters a great deal in how one performs on exams.

Students often make an understandable mistake. They segregate their lives. There are classes, and then there is a beast called exams. So, one goes to class every week, hopefully enjoying the school experience, learning what one can. Then, there comes a time when all that has to stop so one can start to prepare to meet the beast.

Although understandable, this approach is wrong. In truth, the road from class to exams is a continuous highway, everything traveling together in a more or less logical order. Classes feed into outlining, and both feed directly into exams. Exams are the logical conclusion to what you have been doing all semester. That is why *how* you go to school matters a lot, both to exams and to what you get out of law school. In this chapter, we offer some suggestions about an approach to class from day one that can translate into better exam results at the end of that highway.

Before we do, though, here's one thought connected to our insistence that exam taking and law practice are related. Think about the Phantom for a moment. Now, suppose you are a client. You've got a legal problem, something that matters a lot to you, like acquiring a piece of property to build a home, or salvaging the family business, or even a possible prison sentence. You have a choice between two lawyers: one who does all the necessary prep work, even when it is drudgery, and gets to meetings on time, and one who seems quite brilliant, but shows up haphazardly and never quite knows what is going on. Which one are you going to choose? You will want to be the sort of lawyer you'd hire if you needed a lawyer. By the same token, you will want to be the sort of student that will become that lawyer.

Again, we don't mean to sound preachy; we were students, too, and we cut some corners and made mistakes. We confess that there is a bit of "do as we say, not as we do" going on in this chapter. But we were pretty diligent. And most of the people we know who did well in law school were similarly diligent, especially during the 1L year. That is because the 1L year is methodological—learning how to do things— to a greater degree than the following years. Think of all this advice as a chance to learn from our mistakes, and the many we have observed along the way.

PREPARING FOR CLASS: BRIEFING

Class preparation involves reading cases—sometimes several times, especially in the early weeks of your first semester—and "briefing" them. Briefs are just that—brief summaries of the case that will be your guide during class.

When it comes to briefing cases, we can state our position succinctly. *Do it!* There are, and always will be, students who resist this advice. After all, briefing cases is a combination of hard work and tedium, and who wants to sign up for either of those if it's not necessary. But, in our view, it is necessary.

We recognize that this might be a monumental task in the early weeks of school, when you are struggling to get a handle on the distinctive language of the law and have yet to obtain the sort of perspective that will later allow you to separate the important from the unimportant. In the beginning, it might take you too much time to put together the sort of complete brief we are about to describe. That's okay. One way to balance between striving for first-rate briefs and keeping your sanity is to set a time limit for each brief. If you are spending hours briefing a single case, that's not an efficient use of your time. See what you can get together in, say, thirty minutes (not including time spent reading the case). If the brief is incomplete at that point, so be it. You can fill it out later, with the benefit of class discussion.

We do not recommend the collections of ready-made case briefs that are available for purchase. They vary widely in quality, and you should be aware that the person who prepared them could have been working with a different version of the case than you have; cases in casebooks are heavily edited and the authors of casebooks edit them differently. Thus, even if the preparer is terrific, you still might come to class having prepped from a different version of the case than the one that was assigned.

Even if the commercial brief is attuned perfectly to what you have covered, and is well done, it is still a mistake to rely too heavily on it. It's a shortcut that does not take you to your ultimate destination. Students who get seduced by the ease of commercial materials mistakenly suppose that the point of briefing is to collect or have on hand a set of concise case descriptions. If this were all that was going on, however, your professors would just hand out summaries.

It is important that you do the actual work to *prepare* your own summaries. If you were trying to get in better physical condition, it might help to get a book on fitness. But reading the book won't get you fit. Neither will having someone else do your pushups for you. As with physical fitness, so it is with legal reasoning. The value of briefing is in the *doing*, and if you rely solely on commercial outlines, then you aren't doing.

Let's think of this in connection with what lawyers do in their practice. Indeed, this is probably a good place to clear up some confusion you might have about terminology. We suspect you know at this point that, for court proceedings, lawyers prepare and submit to the judge documents called "briefs." And you know that what you are preparing for class are "briefs." But they aren't the same thing. Your class briefs are summaries of cases. Lawyer's briefs are written arguments on behalf of a client that typically cite many cases.

While the two kinds of briefs are quite different, there is a relationship between them. Cases are the building blocks of the common law, and the briefs you prepare for class are *dissections* of those cases so that you learn the rules and how they work. When lawyers write their "argument briefs" they rely on, and in effect have done, "case briefs" of all the cases they cite. Some lawyers, when they do legal research, will actually prepare short case briefs of each relevant case they find, just like you do for class. Then they use their case briefs to write their argument briefs. In fact, back in the day when law books were expensive such that no one had a full set, and there were no electronic databases, lawyers *had* to prepare these case briefs, just like you will, because that was the only way they'd remember the cases when they got back from the law library. Of course, each practicing lawyer will eventually develop his or her own way to summarize quickly. Things are different now; most lawyers have all the cases at their digital fingertips. But the key point is that lawyers know how to take a case apart and put it back together in a way that is helpful, and that is what you need to learn.

The dissection analogy is, we think, terrifically helpful. Medical students have to learn anatomy. They buy big fat books with lots of pictures of the human body in them, and they memorize, memorize, memorize. Then, they dissect. They learn to take apart the human body and actually gain exposure to those body parts they have memorized. They spend years becoming familiar with those parts by examining them over and over. Now, suppose you are a patient of a doctor and that doctor is going to do something with your body. Would you want a doctor who just learned from those books, and then dug into your body? We're guessing the answer is no: You would want someone with experience dissecting, and experience practicing with those body parts (under supervision).

Briefing cases is like dissection and supervised practice for medical students. Briefing your cases and then discussing those briefs in class is the chief way you are going to learn how to *do* law. It will also help you learn the substance of the law, of course. But as you now know, the most important thing you are learning in the 1L year is how to take apart and put together legal doctrine and legal arguments as lawyers do. The way you are going to really learn this skill is by dissecting the cases when you write your briefs, not only to learn what the cases say, but to learn how they fit together, so that you can thereafter pick up any case in any area of the law and make the most of it for your client.

A MODEL FOR CASE BRIEFS

When you brief cases you are doing double duty. You are learning the law, but you are also practicing, indirectly, for exams. A good case brief is ultimately an exercise in legal reasoning. Here we're going to describe for you a model for briefing cases. The model is hardly original to us — in fact, it is quite standard. Where we may be able to add some value is in explaining its features.

Facts. As you begin to brief, ask yourself: What is the "story" at the heart of a judicial opinion? What facts are (or are not) provided? Can you summarize them as succinctly (or more succinctly) than the court? Of course, being more concise than the court means omitting stuff you've read. Which facts were key to the ultimate outcome and which turned out not to be germane? You will find that questions like these are exactly what motivate the hypotheticals your professor is going to ask about the case.

Procedural posture. How did the case come to this court and what court is it precisely? This is critically important not only for explaining the context in which rules are made and applied, but also knowing how much authority the case has. Is this a case from a trial court that exemplifies a rule but carries less binding authority? Or is this a U.S. Supreme Court decision that every other court must follow? Did the parties stipulate to certain facts at this stage, or were factual issues contested and resolved by a fact-finder? Is the court declining to decide the merits of an issue because of the procedural posture?

Issue. What is (are) the legal question(s) at the heart of the case? What was it the parties asked the court to resolve? Stating legal issues with precision is surprisingly difficult. Often the best way to do so is by starting with the term "whether." (For example, in *Baker v. Farmer* from Chapter 4, the issue might be described as "whether an oral agreement can be enforced in court.") Not only is the professor going to demand this of you in class, but you are going to do it again and again on exams (and as a lawyer). Doing it in your briefs is how you get good at it.

Judgment. Who won? What did they win? A motion to suppress evidence? Damages? An acquittal? This might seem too obvious to mention, but it is nonetheless critical to understanding the rule. Put it in your brief.

Holding/Rule. What is the legal rule that was relied on to resolve the legal issue? This is ultimately what you came for. And yet it is sometimes remarkably difficult to pry a rule out of a case. It will take a lot of practice before your dissection easily yields precise and accurate statements of rules. Even then, it will become clear enough in class that rules mutate: They are refined from case to case as they are applied to new facts.

Rationale. Here you distill in a sentence or two the reasoning that the court used to get to its rule and its conclusion. This can be tedious, but it is critically important. If a rule seems to defeat its rationale as applied in a next case (or hypothetical), then maybe the rule needs to be refined or revised. A lot of what is going to happen in class is exploring the rationales for rules, and whether those rationales collapse under the pressure of new facts.

Briefing is not an exercise in rote copying from the case. It is a test of comprehension and of method. As you do it, you should be asking yourself lots of questions. For example, what legal issues are raised by the facts? Do you understand why the court framed the issues as it did? If one or another key fact were changed, would that affect your analysis of the issues in the case? Why? Is this a good rule? Do you see some potential for harm in it? Can you think of a better rule? Would that rule accommodate other fact circumstances you can think of? What policy considerations support or cast doubt on the rules?

BE ACTIVE IN CLASS

Both class and briefing require your active participation. The work you do when you brief a case is exactly what you will do as a lawyer, and this is what you will do on your exams. Moreover, each effort at briefing is not only a mini-practice exam, it's an opportunity for feedback. If you brief cases before class, then class will provide an occasion to go over the work you did, and for you to self-grade it.

The same is true of class discussion. The purpose of the Socratic method is to allow everyone in class to participate in the exercise of thinking through the case and its ramifications. Sure, one student (or a few) and the professor will be doing it aloud. But while they are, you should not only be listening closely and taking notes, you should be playing along in your head. Again, students get confused about this. They think that if they are not on call, their job is just to scribble everything down. But that is wrong. What matters most is participating actively in class even if you are not speaking.

Try to answer a question before the student who is on call does. See if your answer is the same. See how the professor reacts. Does the discussion track what you wrote in your brief? Or is it framed differently, focusing on things you missed or that seemed to you at the time of briefing unimportant or mysterious? The point is not that a good brief will anticipate or track all the issues that get discussed in class — that is asking too much of a brief, and expecting too little of class. Rather, a sign of a good brief is if it flags, perhaps only imprecisely, some of the issues on which class discussion focuses.

The Socratic method centrally is about *dialogue*: actual dialogue between professor and students, as well as metaphoric dialogue between the members of the class and the assigned materials. The learning in a law school class is to be found all around you; it is not just located at the front of the room. Directly and indirectly, you will learn a lot from your classmates. You might think that one of them has asked a silly question, only to be surprised to see the professor take it up in earnest. If so, you will need to rethink why you assumed the question was silly. You might think that another student has answered a question correctly, only to see the professor dismiss it as unsatisfactory. Again, time to review. And, of course, you might disagree with your fellow students about some case, issue, rule, or policy. Depending on how your professor runs the class, you might have an occasion in class to engage with those of your colleagues with whom you disagree, and that is likely to be an illuminating engagement.

Here's where your brief interacts with class itself. Briefing is not just preparation to sit and listen in class. Think of in-class discussion of cases that you have briefed as roughly akin to middle-school classes in which the teacher reviews the previous night's homework assignment. Ideally, your brief will closely track class discussion. But if not, that's okay. Just make sure that you understand why your "homework" turned out to be not quite right. Perhaps you'll even want to mark up your brief as class discussion proceeds, noting where you missed a key fact, framed an issue badly, or misunderstood a rule or its implications. The time you take to do this will be well spent.

TECHNOLOGY AND PARTICIPATION

Even into the 1960s, law students (then almost exclusively white and male) were expected to show up to class dressed in suits. Drinking coffee was not an option. Laptops, PowerPoint, and the Internet were, at best, a glimmer in the eye of research scientists or science-fiction writers. Cold-calling was the name of the game. The on-call student was instructed to stand up so that he could receive a merciless interrogation.

Today there are plenty of professors who still cold-call on their students. But otherwise, the world of the law school classroom has changed dramatically, and generally for the better (we think). The classroom of today is enlivened and enriched by a much more diverse student body. Probably you get to roll out of bed and head to class in sweats, with a fancy coffee drink in hand. Most law professors have moved toward less fearsome pedagogic methods. As we explained last chapter, the latter is in our view mostly a positive development; we cold-call but we also work hard not to terrorize, appreciating how difficult it is for anyone to learn while in a panic. Still, we recognize that there is room for — and indeed benefits to students that flow from — a range of teaching methods and styles. You are probably going to be plenty terrified the first time you negotiate a deal on your own, or stand in front of judges, believe us. And you have to make cogent arguments nonetheless.

A less obviously salutary development is the increasing presence — in some instances domination — of technology. Here we have in mind the all-pervasive laptops and tablets. Some professors allow them, others don't. Our view is that, even when their use is allowed, you should think carefully about whether and how you are going to use them. We are big fans of the new technology, but there are some potential downsides that you need to consider.

First, there is the problem of distraction. If you have an electronic device in front of you, that means you probably have access to the Internet, and if you have access to the Internet you have access to messaging, e-mail, social networking, shopping, gaming, YouTube, and so on. Your intentions might be pure—you might be thinking to yourself that you will only check your messages during a slow moment of class—but you are fighting a losing battle against overwhelming physical and psychological forces. Let's face it, when a notification pops up on your screen, or when a video beckons, you are going to be sucked in. The most enthralling teacher in the world can't compete with the Siren-like powers of electronic media. We say this not because we think law students are immature. We say this because we think law students are human. So are we. As audience members at academic conferences, we try not to turn on our tablets because we know we will soon start answering our e-mail, and that is not the point of attending a conference.

Indeed, on the issue of technology in the classroom, we are unyielding. One of us (Friedman) decrees the "death penalty" for students caught online in class. He tries generally to be mellow about rules and their enforcement, within the demands of the profession itself. But he also tends to wander the room while he teaches, and if he sees the Web or e-mail on a student's screen, fuhgeddaboutit. You can pack up your stuff and leave: The grade is F, thanks. Why is he so hardcore about this? Because it is impossible to participate in the way we described earlier while multitasking. *Impossible*. Yes, we live in a multitasking world. But you cannot seriously engage in a dialogue while you're doing something else. You just can't. If you don't do well in your 1L year and wonder what happened, the first question you should ask yourself is if you were active in class in the way we described, or were instead attending to e-stuff.

We also feel obliged to let you in on a secret, one that you probably know already, at some level. To the extent you use class time for e-mail or entertainment, you are not actually sparing yourself the effort required for thinking and learning. You are merely time shifting, like when you "DVR" a television program. Instead of doing the work in class, you are now going to have to do it after class, most likely in those hyper-hectic weeks leading up to exams. If you think about it, this makes no sense. You are postponing hard work from a less stressful time to a more stressful one. Oh and, by the way, you are helping yourself to a pretty lame form of downtime. Do you really want to spend your scarce "me-time" budget in class? Surely you can think of better places and better ways to amuse yourself.

Second, even when they are not causing distraction, electronics invite a form of classroom participation that is inimical to learning what you need to learn to do well on your exams. When students have laptops in front of them, they tend to fall into the mode of writing down everything that happens in class. You are training to be a lawyer, not a stenographer. Typing out, more or less verbatim, the words coming out of your professor's mouth, is not going to do you a lot of good. What class time adds to your legal education is not primarily information — although certainly some will be imparted. Rather, as we have explained repeatedly, you are being taught how to spot, frame, and think through issues. To get a feel for those skills requires you to listen and think simultaneously, not merely to record. As we have said, even when you are not on-call or speaking, you need to be an active, engaged, self-conscious participant who pays attention to the interactions between your professors and your fellow students. Why is the professor pushing so hard on that question? Why was she not satisfied with the answer given? On what grounds is she defending or criticizing the decisions we are reading? What's the point of her asking that weird hypothetical?

There's a related point to be made here about the problem of in-class stenography. The thought that one's principal task is to record information provided by the professor presupposes that legal education involves a one-way transmission process: Professor speaks, students absorb. Perhaps you will encounter some law professors who teach this way. But we hope that it is clear by now this is not the point of the Socratic method. Rather, we are trying to teach you by example the judgment needed to tell good arguments from bad ones, the skill of practicing lawyers and expert exam takers.

Now, we make one concession to technology. What technology can offer is the ability to organize and synthesize in just the way we say you will have to for your outline. There is something elegant about having all your materials in bits and bytes so you can cut and paste, and so you can quickly consult your case and your brief and maybe even last week's notes. We can see the advantages.

Still, we really do suggest you give the issue thought. We hope you don't think we are Luddites. Just like you, we live much of our lives on computers and dealing with technology. But we can't walk into the classroom and type and teach at the same time. And you can't type frantically and learn. Try some experiments. Trade off with a buddy on 'typing duty'. See which way you learn best. Organize in groups to do this.

But whatever you do, be present in class. You are probably paying insanely good money for this, and the classroom give-and-take is what is at the heart of what you are paying for. You aren't going to get the judgment to think like a lawyer in any other way.

GUNNERS

Those of your classmates with their hands in the air all the time have traditionally been called "gunners" and most of you do your best to avoid this label, even at the cost of not putting your arm in the air when you have a question, or something to contribute. We should say up front that we intensely dislike the tendency of law students to divide the world into regular students and gunners. (Yes, folks, it's time to move past high school.) Class is not a game in which a small group performs and everyone else tunes out, or makes fun of those who raise their hands and speak.

One of our overarching themes is that law school actually has a lot to do with law practice. Nowhere is this truer than when it comes to class participation. You should relish the opportunity to participate, either when you are called on or when you volunteer, because that is what you are going to be doing as a lawyer. If you are thinking that the "public speaking" aspect of law is only for courtroom litigators, you are wrong. Whether they are doing deals, arbitrating disputes, or persuading regulators, all lawyers spend a good chunk of their time talking about the law. And guess what? Senior lawyers and clients notice useful contributions to conversations. If you expect them to throw good work your way, you are going to have to show them that your head is in the game, and that you have valuable things to say. Now is the time to begin to get the hang of it. Of course that doesn't mean you need to or should raise your hand every time a professor directs a question to the class. Pick your spots. But to give up this opportunity is to squander your tuition dollars.

The classroom is an intellectual community. Everyone is in it together. If you are the person who doesn't participate, you are free-riding. If you are someone who can't stop interjecting, you are crowding out your colleagues. If you lean to the quiet side, force yourself to do your part, put your hand in the air a bit more often. And if you are the one sitting in the front row with your hand up all the time, here's a suggestion: Your classmates probably don't want to hear from you *that* much. The key here is the happy medium, with everyone playing a part.

Finally, be strategic. When you get yourself out of law school you will want a job. Maybe a clerkship. You are going to need reference letters. Who is going to write them? The professor at the front of the room calling on you, that's who. We tell our students that sitting quietly in class all semester and then getting an A on the exam — assuming an A is what they get — is not going to make for strong references. It is just human nature: Professors really get behind students who take the endeavor seriously. One can over-participate as well as under-participate, to be sure. (We get annoyed at people with their hand up constantly, too.) What we are looking for are smart, engaged, mature people with good judgment. So are employers. Now is the time to work on being that sort of person.

"PSYCHING" THE PROF

The first-year law school curriculum is fairly standardized. Some schools include a course on legal methods, or legislation and regulation; others don't. Some have spring electives; others don't. But pretty much everywhere, you are going to be taking classes in Civil Procedure, Contracts, Criminal Law, Property, and Torts. And yet if you happen to talk about one of these core courses to a friend in another section at your school, or at another school, you will likely discover that he or she is learning it differently than you are. The syllabus for your Torts class includes week after week on negligence and strict liability, and only a week at the very end of class on intentional torts. Your friend's Tort class starts with a month on intentional torts. Your Civil Procedure class is all about pleading, discovery, joinder, and motion practice, with passing mention of personal and subject-matter jurisdiction. Your friend's is the opposite. That there is such variation is neither surprising nor a cause for concern. Each of these subjects is too complex to cover in its entirety in a single course, and different choices can reasonably be made about what will constitute representative and pedagogically useful materials. (Remember, the method you are learning is as important as the substance.)

You can help yourself, though, by thinking about why your professor has chosen to present the subject of a particular class in the way in which she has presented it. It will pay to make an effort to get inside the head of your professor — to get a sense of how he thinks about the subject.

Different professors come to their courses with different training, different interests, and different aspirations. Some will want only to teach particular doctrines or rules as discrete, self-contained units. Others will have a broad "take" on the subject, a view of how all of its parts fit together as pieces in an intricate puzzle (e.g., Criminal Law is best understood as a scheme for deterring antisocial conduct, not as punishing culpable wrongdoing). Others will emphasize a special set of tools to be used in analyzing problems within the field (e.g., to understand Contracts, one must understand and apply principles of microeconomics). Others will highlight recurring themes (e.g., Torts teaches us first and foremost about the open-endedness and malleability of legal rules).

For each of your classes you should work to get a sense of where your professor is coming from. We recommend this in part because knowing the law requires recognizing forests as well as trees: Arguments about particular issues or doctrines in criminal law connect to larger views about what criminal law is, and what it is for. We also recommend it because it will probably give you some guidance on how to focus your efforts at studying. If you hear from your Constitutional Law professor regular expressions of concern about judicial subjectivity and the value of interpretive approaches that (arguably) constrain discretion, such as textualism or original- ism, then you probably can expect to get a set of questions that invite you to discuss the role of discretion in courts' constitutional decisions, and perhaps the legitimacy of the institution of judicial review. Likewise, if you have a Contracts professor who is fond of pointing out ways in which doctrine does or does not permit the allocation of scarce resources to the user who most highly values them, you can expect that you might be asked to argue for or against the application of a given rule on the ground of efficiency.

We are not advocating that you try to mimic or parrot your profes- sor on her exam. She might be unimpressed to see a version of her own thoughts being thrown back at her. Rather, we mean that you ought to engage issues and questions that your professor explicitly or implicitly highlighted during the semester as central to the subject. To do so is to demonstrate that you have a sense of the forest as well as the trees. That sort of showing might earn you some exam points in its own right. It might also give the professor some confidence that you have a handle on the subject, which in turn might get you the benefit of the doubt when she is trying to determine how to score particular parts of your answers.

OH, AND HAVE FUN

1Ls often view the classroom experience with stress and terror. 3Ls sometimes harbor a sense of monotony and boredom. Both extremes are a mistake. Be engaged. Make your professors and your classmates help you. Interact with the material; don't expect it to just happen to you. Prepare for class, milk class for all you can, reflect after class on how you can do better. Experience tells us you are going to be sitting in our office in fifteen years reminiscing about how great that classroom experience was. Why wait? Enjoy it now.

The Bottom Line

- ☑ Be "present" in class.
- ☑ Brief cases.
- ☑ Look and listen for the right things in class; don't transcribe.
- ☑ Be thoughtful about technology (maybe even skip it).
- ☑ Try to adopt the perspective of the professor: What's his or her take on the subject?

PART II

EXAMS 101: NO POINTS LEFT BEHIND

Chapter 7

IRAC: A FRAMEWORK FOR ANALYSIS

☑ IRAC is a framework for legal analysis.

☑ IRAC divides legal analysis into four steps: Issue, Rule, Analysis (a.k.a. Application), Conclusion.

☑ Follow IRAC's steps to succeed on exams.

We've spent some time on classes. Now it's time to focus on exams: what they are testing for, and how to tackle them.

In this, the first chapter of Part Two of the book, we are going to describe in more detail something we've already discussed: IRAC. IRAC is often encountered in legal writing courses, where it is presented as a framework for organizing the legal analysis contained in a memo or brief. Unsurprisingly, it's equally useful as a framework for analyzing exam questions. The next chapter will provide you with a simple analogy that will help you grasp what law school exams are all about. Then, in the remainder of Part Two, we are going to take apart the exam-taking process in meticulous detail.

By way of reminder, IRAC stands for: **Issue, Rule, Analysis,** and **Conclusion.** (Sometimes people say the "A" stands for "Application," because you are applying the facts of the case to the applicable legal rule, to make legal arguments. "A" can also be said to stand for "Arguments.")

The key to doing well on exams rests in learning how to *use* IRAC. In the context of exam-taking, you will need to demonstrate that you can: (1) *identify and frame the issue(s)* posed by the fact pattern; (2) *identify as relevant* (and sometimes make the case for the use of) one or more legal rules that will govern the resolution of the issues that you have identified; (3) *argue cogently about how the rules apply to the issues raised by the facts*; and (4) accurately *assess the likelihood* of a given argument prevailing. Moreover, at each step, you must be prepared to anticipate and respond to analysis that runs counter to your own. This is what it means to "think like a lawyer" and this is what will get you points on your exam answers.

In this chapter, we are going to keep the discussion of IRAC very simple — refinements will come later. To see how it works, let's return to a basic claim of this book: Taking exams is like practicing law. In a law school essay exam, just as in law practice, you typically start with a problem presented in narrative form. Your job is to *translate* that narrative using the concepts and categories of the law. A lawyer cannot give a client legal advice until she specifies precisely what the question is that the client needs answered. But this question must be framed and resolved through the use of legal concepts and rules.

Here's an analogy that might help to put exam-taking (and legal reasoning) in perspective. In one way, although not in others, law practice and law school exams resemble word problems on a middle-school math test. You remember those, right?

> Jill leaves the train station on a train heading east at an average speed of 40 mph. Julie leaves an hour later from the same station heading west at 50 mph. At what point in time will they be equidistant from the station?

Now you've probably heard from your professors — and you have definitely heard from us — that the application of legal rules differs fundamentally from the application of basic math rules. Basic math is mechanical and, if the problem is set up properly, generates a right answer. Rule application in law, on the other hand, requires judgment and argumentation and permits multiple plausible answers. And yet, law practice and law exams are like word problems in the following respect: *The crucial first step is to take a problem phrased in ordinary English and translate it into a specialized language that has been developed to enable more precise analysis.*[13]

---

13. As we discuss later, law school exams are like math word problems in a second respect; namely, it is very important to not simply provide answers but to "show your work."

In math, the need for translation is obvious. This is because its specialized language looks so different from ordinary English, consisting as it does of symbols and formulae (e.g., $R \times T = D$, where R is rate, T is time, and D is distance). In law, the need for translation is sometimes equally apparent: We doubt you had much occasion to use the word "estoppel" or "escheat" before attending law school. (Or even the word "egregious," which seems quickly to become every law student's favorite word to bring home to everyday life.) Often, however, the need for translation is obscured because lawyers have taken a standard English word—"nuisance," for example—and infused it with a special and relatively precise meaning. Law school, particularly the first year, immerses you in the specialized language of the law so that you can properly analyze real-world problems. What your professors want to see from you on your exams is that you are mastering the language of the law. Keeping IRAC in mind will allow you to demonstrate that you have.

"I" IS FOR ISSUE (OR ISSUES)

As you understand by now, the biggest difference between law school classes taught via the case method, and law school exams, is that, as you read cases, the issue is relatively apparent, while in taking law school exams, spotting issues is perhaps the hardest task. That is why, although we are going to cover all of IRAC in this and the successive chapters, we are going to give most attention to issue spotting.

Let's begin with a simple scenario. (We realize many of you have not yet begun law school, so we are keeping the examples here easy. Still, as we mentioned earlier, law school is a full immersion experience. Might as well get started now!) Imagine you are a newly hired associate at a small law firm. You arrive at the firm, are shown your desk, the coffee room, and the restrooms. Now what? For many new lawyers, their first assignment will involve a request from another lawyer to do some research. For example, one of your colleagues might call you into her office and tell you something like this.

SEYLA'S STORY

We have a client named Seyla who lives on a two-acre parcel of land. This parcel at one time formed half of a four-acre parcel. However, twenty years ago, Seyla sold the other half of that larger parcel to Trace, the person who is now her next-door neighbor. Trace still owns that land today.

Sometime after the division of the parcel, maybe ten or twelve years ago, Trace began regularly driving his pick-up truck across one corner of Seyla's property to a nearby public road. He has done this often enough that the route is now marked by a dirt path. It turns out that there is another dirt path that Trace could use to gain access to the same public road. This other path is located entirely on his property, and does not cut across Seyla's. But this path feeds into the public road awkwardly, and so Trace does not like to use it.

Seyla tells us that she has never explicitly given Trace permission to use the dirt path cutting across her property. On the other hand, she also tells us that she has not been particularly bothered by his doing so. (She has no use for the path because she has a separate driveway that connects to the public road at a different point.) According to her recollection, Trace has used the path pretty regularly, although she remembers that there was a six-month period a couple of years back in which he could not have been using it because he was recovering from a serious illness and was housebound.

Seyla recently received an inquiry from a prospective buyer of her property. The prospective buyer noticed the dirt path running across Seyla's parcel, and wants to know if Trace will be legally entitled to use it even after the sale of the parcel. I'm going to give you some documents pertaining to the history of the property. Please write a memo analyzing whether Trace has an entitlement to use the road that will survive Seyla's sale of her property.

There it is: your first legal assignment! Notice that, in giving you this assignment, your colleague has said nothing about how to look for the answer to the question that she has posed. She's relying on you to figure that out. This is because the expertise of lawyers, even novice lawyers, begins with recognizing how to translate real-world problems into the language of the law. And just as this is always the lawyer's first step, it's also the first step for the law student on an exam. To "issue-spot" is to translate narratives into the language of the law. As we've explained, traditional law school exams are a bundle of legal issues contained within fact patterns that are stylized versions of the sort of stories and problems that real clients present to real lawyers.

So what are the legal issues raised by the assignment just imagined? If you are reading this with some Property classes under your belt, you might recognize that Seyla's situation calls for the application of the law of property. (No worries if you haven't; our explanation here will speak for itself.) Specifically, it raises the issue of whether Trace has acquired an *easement* appurtenant to his land—a "use-right" that is as much a part of his ownership of his property as his right to exclude others—or whether it is a mere license (or permission) granted by Seyla that can she can revoke at any time. In short, if it is an easement rather than a license, Trace's right to use the road will continue even after Seyla's sale of her property.

"R" IS FOR RULE

After a lawyer identifies the issue or issues presented by a client's story, the next thing she needs to do is determine the rule or rules that provide the frame for the resolution of the issue. These are the rules that you learn in your classes. They are the same rules that often are summarized in treatises and study aids. A real lawyer might not know the precise rules that apply to a particular client's problem, but she knows where to look for them—that is, how to do the legal research necessary to find the applicable rule(s). On exams, however, you will typically not be asked to do legal research. Rather, you are simply expected to demonstrate how the rules you learned during the semester apply to the issues you identify.

Sometimes the identification of the relevant rule will be very straightforward. In other instances, however, the job of identifying the relevant legal rule will be more difficult. Seyla's story invites application of a particular rule for determining whether an easement has been established; namely, the rule governing "prescriptive easements."[14] According to a common formulation of this rule, the user of a portion of another's property is said to gain an easement by prescription if that use is: (1) without the permission of the owner of the land being used; (2) known to the owner; and (3) open, continuous, and under a claim of right for a specified period of time (the "prescription period").

Note how the test has three "elements." It is very common for legal rules to take a multi-step form like this. As a new attorney, you wouldn't necessarily be expected to have this rule at your fingertips, although as a student taking a Property exam you might well be. Regardless, you will be expected to have enough of an understanding of property law to know that there are rules governing the formation of easements that apply to situations like the one facing Seyla.

"A" IS FOR ANALYSIS (or APPLICATION)

Let us suppose that you have properly isolated and defined an issue, and located a rule (or set of rules) that seems to speak to the issue. By now you surely understand that if there is one thing your professors will be looking for you to demonstrate, it is awareness that rule application is typically not mechanical or automatic. That there are arguments to be made; commonly, arguments on both sides.

Sometimes, life for the legal analyst is simple. For example, as you might have learned in Torts, the common law in many states includes a rule stating that a child under seven years of age is — so far as the law is

---

14. As this example indicates, we are using the term *rule* as shorthand for "rule or standard." If you haven't already, you will soon learn that nothing so engages the attention of law professors as the distinction between rules (which are relatively clear and specific) and standards (which are relatively open-ended and ambiguous). Whatever the importance of this distinction in other contexts, it is not important for present purposes. Pretty much everything we say about rules applies to standards as well.

concerned—incapable of acting negligently. Thus, if a suit is brought against a child alleging that the child committed the tort of negligence, and if her birth certificate establishes that his age at the time of the allegedly careless acts was four, then there's really nothing for the trial judge to do but to grant the defendant's motion to dismiss. (Even here, the trial judge might think that the rule is so foolish, or otherwise so ripe for rejection, that she could conceivably refuse to apply it. Perhaps more appropriately she might write an opinion inviting her jurisdiction's high court or legislature to overturn it.)

However, it is more often the case—particularly on law school exams—that you will be confronted with some combination of easy and difficult instances of law application. Seyla's story offers some of each. For example, imagine that you are told in the instructions to your Property exam that the prescription period for easements is ten years. The application of that facet of the rule to the facts of Seyla's case would seem to be simple. The facts of the problem seem to make clear Trace has been driving across Seyla's land for at least ten years. On the other hand, there'd be more of a judgment call to make as to whether the six-month period in which Trace ceased to use the dirt road because of his illness counts as an "interruption" that would defeat his claim to an easement. (In other situations, discussed in later chapters, there will be uncertainty—and hence a need for argument—as to which of two or more rules to apply.)

As we stress in the subsequent chapters, when it comes to rule application, your professors are typically going to expect you to make arguments on both sides of the issue to which the rule is being applied. This, too, mirrors actual law practice. Even when you are representing one side or another to a transaction or dispute, to do so effectively you must anticipate and develop responses to the other side's arguments. That is precisely why so much of the classroom experience in the first year is given over to developing and making arguments on both sides of a legal question.

"C" IS FOR CONCLUSION

Finally, there is the "conclusion." We put quotes around this word because it is so often the case on law school exams—as in the real world—that there is no pat answer to a legal question. Sometimes one argument is obviously stronger than another, whereas at other times a question will be closer. Even if questions with clear answers predominate in the real world, in the sense that many legal disputes are resolved before there is litigation, they certainly do not on exams. Professors almost always include a host of issues that have respectable arguments on both sides. This is why your conclusions will and should typically be expressed in qualified or probabilistic terms. In analyzing the easement issue in Seyla's case, for example, one might conclude by saying something like this: "It is likely that the issue of whether Trace has gained a prescriptive easement to use the road running across Seyla's land will need to be resolved by a jury, which will have to determine, for example, whether the facts support the conclusion that Trace's use of the road was uninterrupted."

IRAC REFINED

We've now run through a very simple application of IRAC, just to give you a feel for the analytic framework it provides. The following chapters focus more intensively on each IRAC element as it applies in exam settings, and demonstrate in more concrete ways, and more complex settings, how to use IRAC to hit bumpers. But first we want to help you appreciate what is really expected of you on your exams. The best way to do that, we have found, is through a metaphor that might seem a little odd at first, but actually makes a lot of sense . . . .

The Bottom Line

☑ IRAC: Issue, Rule, Analysis, Conclusion.

☑ IRAC is a framework, not a formula: It *guides* analysis.

☑ Use IRAC to break down and analyze fact patterns.

Chapter 8

THE PINBALL METHOD OF EXAM TAKING

☑ Taking exams is like playing pinball: You score only when you hit the bumpers.

☑ In exams, you hit bumpers by using the elements of IRAC.

☑ Find the bumpers and "hit" (i.e., analyze) them; everything else is wasted time and effort.

As we said at the outset, we're not much for cute tricks or shortcuts. At the same time, though, our approach to exam taking relies on a few simple ideas and methods. We often illustrate them by using an analogy or metaphor, something easy to remember. For example, in the last chapter we compared an exam to a simple mathematical word problem to make the point about the importance of translating ordinary language into law.

We are about to offer you our most important analogy. This analogy, which will recur throughout the remainder of the book, involves the game of pinball. Pinball was and is an arcade game, although now of course it comes in digital versions. For those readers unfamiliar with pinball, we'll provide a (clunky) description. But we encourage you to try it for yourself—it's fun!! **Open Book Digital** has an example of a pinball app—check it out!

As we proceed with the pinball analogy, please keep in mind that it is only an analogy. We don't think that law school exams are games.

Quite the opposite: This book is premised on the idea that exams test for real abilities that figure centrally in the actual practice of law. (Also, for readers with two left thumbs, no worries. You don't have to be an actual pinball wizard to ace your exams.) Still, we think this analogy tells you something extremely important about exam taking, something—in our experience—students often miss.

HOW PLAYING PINBALL IS LIKE TAKING LAW SCHOOL ESSAY EXAMS

In arcade pinball, the player pulls back a handle connected to a spring-loaded plunger and then lets go, which propels a small metal ball to the top of a tilted playing field sitting under a pane of glass. (There's a picture below, one of many illustrations here by the talented Claire Suni, formerly a Harvard law student and now a practicing lawyer.) The ball then rolls down the field with the pleasant whirring sound of metal on wood. The field is cluttered with "bumpers"—targets that the ball hits, and then bounces off of. When the ball hits a bumper, the machine makes some sort of noise—beeps or clangs or chirps or jangles—and the player scores points. But beware! Gravity is always pulling the ball downward. At the bottom of the field, in the middle, there is an open hole. When the ball goes through that space it disappears into the bottom of the machine, and your turn is over. (Usually you get multiple turns per game.)

So where's the skill component? You have some control over where the ball goes. There are two push-button flippers on either side of the space that "guard" it, which you operate by pressing buttons on the sides of the pinball machine. As the ball rolls toward the hole, you try to press the buttons that control the flippers at just the right time, so that one or both of them flip the ball back up into the playing field, where it can hit more bumpers and you score more points. Got it?

Here's the thing about pinball, and the reason why we rely so heavily on this analogy. *The pinball player scores points **only** by hitting the bumpers.* Given the description we have provided, it

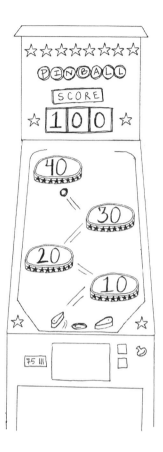

would have been perfectly reasonable for a person unfamiliar with pinball to believe that the goal is to keep the ball from going down past the flippers for as long as possible. But it isn't. The only reason not to let the ball go down into the machine is so that one can continue to hit bumpers. On a well-constructed pinball machine, the ball can wander around a great deal without hitting bumpers, but hitting bumpers is all that matters in the game of pinball.

What goes for pinball goes for exams. *Nothing matters but hitting the bumpers!* This is the only way to score points. There are certain things the professor is looking for. When you write about them, you score points. When you don't, no points are given. We will talk more about how professors go about scoring exams in a moment, and, as we noted earlier, on **Open Book Digital,** you can find actual graded law school exam answers. For now, though, this is the fundamental lesson: Points are given only for hitting the bumpers that the professor has built into the fact pattern.

This may seem obvious to you, but believe us: it isn't. Students frequently spend precious exam time (and precious words if the exam is one that limits your word count) talking about things that do not constitute bumpers. We're about to tell you what counts and what doesn't but we want to say it one more time: *You only get points for hitting bumpers.*

WHAT COUNTS AS HITTING A BUMPER

Now we come to that moment you've been waiting for: when taking an exam, what counts as hitting a bumper? How do you hit them?

There's a short answer and a long answer. Here's the short answer (drum roll, please) . . . It's IRAC.

We can see you sitting there scratching your head in frustration. You've read this far to hear us say IRAC? That's the big secret?! Oh please.

Don't go away yet! We warned you that there is no magic here. Remember the conclusion of the old movie, *The Wizard of Oz?* There was no magic there either, but things worked out just fine. To paraphrase Glenda the Good Witch, you've always had within you the power to do well on exams. Our job is to help you to see that everything you need is already here, right in your own "backyard."

But we do want to say one more time the most important of things, which is that if this seems obvious to you now, be careful. Again, as much as this may seem obvious to everyone, we promise you that, come exams, this is one of the first things that goes out the window. Every moment that you are taking an exam, you should be asking yourself: am I using IRAC or doing something else? Because when we grade the exams of our lovely and excellent students, we spend lots of time reading something else.

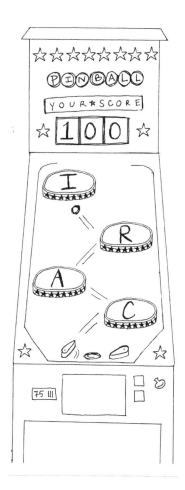

WHAT DOES NOT COUNT IN TAKING EXAMS

It will help if we take a moment to tell you some things that do not matter when taking exams. We can think of three important ones.

First, it does not matter, in and of itself, how quickly or slowly you finish an exam (although you cannot go over the time limit, of course). You should see this by now, but it bears emphasis. Someone might find an exam easy and complete a scheduled four-hour exam in three hours. This is not a wise idea, though. Who finishes first does not matter, only how many bumpers they hit. You can always take that extra time looking for more issues to discuss or more arguments you have not made.

Second, it does not matter how many words or pages you write (again, subject to the need to comply with word or page limits). A very long exam answer might score poorly, and a short one could score well, simply because the short answer is constantly hitting bumpers. In fact, *writing too much on any given issue on an exam can be counterproductive*, a point to which we will return later. Most professors will only award so many points for any given aspect of an exam question. Typically, all those points can be obtained with a few well-chosen words or sentences. Write anything else and you are using words and time to no good end. Particularly in a word-limited or time-limited exam, lengthy explication is not always best.

Finally, and perhaps most important, it does not matter how brilliant your exam is in some abstract sense. One exam could be full of truly stunning insight about the world and the law; another might be mundane. But mundane might well score higher if that answer addresses all the things the professor is looking for. Hitting the bumpers is everything.

BUMPERS ARE SPECIFICS

There's nothing generalized or abstract about bumpers. Professors typically grade using some sort of key. They are looking to find some very specific things in your exam answer.

To see what might be unique about law school exams, start by thinking about certain kinds of exam answers you wrote in college. These likely were quite different from exam answers that follow the approach outlined in this book. In college, you were perhaps often asked to assimilate huge amounts of information. In turn, you might well have been rewarded on your exams for displaying great breadth and depth of knowledge—for showing that you had done the reading and really understood it. And you might do particularly well if in your own freestyle way you showed that you had an interesting perspective on the course material.

In law school, however, you are no longer being tested on general comprehension. Professors expect everyone to have that. Nor are you being tested for pure imagination or creative spark. Rather, exams will put you in the role of being a lawyer, or perhaps a judge. You will have a case, or a client, and a fact pattern that presents a legal problem. You will be asked to demonstrate that you can recognize the issues and make the arguments that a top-notch lawyer would. Knowledge of the course that does not bear on that specific legal problem is irrelevant. Insight about the law that does not help solve the legal problem is worse than worthless—it is taking up space that could have been devoted to the problem at hand. It is the equivalent of the pinball running round the pinball field without hitting any bumpers. When we talk about hitting bumpers we mean identifying legal issues and analyzing them properly by making good arguments.

Just to ward off a possibly misleading aspect of our pinball analogy, we should mention that, in emphasizing the need to hit bumpers, we do not mean to suggest that the best exam answers are merely scattershot efforts to hit any bumper one spies. To get a high score in pinball often requires the player to proceed methodically, hitting bumpers in a certain order, for example. As we will see in coming chapters, the same is true for exams.

HOW HITTING BUMPERS (OR NOT) AFFECTS GRADES

To further appreciate—and underscore—the importance of bumpers, it is useful to think for a moment about grades and grade curves. Rare is the professor who reads an exam and instantly concludes, "This is an A," or "This is a B+," and simply records the grade. Rather, professors typically grade on points. They read an exam and score it, issue by issue. Then, they total up the points for all the issues. Next, they prepare a list of all the exams and the points received, then another list of all the point totals, so they can see the frequencies. (Typically this is all done anonymously.) Finally, all the point totals are placed on a curve. The top X% get a grade of A, the next Y% get A-minus grades, and so on. Often grades are allocated based on a mandatory or recommended curve.

It is worth emphasizing the takeaway here: *picking up a few additional points can make a real difference in your grade.* There are "easy" points on an exam and "hard" points. We do not mean that some questions are easy and some are difficult, although that might be true. Rather, think about it this way. Suppose an exam has 80 possible points. Virtually everyone in the class is going to get some threshold number of points, say, 25. The top exam is perhaps going to get 65. So, the entire curve occurs in the range between 25 points and 65 points. How many people are there in your class? If you are in a typical law school, this number might be between 50 and 120. So, all those people are going to spread out between 25 and 65. Easy points are the ones everyone gets up to the threshold. Then, each additional point is "harder" in some sense. But by picking up just a few of the "harder" points, or points above the threshold, you might raise your grade one entire level. (Another analogy here might be sit-ups or push-ups. The first few are relatively easy, and then they gradually get more difficult. But adding even a few "reps" at the end of your routine can make a meaningful difference in your fitness and strength.) That is why we continually stress hitting bumpers and picking up points: A few additional points can translate into a higher grade. And that is why we so strongly believe that if you follow the methods in this book, you have a good chance of raising your grade, for all the right reasons.

Exam Number	Raw Score	Grade
3124	63	A
2395	63	A
2284	61	A
2342	61	A
4944	59	A-
5004	59	A-
3378	59	A-
4455	59	A-
5374	58	A-
3448	57	A-
2826	57	A-
4902	57	A-
2233	57	A-
2481	57	A-
5103	56	A-
2568	56	A-
2627	56	A-
2755	56	A-
3630	54	B+
4757	54	B+

All this might sound rather obvious. Based on our experience, however, it is not. Students constantly write exams they believe to be wonderful. Their answers might indeed display a great knowledge of the material, they might be full of insight, they might be well written, and still they could yield a disappointing score. Students come to our offices all the time and insist that their exam answers had all of these virtues. And we are forced, sadly, to explain that none of it mattered. What mattered was addressing the questions raised by the fact pattern.

In the next chapter we begin to tell you quite precisely how to find and hit the bumpers on your exams. But first we want to reemphasize the fundamental point of this chapter. You must find what the professor is looking for you to find, or you won't score the points you need to get a good grade. This is not some arbitrary tyranny on the part of the professor. Rather, if you think back to Chapter 1, you will see that it reflects a perfectly reasonable insistence that you do what good lawyers do. What matters is not abstract brilliance or information dumping. What matters is making the kinds of arguments that good lawyers make.

None of this is cause for the cynical thought that exam grades are arbitrary. As you know from applying to law school, you and your classmates for the most part have similar academic profiles. To the extent it makes sense to view grades in terms of a competition, you are competing against true peers. It's no surprise, then, that the margin that separates one grade category from the next is relatively small. Moreover, in our experience, the grade lines that professors draw tend not to be random or idiosyncratic. Rather, some students just do a better job of consistently hitting bumpers; that is, identifying the legal issues and making the legal arguments as would a focused, steady, thorough, and clear-headed lawyer. That's what we want to teach you to do.

The Bottom Line

- ☑ Law school exams are not general knowledge exams.

- ☑ You earn points by spotting the issues that the professor has built into each fact pattern, and then analyzing them properly.

- ☑ Hitting even a few extra bumpers can make a real difference in your grade.

Chapter 9

ISSUE SPOTTING AND ISSUE SORTING

☑ The difference between spotting and sorting.

☑ How to make and use lists to spot issues thoroughly.

☑ When to write more, when to write less.

W e have likened exam-taking to a game of pinball, in which players are rewarded for keeping the ball in play so as to hit as many bumpers as they can. We have also explained that the IRAC framework can help you to convert narratives (fact patterns) into a format that permits methodical analysis. Now we begin to refine the story, focusing on the "I" element of IRAC.

Traditional law school exams are often described as "issue spotting" exams. This is an apt description. Of the total points one might earn on an exam, a large percentage often can be obtained — depending on the Professor's grading criteria — by correctly identifying and framing issues, *irrespective of how those issues are analyzed.* So if you can do a good job of issue spotting, you will probably do reasonably well on your exams. This is less odd than it sounds. When it comes to legal analysis, the ability to isolate issues is the necessary first step.

Closely related to issue spotting is *issue sorting.* Issue sorting requires judgments as to which issues require more of your time and attention, and which require less.

To give you a better sense of what we mean by issue spotting and issue sorting, it will help to return briefly to the pinball analogy. Imagine yourself staring intently at the game in front of you, trying to track the motion of the ball as it rolls around the playing surface. One of the challenging aspects of pinball is that the flickering lights and sounds are distracting. It's easy to lose sight of bumpers. To earn a high score, you need to remain aware of all the bumpers — all of the opportunities to score points — even amidst the stress of keeping the ball in play. This is the pinball analogue to issue spotting.

In addition, as you play, you probably will discover that certain bumpers or targets are worth few points or none at all — the field of play sometimes includes inert posts that merely serve as obstacles — whereas others are worth many points. Not surprisingly, the more valuable bumpers tend to be located in positions that require you to wield the machine's flippers with more precision and better timing. And yet these are bumpers that you will want to try to hit to increase your score. Here we have the analogue to issue sorting. Having surveyed the entire field of bumpers, you will next want to think about which are likely to be the most valuable ones and hone in on them, *although not to the exclusion of the easier targets*. The trick is to do both: Spot all the issues and then sort them.[15]

MATCHING

When it comes to issue spotting, it is far more common for students to err by failing to spot an issue than by spotting one not raised by a fact pattern. This type of failure often results from skipping steps, and therefore missing the opportunity to hit bumpers and rack up points.

Take, for example, a question that appeared on a constitutional law exam Friedman once gave. It presented to students a statute that discriminated among people on the basis of their ability to speak English. It also informed students that a person's English-speaking ability correlates with his or her place of national origin. Here there were *two* issues to be addressed: whether a law that

---

15. One can also think of issue spotting and issue sorting as analogous to fishing with a net. In the first instance, you want to cast as wide a net as is feasible so as to catch as many fish (issues) as possible. Then, once you have pulled in the net, you want to sort through the issues and decide which ones are the most valuable (i.e., call for the most extensive analysis), which ones have some value (i.e., call for some analysis), and which ones should be tossed overboard (i.e., at most mentioned, or perhaps ignored).

discriminates on the basis of *language ability* violates the Constitution's guarantee of "the equal protection of the laws," and whether a law that discriminates on the basis of *national origin* violates that guarantee. Although these two issues obviously are related, they are distinct. Under existing precedent, the more novel and difficult question was whether the Constitution forbids discriminating on the basis of English-speaking ability. By contrast, it is fairly well-settled that discrimination on the basis of national origin is impermissible.

As it happened, almost all of Friedman's students discussed the issue of discrimination on the basis of language ability. But only about half the students *also* analyzed the question of discrimination on the basis of national origin. In other words, half of the students missed the "easy" issue that surely *everyone* knew about. So, half of the class got more points than their colleagues just for being thorough and careful—for not "locking in" on one issue so as to miss others standing right nearby.

Unfortunately, it is not unusual for eager and time-pressured law students to miss easy issues. The good news is that this sort of error can be avoided with some preparation and care. In particular, it will help to think of issue spotting as an exercise in *matching*. Once again, law school is in some respects not so different from earlier phases of your education. When you were in grade school you probably encountered a puzzle that looked like this:

Subject List	*Issue List*
Elephant	Barks and likes to be petted
Cat	Woolly coat and says "baa"
Dog	Moos and people drink its milk
Cow	Long trunk and very large
Sheep	Meows and likes to be petted

Your task was to draw a line from the items on what we will call the "Subject List" to the corresponding items on what we will term the "Issue List." Simple, right? Well, it seems so now, but there was a time when this sort of thing would have been challenging for you. So it is with issue spotting.

Issue spotting is a lot like grade-school matching, even though it of course has more nuances. For a law school exam, the Subject List includes, ideally, the law covered in the course. The Issue List contains the issues hiding in the fact pattern(s) you are given. As you did in grade school, it is your job on a law school exam to draw the right connections between the Issue List and the Subject List. Successful matching thus involves these essential steps: having a complete-yet-usable Subject List, getting a knack for extracting the Issue List from facts that are given to you, matching one to the other, and keeping track of the matches that you have found. In this chapter, we'll give you a general sense of what it means, in the context of law school exams, to generate lists and to match. A more thorough discussion of how to make these lists, and the all-important task of keeping track of matches, can be found in Chapter 14. For now we simply want to stress that getting these two lists right is a huge part of succeeding on law school exams.

THE SUBJECT LIST

The critical first step to identifying issues on an exam is to put together a first-class version of the Subject List. When you take an exam you must have at hand a comprehensive and workable list of what was covered in the course. The importance of this list cannot be overstated: It is going to be your guide during the exam-taking process and it is going to help you avoid missing issues that you should spot.

Where does this list come from? It is a summary of your *course outline*. This is why outlining your courses is absolutely critical. (Chapter 13 is all about outlines.) When you outline, you are going over everything you learned (and, ideally, committing a lot of it to memory). For now, the important point is that the Subject List comes from sources such as your outline, supplemented by the syllabus provided by your professor, and the organization imposed by your textbook.

When we say the Subject List is a synthesis, we mean that it summarizes all the material covered in the course. But the summary itself can get long and complex, so much so that it, too, needs to be summarized. Essentially, what you need to do is prepare a Table of Contents for the entire course, arranged in a logical order. We'll say more about this in Chapter 13. For now it is enough to say that during the exam you will use the Subject List to remind yourself about the issues you should be looking for in the fact pattern.

THE ISSUE LIST

We said earlier that the Issue List comes from the fact patterns that you will be given on your exams. This might have struck you as odd. What does it mean to find a "list" in fact patterns? To understand this idea, it will help to get into the head of a law professor drafting an exam.

Each professor has his or her quirks and tricks, but there is a lot of commonality in what we do. When drafting an exam, most of us try to cover as much as possible of what was taught in the course. It is nearly impossible to draft an exam that covers 100 percent of those materials. And it would be unfair, most of us believe, to give students an exam that covered less than 50 percent of the course. The "sweet spot" is somewhere around 70 to 80 percent.

In other words, your exam most likely will test you on roughly three quarters of what you learned in the course. In this respect, law school exams are not like the grade-school matching exercise we provided earlier, because not every item in the Subject List will have a counterpart on the Issue List. Also, it might be the case that an item on the Subject List will match two different items on the Issue List.

The fact patterns on each exam thus provide the vehicle for raising most or all of the material you learned in your course. In this sense, each fact pattern is as much of a "list" as your outline. The catch, of course, is that the Issue List comes in the form of a narrative rather than a simple enumeration. Your job, as you read through a fact pattern, is to convert it into a list of issues that call for the application of rules and principles that you learned in your course. Naturally they are hidden, but they are in there! We're about to explain how to unearth them.

SCROLLING

One way to think about the matching process is in terms of scrolling. As you write your answer to a question you should be scrolling down the Subject List looking for the issues contained in the Issue List. In every instance you are asking, "Do these facts call for the application of this rule, or that principle, that is on my Subject List?" In other words, "Do these facts address something that was taught in the course?"

Suppose you are taking a Contracts exam. The fact pattern describes an interaction between X and Y. Begin scrolling! (Here we're going to use some words and concepts you will probably encounter in Contracts class, if you have not already.) Are the parties contemplating a sale of goods, such that Article 2 of the UCC controls? Or is it a sale of land or a services contract governed by common law principles?

Now, more facts and more issues: Do the new facts suggest formation problems? Was there an offer or a mere solicitation of an offer? An acceptance? Was the acceptance prior to revocation? And so on.

If the facts suggest an agreement, is it the sort that needs to be in writing to be enforceable? Does the agreement involve a genuine bargain, such that there is consideration for each party's promise or performance? If not, is there foreseeable detrimental reliance by the party seeking to enforce the agreement, such that promissory estoppel might apply?

Are there grounds for interpretive disputes as to the content of its key terms? If so, is there any other reason that the bargain might be unenforceable by a party who might want to enforce it?

Has there been a failure to perform? Is the failure complete or partial? Was performance contingent on the existence of a condition, the absence or presence of which excuses nonperformance? Is there an issue as to which damages measure should apply, or how to calculate damages?

You might fairly complain that the approach just described is somewhat mechanical. True! We have merely been ticking off many of the key subjects covered in a standard 1L Contracts course, and asking if any facts provided in a fact pattern raise issues under one or more of those subjects. *Law school exam answers tend to be judged in the same way that a careful shopper assesses his trip to the grocery store — by checking off the items that have been purchased to make sure nothing is overlooked.* As we explained previously, professors grade you for spotting the issues presented by the exam. *These* are the bumpers that matter. So, you must devote your energies to carefully unearthing these issues. If we had a dollar for every time a student has told us after an exam, "I can't believe I didn't discuss that issue!" we'd be rich. (Okay, not rich, but you get the point.)

Again, we'll have more to say about matching in Chapter 14. For now it is enough to appreciate that the trick for the issue-spotting dimension of IRAC is to be meticulous, and that the key to being meticulous is to create lists and devote careful attention to them.

IGNORE, MENTION, OR ANALYZE?

As exams approach, students often ask, "Which is the better strategy? Should I try to spot as many issues as possible? Or should I focus in depth on a few issues?" The answer is easy, we say: "Do both!"

Understandably, students find our answer frustrating. How is it possible, given time limits, word limits, or both, to provide answers that are both "wide" and "deep"? In this respect, exam taking is once again tied to the practice of law. Real-life legal problems tend to be messy. Yet they also tend to revolve around, or be driven by, a central set of issues or problems.

A good litigator can stand up in court and, notwithstanding the many complexities of the case, present to the judge or jury a very succinct and powerful statement of its gist. ("Your honor, at its core, this litigation boils down to three issues.") A good lawyer advising a client on a transaction or a business move can do the same. ("At the end of the day, this decision comes down to whether you are comfortable running risks a, b, and c to have the chance to obtain benefits x, y, and z.") Exams are no different. If you are on your game, you will find lots of issues, but they will not be equally important, and it is essential for you to separate the wheat from the chaff.

Some issues are not worth raising. Indeed, you might get docked points for raising them. These include issues that emerge from a fact pattern only if one adds to it unrealistic additional facts not provided in the exam itself. An informational void—just because it is a void—raises a spectrum of possibilities running from the plausible to the ridiculous.

Imagine that, on a Criminal Law exam, you are provided with facts indicating that O is the owner of a residential drug rehabilitation center that has burned down, tragically resulting in the death of some of the residents. You are further provided with testimony from residents who managed to escape by crawling through a window that the home's fire exits were locked. You are almost certainly being invited to assess whether O can be convicted for murder (causing another's death through recklessness demonstrating a "depraved heart" or "extreme indifference" to human life), involuntary manslaughter (causing death through "ordinary" recklessness), or negligent homicide. Still, nothing in the presentation of the facts explicitly negates the possibility that an unknown malefactor surreptitiously locked the center's fire exits without the owner's knowledge. Should your exam answer discuss the significance of this mysterious person? No. Unless you have an explicit invitation from your professor to speculate broadly, when you issue-spot, you should not waste your time on remote possibilities just because the facts fail to negate those possibilities.[16]

Leaving aside issues not worth discussing, the key issue-sorting task is to distinguish issues that, based on the given facts, can be disposed of with a conclusory statement, and those that require more substantial analysis of the sort discussed in the next chapters. To appreciate this distinction, it will help to introduce a new example. Imagine you are given the following fact pattern on a Contracts exam.

ALAN'S DEAL

Alan owns Alan's Pet Shop. He decides to sell the business, including the building that houses it, to PetDepot, a national chain. Under the terms of their written agreement, PetDepot agrees to pay Alan $2 million. Half is payable upon the signing of the agreement. The other half is to be paid a year from the date of the agreement.

The signed agreement includes the following provisions, among others:

(1) PetDepot promises to continue to operate the business under the name "Alan's Pet Shop";

(2) Alan promises that, for two years from the date of the agreement, he will not operate a pet-related business within a twenty-mile radius of the location of Alan's Pet Shop.

---

16. That is, unless you are using unlikely possibilities to good rhetorical effect, the way a defense lawyer might do so to emphasize to a jury how much the prosecution's case rests on surmise and conjecture (e.g., "For all we know, this could have been the work of a third party").

Shortly after the agreement is signed, PetDepot concludes that it cannot run the business profitably without expanding it. It therefore buys the building adjacent to Alan's and remodels the combined space. Six months after the date of the agreement, it holds a grand reopening, with the store now operating as a "PetDepot Superstore."

Alan, furious that PetDepot has not honored the name-retention provision, proceeds to open a small pet shop two blocks from the Superstore. One year after the date of the signing of the agreement, PetDepot notifies Alan that it will not pay him the second of the two $1 million payments because of Alan's violation of the agreement's noncompete provision.

Discuss the rights of Alan and PetDepot.

Let's first review issue-spotting, then turn to issue-sorting. Recall the simple exercise in matching with which we began this chapter. Let's try that exercise again, except now, instead of listing animals and their attributes, we're going to list some of the facts provided to you in the story of Alan's Deal (the Issue List) and some of the subjects you will probably cover in your Contracts class (the Subject List).

Start with the Issue List. You will see that it summarizes facts contained in the narrative of Alan's Deal that raise possible legal issues under the rules of contract law. (Note: this is a partial list—probably there are other relevant facts and issues that would need to be mentioned and analyzed on a real exam.) If you haven't taken Contracts yet, there'd be no reason for you to know that the facts summarized on the Issue List raise issues of law. There's a reason for that. *Part of what it means to learn the law is to learn when and how the law's rules make certain facts salient, even though they wouldn't be salient if the law used different rules.*

Talk of rules brings us to the Subject List. You will see that it names various concepts or doctrines that you will probably encounter in Contracts. These are the rules that courts have fashioned that determine when an agreement is legally enforceable, and what counts as the breach of such an agreement.

As it is with elephants and cows, so it is with "consideration" and "impracticability." When it comes to issue-spotting, your job is to match facts/issues with subjects/rules. And that is exactly what is happening in the chart below. Here, the straight black lines are doing the matching for you. Soon enough, you'll be doing it on your own.

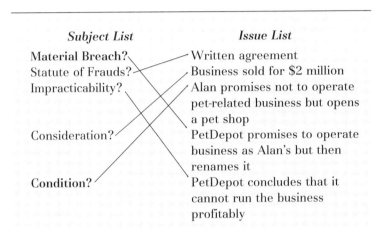

Okay, now let's shift from issue spotting to issue sorting. You'll notice that, on the above list, two items on the Subject List are in bold font, while others are not. This is our way of representing the idea of issue-sorting.

Once you become familiar with contract law, you will realize pretty quickly that the facts provided in the narrative of Alan's Deal leave very little room for the analysis of issues pertaining to contract *formation* (i.e., offer and acceptance, consideration, statute of frauds, etc.). The facts describe a contemporaneous exchange of money for tangible and intangible property that is memorialized in definite terms within a writing. On an exam, therefore, you'd at most want to mention this conclusion in passing. Doing so would demonstrate that you are methodical, but also capable of exercising judgment.

At the same time, you should realize that there are more likely to be contentious issues about whether PetDepot or Alan has committed a material breach, whether to construe the "noncompete" clause as a condition of performance, such that PetDepot was entitled to refrain from paying Alan, and so on. It is these latter topics that the professor wants you to discuss in greater depth.

Here's one way to think about the different treatment appropriate to the different issues raised by this hypothetical. Suppose that your Contracts professor were to call on you in class and ask you to present the issues raised by Alan's Deal. If you spent two minutes of class time discussing formation issues, your professor and your classmates would be irritated. Is this really the crux of the case? Or are you just running through your list of possible issues in an over-inclusive manner for completeness' sake? By contrast, if you asserted that Alan was free to open the new store because PetDepot's renaming of the store constituted a material breach that relieved Alan of his obligations under the noncompete provision, your professor would surely acknowledge that you were making a relevant argument. Whether the argument is right, or the strongest possible one to make, is beside the point. It is precisely this distinction between a good argument and a trivial one that is at the very heart of issue sorting.

DECIDING HOW MUCH TIME TO SPEND ON AN ISSUE

The advice we have offered so far has presupposed that the facts presented to you on an exam will permit a sharp contrast between frivolous issues that require no attention, easy issues that require only a brief mention, and hard issues that require extensive analysis. So far, so good — but you will undoubtedly face more difficult judgments as to where on this spectrum particular issues lie.

For example, as you read about Alan's Deal, it might have occurred to you (depending in part on whether you've covered the issue in Contracts) that PetDepot could argue that its failure to abide by the name-retention provision should be excused under the doctrine of "commercial impracticability." After all, PetDepot's decision to rename the store was a response to the nonviability of the business conducted under the terms of the agreement with Alan. And yet a bit of reflection reveals that this argument is weak. As you have learned, or probably will learn, in Contracts, impracticability is not a robust doctrine to begin with — courts are reluctant to apply it. And (as we discuss below), the fact that PetDepot misjudged the economic viability of its original plan for running the business does not by itself call for the doctrine's application. So you've spotted this issue, even though it seems only faintly raised by the facts, and even though it calls for one-sided analysis. Should you say anything about it?

Our advice is to *err on the side of inclusion,* within reason. Remember, professors are usually trying to cover roughly 70 to 80 percent of the course materials, and probably won't be able to craft an evenly balanced set of facts for each and every part of that material. Some of the issues on an exam will be subtle, and some not.

However, we stress that this rule operates only at the margin. If you are constantly identifying implausible claims as real issues—"shotgunning"—then you are probably going to annoy the professor and suggest to her that you can't tell a good argument from a bad one. Similarly, if you are facing a word limit, it is best to use your words where you are more certain there are bumpers. Don't waste limited words on issues that might not really be there. (Here, too, though, there is a balance. Typically, there are only so many points you can get discussing any given issue. If you are going on and on about one, then you might be wasting words when you could do better to find an additional issue.)

There is a strategic way to handle situations involving borderline issues. The best thing to do is to mention the issue, explain that, although there are colorable arguments on each side, one is much stronger than the other, and then quickly dispose of it. For the impracticability issue, one might write something like the following: "Impracticability excuses nonperformance and PetDepot could argue that they were taken by surprise when they discovered that the store could not operate profitably. However, courts are suspicious of this doctrine. And even if they weren't, these facts do not support its application. Impracticability is meant to deal with dramatic, unexpected 'shocks' in the business environment, not to provide insurance against ordinary business risks."

Addressing the issue in this way might even earn you double credit. It shows the professor that you are comprehensively analyzing the issues presented by the fact pattern, but also that you can distinguish among issues that are easily resolved and those that are closer calls. This sort of demonstration is valuable in its own right. It also might work to your advantage in other parts of the exam by instilling in the professor the (justified) confidence that you know what you're talking about, and therefore should be given the benefit of the doubt on any close grading calls.

Issue sorting is a matter of training and talent but technique matters, too, as we have tried to explain here. Working on your mechanics and your "feel" for judgment calls will get you a long way toward the goal of knowing which bumpers to lock in on, and which ones merely to mention.

The Bottom Line

☑ Methodical issue spotting is essential to strong exam performance.

☑ Use your "Subject List" and "Issue List" to be methodical (*see* Chapter 14).

☑ Sort issues into those that deserve more or less attention.

☑ Pick your battles: Move quickly through one-sided issues, dwell on "meatier" ones.

RULES

☑ The role of rules: Frameworks, not answers.

☑ What to do when rules conflict.

☑ Working with rules and their rationales.

T his chapter is one of the shorter chapters in the book. That might surprise you. Most students come to law school expecting to learn a body of rules.[17] And they do. Yet one of the most common mistakes we see on exams is a student trying to earn points merely by reciting, for example, the elements of the tort of battery, or for accurately summarizing the test for analyzing the extent of Congress's power under the Commerce Clause of Article I of the U.S. Constitution. This is no way to hit bumpers.

To help illustrate this point, let's return to our running theme: that law school exams really do connect to law practice. Recall Seyla's Story from Chapter 7, which raised the question of whether a neighbor's regular use of a dirt path on an owner's property had created an easement. If, as an associate, you were assigned that case, you would

---

17. We use the term *rules* broadly to include clear rules (e.g., "It is unconstitutional for a court to impose capital punishment on a criminal defendant for a crime she committed while a minor"), looser standards (e.g., "An actor will be deemed to have acted carelessly if she failed to act in the manner that a person of ordinary prudence would have acted under the circumstances"), and doctrines that can contain clusters of rules and standards (e.g., the doctrine of felony murder).

be required to do some digging. Specifically, you would have to dig into facts (e.g., look at documents for facts as to prior purchases and sales of the land, and any formal or informal agreements reached among the relevant landowners), and you would have to dig into law (e.g., the rules for prescriptive easements). Notice that these two jobs are closely connected. The colleague who assigned you the case would be annoyed, to say the least, if your legal research led you to write a mini-treatise that covers all the possible circumstances that might create an easement. You are expected to identify rules that are likely to have some bearing on the client's situation, given the known facts about it (and perhaps facts not yet known).

The same is true for exams. Remember, "rule" is but one element of the IRAC framework. IRAC invites us to think about rules in a certain way. On a law school exam, rules are invoked not for their own sake, but as a step in the analysis of issues. Rules provide the *structure* for your analysis of issues that you have spotted. On exams, you will not be rewarded for reciting rules so much as for using or applying them. Chapter 11 discusses application in depth. The goal of this chapter is to explain how rules, properly conceived, set the stage for analysis. This in turn requires you to adopt a particular stance toward legal rules. *You must simultaneously embrace them and yet be prepared to question them.*

FOLLOW THE RULES!

As you may have noticed, we think there is value in stating the obvious. Here's another instance of that. You are in *law* school. You are learning the law. You are training to be a lawyer, and your clients will want to know one thing from you primarily: the law. So, it should come as little surprise to learn that the driver for your exam answers should be the law.

Still, legal rules rarely provide algorithms that spit out answers. They more typically provide frameworks of analysis. For example, a tort claim for negligence ordinarily requires the claimant to prove duty, breach, factual cause, proximate cause, and injury. These "elements" have been identified by courts and commentators for a reason: They help to focus and structure analysis even though they also generate ambiguities. And yet it is very common to find answers to Torts exams in which students analyze negligence problems without working their way through these elements. Under the pressure of exam writing, some students seem to forget or abandon the very rules that can guide their analysis, instead falling back on a loosey-goosey form of writing that leads them to miss bumpers. In this sense, legal rules and tests are just another kind of checklist that you need to follow.

Do not fight the structure of the law. If you have a promissory estoppel question on a Contracts exam, then you should proceed systematically through the elements of promissory estoppel, most likely in the order provided by its definition in case law or other authoritative materials, such as the Second Restatement of Contracts.

Begin with the first element of the doctrine: the promise. A standard trick of Contracts professors is to give facts that describe a sympathetic actor who relies to his detriment on something less than a promise, such as a mere prediction as to how things might turn out in the future. In doing so, they are counting on some students to skip the initial analytic step of determining whether any promise has been made. If there is no promise, then—depending on one's understanding of the proper scope of the doctrine of promissory estoppel—there is either no basis for invoking the doctrine, or at least a need for a further explanation as to when and why it can be invoked in the absence of a promise.

Promissory Estoppel:

1. One who makes a promise
2. That reasonably can be expected to induce detrimental action or forbearance
3. By the promisee or a third party
4. And that does induce detrimental action or forbearance by that person
5. Shall be bound to the promise
6. To the extent necessary to avoid injustice.

It might turn out on reflection that not every element in a test requires as much analysis. On a particular negligence problem, the issue of duty might be fairly well settled and can be disposed of quickly, whereas the issue of breach or causation is tricky and requires further attention. This is consistent with what we told you in Chapter 9 about sorting issues. But in sorting them, you do not want to skip steps. Even elements of a test for which the answer is fairly clear at least deserve mention. Analytic thoroughness, as well as the right amount of attention to each issue, will earn you points.

SPLITS OF AUTHORITY

Splits between or among different jurisdictions as to the adoption or rejection of certain doctrines are staples of law school. As you might have learned, or might yet learn in Criminal Law, the California Supreme Court, out of hostility to the felony murder rule, adopted a relatively restrictive test for what can count as the sort of "inherently dangerous" felony that, if it leads to a death, will support a felony murder conviction.[18] Other courts, such as the Georgia Supreme Court, are more accepting of felony murder and thus have adopted a broader definition of what counts as an inherently dangerous felony.[19] The Model Penal Code, for its part, declines to recognize felony murder as such, and instead states that one who causes the death of another while engaging in certain enumerated crimes, such as robbery or attempted robbery, is subject to a rebuttable presumption that he has acted with the sort of "extreme indifference" to human life that will support a murder conviction.[20] This is all fine and good: Reasonable people can reach different conclusions about what the rule should be. But what is a law student to do on a Criminal Law exam? Apply the rule she thinks best?

The good news here is that your professor will probably give you guidance on this question, either in class before the exam, or in exam instructions. Indeed, it is very common for exam instructions to inform you that you are to apply the law of a fictional jurisdiction ("Ames," for example). Typically, you will be further instructed as to where the courts of Ames stand on issues that have divided the courts. Here,

---

18. *People v. Phillips*, 414 P.2d 553 (1966).
19. *Hines v. State*, 578 S.E.2d 868 (Ga. 2003).
20. Model Penal Code § 210.2(1)(b).

of course, one need only follow the instructions given. For example, you might sometimes encounter an exam instruction like this:

> For purposes of this exam, you are to apply the law of the mythical jurisdiction of Ames. Ames law follows the settled black-letter law that we learned in class. Where we encountered disputes between or among courts you should assume that each of the relevant conflicting decisions was issued by an intermediate appellate court of Ames, and therefore that there is not yet an authoritative rule of Ames law.

This sort of instruction directs you to treat splits of authority you encountered in class as positions that have support in Ames law, but have not yet been finally adopted by the Ames Supreme Court. Now what?

Typically, when you get this sort of instruction you are being issued an invitation. The invitation is to show that you understand why disagreements that you have encountered in class might matter for the resolution of an issue or set of issues raised by a fact pattern on your exam.

Return, for example, to felony murder. If you were to receive an instruction like the one just given on a Criminal Law exam, and were given facts that reveal a death caused during the commission of a particular felony, it is probably the case that you are being invited, first, to point out that the choice among the California, Georgia, and Model Penal Code approaches could determine whether or not a given defendant or set of defendants can be convicted of felony murder.

Second, it is possible that you are also being invited to express a view on which rule ought to apply. If so, your view should be informed, of course, by law and by the facts of the case rather than mere opinion or preference. It's okay to say something like, "Felony murder is harsh, therefore the California rule should be adopted by the Ames Supreme Court." Better, though, to tie your judgment to the particular case ("A felony murder conviction, and the possibility of life in prison for this felon, is so disproportionate to the wrong done, and so unlikely to deter future killings, that it demonstrates the superiority of the California approach") or to other aspects of the law that you have encountered in class ("A narrow approach to felony murder is most in keeping with the rule of lenity . . .").

MINORITY OR OUTLIER RULES

At some point in your classes, you will read a particularly interesting and perhaps compelling judicial opinion, only to learn in class that the opinion is an outlier: Its result and rationales have been rejected by most other courts. To return to the example of promissory estoppel, you might read in your Contracts class the Wisconsin Supreme Court's 1965 decision in *Hoffman v. Red Owl Stores, Inc.*[21] Although the matter is not free from dispute, many contracts scholars regard *Hoffman* as an outlier because of its willingness to recognize a claim for detrimental reliance on something less than a full-blown promise.

Suppose your Contracts professor assigns you *Hoffman* and then takes the position in class that it is "bad law." You might understandably be puzzled or even resentful: "Why did we read that case if it sets out the wrong rule?" The answer, of course, is that one can learn something about the path on which one is traveling by considering paths not (yet) taken. To learn about decisions regarded as "wrong turns" is to appreciate at least some of the reasons for the rules that we now have.

Hoffman, for example, seems to suppose that promissory estoppel is best understood as a doctrine that is concerned to ensure a kind of fairness in business dealings: Even for a promise unsupported by consideration, fairness calls for liability if the promise foreseeably induces detrimental reliance by another. But then—reasons *Hoffman*—fairness likewise calls for liability when a statement falls short of a promise; for example, a prediction of how a business might develop in the future induces foreseeable detrimental reliance. And yet, as noted, later courts seem for the most part to have been unmoved by this line of reasoning. To think about their resistance is to think about what, if anything, might justify their different understanding of promissory estoppel. Is it because contract law is simply deaf to fairness? Or is there a more nuanced rationale? For example, in this domain, is a concern for fairness outweighed by the need to leave parties with room to engage in preliminary, nonbinding negotiations—room that would be lost were promissory estoppel to be extended beyond promises to predictions?

---

21. 133 N.W.2d 267 (Wis. 1965).

Understanding why you spend class time on outlier decisions can help you think about the place of rules in exam answers. You are given facts on a Contracts exam that look similar to those that would support a "clean" application of the doctrine of promissory estoppel, but differ in some important respect. There is foreseeable and detrimental reliance by one party on statements made by the other, but the statements don't seem to add up to a full-blown promise. Your job in the first instance is to apply the rules. Under the majority approach, the claim of the disappointed party will fail. But it certainly won't hurt to convey your awareness that the facts present a case that invites consideration of the limits and justifications of the rule. One easy way to do this is to adopt the predictive voice we earlier mentioned in connection with Holmes's Bad Man. Thus, you might say toward the end of your analysis, "Plaintiff's claim for damages based on promissory estoppel will probably fail, unless he is in front of a court, like the Wisconsin Supreme Court in *Hoffman*, that is willing to treat contract law as law that allows recovery to avoid injustice whenever an actor foreseeably induces detrimental reliance by another."

The Bottom Line

- ☑ Don't just recite rules; use them to structure your analysis.

- ☑ Be thorough: Consider and perhaps discuss each aspect of the rule.

- ☑ Discuss policy rationales behind rules when close issues invite you to do so.

- ☑ Acknowledge splits of authority where disagreements among courts might make a difference, but make sure to identify the majority rule where there is one.

Chapter 11

ANALYSIS (APPLICATION)

☑ Using rules to analyze the issues raised by the fact pattern.

☑ How to identify and make the most of "forks" in the road.

☑ The importance of arguing both sides of a question.

☑ How to deal with gaps in fact patterns.

I f, for purposes of hitting bumpers and scoring well on exams, issue spotting is the most important of IRAC's elements, analysis, also known as application, is a close second. It is also probably the most commonly mishandled. In the pressured setting of an exam, students are keen to reach the proper resolution of the issues they have spotted. Unfortunately, they are sometimes so keen to get to their conclusions that they skip steps, and ignore or dismiss possibilities that they would have been rewarded for discussing. Remember, legal analysis is argument!

Imagine a novice pinball player overwhelmed by the many possible targets on the table in front of him. In response, he decides to aim for only one, or a few. After hitting it (or them), he lets out a contented sigh and allows the ball to fall through the space between the flippers, ending his turn. Then he starts the next ball and aims only for one other target. This approach won't earn a lot of points in pinball, and it won't earn a lot of points on law school exams either.

The goal of the spotting and sorting techniques discussed in Chapter 9, and of our admonition to follow the rules in Chapter 10, has been to enable you to break down issue-spotting questions into small, orderly steps that you can easily take and track. Now comes the payoff. You've spotted an issue, you've determined it's worth more than cursory attention, and you've located doctrines or concepts that provide a framework for analyzing it. There's one more task. You must apply the rules in a thoughtful and thorough manner.

There are two keys to the analysis phase of IRAC. The first is relentless scrutiny of the *facts* that have been provided to you (and even some that have not). Your professors will not reward you for spewing information or reciting legal rules. They want to see you *use* the rules that you have learned. The second key is to remember that, when it comes to the application of law to all but the most straightforward issues, *argument* is the name of the game. Even if the exam instructions ask you to defend one side of these issues, you must identify and discuss considerations on each side of any issue.

FACTS AND ISSUE REFINEMENT

To get a sense of the application element of IRAC it will again help to connect the taking of exams to the practice of law. Imagine that you are a lawyer with your own practice. A 30-year-old person, Tia, comes to your office with the following story.

TIA'S TALE

This is embarrassing. I had some laser treatment for my skin and it's been a disaster and I'm wondering if I can sue someone.

I used to have a tattoo on my back. I got it when I was a teenager. It made me self-conscious—when I went to the beach I'd wear a T-shirt. I read somewhere that tattoos can be removed by lasers, so I called a dermatologist. I was going to schedule an appointment, but when the receptionist quoted me the price, I couldn't believe how expensive it was. I checked with my insurance company, but they told me that this kind of procedure isn't covered. So I dropped the whole idea.

Then I saw on the Web that there are laser treatment centers that are not run by dermatologists with medical degrees, but instead by technicians trained to use lasers. They use the same equipment but are a lot cheaper. So I decided to go to one of these places, called Laser Treatment Systems. The treatment was really painful—as the LTS technician said it would be—but I figured it would be worth it. Soon afterwards, however, I noticed that my skin was blistered and discolored.

This time I went to the dermatologist. He said that the laser treatment had caused something called "hyper-pigmentation." That was the first time I had ever heard that word. Basically, the skin that was zapped reacted by producing extra pigment, making it dark and splotchy.

The dermatologist told me that there's always a small risk of hyper-pigmentation with any laser skin treatment, but that it is also possible that my condition resulted from the LTS technician setting the energy level on the laser too high. He said that, unfortunately, laser operators sometimes forget to check the settings on their machines before using them.

I went to LTS to complain. The technician said not to worry—that the hyper-pigmentation would go away after six to twelve months. It's been more than a year now and my skin where the tattoo used to be still looks horrible. If I had known that this might happen, I would never have done the treatment. Can I sue LTS?

Oh, one other thing. When I first went for treatment LTS had me sign a form. I didn't really read it at the time, but I kept a copy.

You read the form. Its concluding paragraph states:

> By signing this contract, I agree that, for any legal claim I might bring against LTS alleging an injury caused by the carelessness of LTS or an LTS employee, LTS's liability shall not exceed an amount equal to two times the amount that I have paid to LTS under this contract for its provision of services.

Although our present focus is on analysis, this example also provides a good occasion to practice issue spotting. Go ahead. Re-read the example. What issues can you spot? Do some sorting, too. Which are likely to call for more extended analysis?

ISSUES: _____

_____

_____

_____

_____

Here are the most important issues presented by the fact pattern.

- *A potential statute of limitations issue.* Tia has told you that it's been more than a year since her treatment. Has she waited too long to sue?
- *A breach issue.* Tia has told you that she received treatment that resulted in a bad outcome. Given her disappointed expectations, she perhaps presumes her treatment was substandard. But of course her views don't settle the question. The issue is whether LTS met the applicable standard set by tort law.
- *A causation issue.* Tia has told you that there is some reason to think that, if she received substandard treatment, it caused her to suffer an injury. But it is not certain that this is the case.
- *A contractual limitation of liability issue.* Tia has signed a form that purports to limit her right to sue for damages in the event of an injury received as a result of treatment.

For purposes of discussing the analysis element of IRAC, let's focus on breach. Look closely, again, at the scenario described by Tia. What are you told that might be relevant to the issue of whether LTS's employee failed to act with ordinary prudence in treating Tia? What are you *not* told? You must pay attention to both.

As to the facts provided, you will notice that Tia reports a remark made by her doctor, informing her that hyper-pigmentation is sometimes a product of laser treatments given at too high an energy level. Now ask yourself: Why has that bit of information been provided? What 'work' is it doing? The answer, of course, is that it is presenting a possible line of argument on the issue of breach. It suggests that there might have been something improper about Tia's treatment, given that she is now suffering from symptoms that, at least on some occasions, are caused by mistreatment.

Now consider another fact. You are told that Tia first heard the term "hyper-pigmentation" when she was talking to her doctor after receiving treatment. Again, ask yourself: "What is that fact trying to tell me?" Perhaps by now you have hit on the answer. It suggests that Tia did not know at the time of her treatment about a possible bad outcome that might be associated with her laser treatment. Ring any bells? Have you encountered rules of negligence law concerning the information that recipients of certain kinds of treatment are entitled to receive before deciding whether or not to undergo such treatment?

Notice what has happened here. If you've covered negligence in Torts, it was probably pretty easy to see that Tia's story suggests a possible claim for negligence, which in turn would naturally raise an issue of breach. Less obvious, but perhaps now a bit clearer, was the presence of not one but *two distinct breach issues*: (1) was the technician sufficiently careful in operating the laser, and (2) even if he was careful, did he give Tia enough information about the risks associated with the treatment?[22]

Notice how little it took from us, in the role of exam writers, to raise these two possibilities. We needed only to have Tia's dermatologist tell her that hyper-pigmentation is sometimes caused by mistakes in setting a laser's energy level, and have Tia tell the dermatologist that she had not heard of hyper-pigmentation before his mentioning it. Let this be a lesson. *Facts in fact patterns are usually there for a reason.*

---

22. We are assuming that your Torts class has covered or will cover these two different kinds of carelessness. Most classes do so when contrasting standard medical malpractice with informed consent malpractice.

True, they sometimes serve as red herrings, and some professors use this tactic more than others. But whether your professor is one who never sticks in an extraneous fact, or one who likes to send students on wild-goose chases, issue spotting and issue analysis is all about thinking to yourself as you read a fact pattern: "Now why is that fact here? Is it relevant or germane to a legal issue?" (This is just an example of the scrolling we discussed in Chapter 9.) If you think about it, this is analogous to what a lawyer must do when listening to a client's story.

We've just seen how close attention to facts can require you to disentangle or refine your analysis of an issue—in this case the "breach" or "fault" aspect of a negligence claim. The same attention to facts can sometimes reveal a similar need to disentangle potentially applicable legal rules.

Let's look only at the issue of whether the LTS technician committed negligence by administering the laser treatment to Tia in an unsafe manner. You have learned (or will learn) that in negligence suits against licensed professionals such as doctors and lawyers—malpractice suits—a special rule applies for determining whether professional services have been rendered with due care. Roughly speaking, so long as a professional follows procedures accepted as proper by his peers, he will be deemed as a matter of law to have acted with ordinary prudence, and therefore will be spared liability. (Call this the "malpractice rule.")

But, as you also know (or will learn), the rule is different outside the domain of professional malpractice. For negligence in the delivery of nonprofessional services, the rules or standards of conduct embraced by one's peers are relevant, but not dispositive: It is open to the fact finder to conclude that even a well-accepted way of doing things among nonprofessionals is sufficiently risky to fail to count as ordinary prudence. (Call this the "nonprofessional rule.")

Thus, when it comes to identifying the rule that will determine whether the LTS technician provided substandard treatment to Tia, there is a degree of uncertainty. Harkening all the way back to Holmes's Bad Man—and back to our initial fictitious case of *Baker v. Farmer*—one can suppose that a judge might conclude that the decisions that applied the malpractice rule to physicians favor the application of the same rule to a laser technician who: (a) has some professional training, and (b) is administering a service that is also provided by licensed dermatologists. But one could also predict that a court will conclude that laser technicians, because they are not licensed physicians, should be judged under the standard for nonprofessionals.

As we have noted before, law professors delight in finding just these sorts of borderline instances. *The good news for you is that, in an exam setting, you typically won't be graded on whether you get the answer right.* Most times, there won't be a clear right answer. Instead, when confronted with a borderline case, it will be your job to recognize the choices a legal decision maker such as a judge will face, analyze the significance of the choice — how it might affect the outcome of the problem — and argue for one or another approach as preferable *while acknowledging that there is something to be said on both sides.* In making these arguments, you will want to address questions like the following: Why do we have these distinct rules? What do these reasons tell us about which rule ought to apply in this instance?[23] Where there is no way to avoid a contestable judgment as to whether a given legal concept fits or doesn't fit an event or situation, you will score points by making arguments.

ARGUING BOTH SIDES, AND WHEN TO DO IT

This brings us quite naturally to the importance of legal reasoning to law application. As we have said from the outset, legal reasoning is a distinctive form of reasoning. It is framed in the first instance by sometimes elaborate legal rules. It is highly fact-intensive. It is probabilistic. Your application of rules to issues must have each of these characteristics.

---

23. Notice that the second of our two standard-of-care issues — informed consent — poses a version of the same kind of problem. The original "home" of informed consent doctrine is the law of medical malpractice. It is based on the idea that even a patient who is properly treated can hold a physician liable if she can show that the doctor failed to provide information about material risks that accompany proper treatment, and if she can prove that, had she been made aware of those risks, she never would have agreed to the treatment in the first place. In suggesting that the "standard-of-care" issue actually breaks down into the issues of substandard treatment and informed consent, we are assuming that a court would allow someone other than a medical patient to invoke informed consent doctrine. It's possible that a court would say that the doctrine operates only in the domain of medical malpractice.

We've said it before and will say it again: Law school exam writing correlates with real-world law practice. When it comes to applying law to a complex, contestable, open-ended issue on an exam, this means first and foremost recognizing the need for arguments on both sides. This is what lawyers do.

To win their cases, good lawyers spend a great deal of time thinking about how they will *lose* them. They try to figure out what the other side's arguments will be. When a case ultimately comes before a judge or jury, the decision maker will listen to the arguments of both sides and determine which she believes is best. Even when an exam instruction tells you to take a side (e.g., by asking you to play the role of counsel for one of the parties), your professors are looking for you to be deliberative. You must consider the arguments on both sides about why, under the relevant rule, one party or the other should win. Only by recognizing these arguments and weighing them can you reach any sort of conclusion. You can't advise your client knowing only one side's arguments. So the first and most straightforward lesson about rule-application on an exam drawn from real-world legal analysis is that your answer should identify and argue both sides.

"If I argue X, she'll counter with Y . . ."

We should qualify this point by returning to some advice we offered in Chapter 9, on issue sorting. Not every issue you spot on an exam will be an occasion for elaborate argument. Some are so tangential or improbable as to deserve only a quick mention. Others are so straightforward that the analysis can be provided in a sentence or two. For this kind of issue it doesn't hurt, and might help, at least to mention possible arguments in favor of the weaker side of the argument. Just be quick about it. (This was the lesson of the "commercial impracticability" issue that we mentioned in Chapter 9 in connection with Alan's Deal.)

As with issue sorting, arguing both sides is as much art as logic. It is where you have to exercise judgment about what is or is not a good argument. However, much of the first semester of law school has been given over to discerning good from bad arguments, so you should have a lot of experience with this aspect of exam taking.

Here are three examples of when you should be arguing both sides:

(1) *Depending on the facts, the issue could go either way.* Probably the most common instance on exams of the need to argue both sides is when there are grounds for disputing how a legal rule applies to a particular set of facts. The "breach" issues raised by Tia's claim, discussed earlier, clearly fit this description. What the laser technician did, and precisely how, will determine whether there was a breach, which is in turn integral to the determination of whether LTS committed negligence. In a real trial, counsel for both sides would spend much of their time trying to convince a judge and jury that the LTS technician did or did not act carelessly under the circumstances. This is not an argument about negligence doctrine in the abstract, but how that doctrine applies to the facts at hand. If in your answer you failed to argue both sides of the breach issue, you would stand to lose as many as half the points to be had.

(2) *The rule as applied produces bizarre result.* Another common situation that calls for argument on both sides is when the application of the rule to the facts seems straightforward, yet the circumstances calling for the application of the rule, or the result that will follow from its application, are so strikingly different from those that probably were contemplated when the rule was fashioned, that there is a basis on which to argue for an exception to the rule, or perhaps even for its outright rejection.

Riggs v. Palmer[24] is a justly famous nineteenth-century decision in which a grandfather had written a will that, upon

---

24. 115 N.Y 506 (1889).

his death, would have transferred much of his property to a grandson named Elmer. However, the grandfather at some point contemplated changing his will in a way that would cause Elmer to inherit less. Desperate to protect his inheritance, Elmer poisoned and killed his grandfather before the will could be changed. Elmer was sent to prison for his heinous crime. And yet he argued that, under the law governing inheritances, he was still entitled to inherit as specified by his grandfather's original will. After all, that will had never formally been changed—Elmer had seen to that!

Elmer's argument might strike you as revolting. But it was a credible legal argument. Indeed, two judges on New York's highest court accepted it. A valid will is a valid will, they reasoned, and the law of inheritance is not concerned to punish wrongdoers—that's the job of the criminal law. If the New York legislature wanted to punish murdering heirs by adding a forfeiture penalty to their prison time, that option was surely open to it. But the legislature had not enacted such a law.

In the end, though, a majority of the judges on New York's high court rejected Elmer's argument. They reasoned that, even though the grandfather's will seemed to be valid under the plain terms of the state's inheritance laws, those laws ought to be interpreted in light of basic principles of justice (or common sense). It can't be the case, they reasoned, that the legislature had *this situation* in mind when they set the rules that determine what counts as a valid or invalid will. Rather, interpreted in light of ordinary morality, the statute was best read implicitly to deprive murdering heirs of the right to inherit.

The point of mentioning *Riggs* is not to convince you that the majority got it right and the dissent got it wrong. Rather, it is to illustrate a kind of situation in which you might be expected to argue two sides of a rule, even though the rule's application to the facts seems relatively straightforward.

(3) *The rules invite policy analysis.* There are certain issues for which the legal standard expressly invites policy analysis. Consider the clause in Tia's contract that purports to limit the damages that she might recover from LTS. On a Torts

exam, this provision raises an issue that closely resembles the issue of "express assumption of risk"—that is, when a contract can be invoked to defeat what would otherwise be a valid tort claim. Most courts say that the enforceability of contractual liability waivers boils down to two questions: (1) whether the waiver is valid (i.e., whether the victim who is now suing in tort actually understood and consented to the waiver, whether the waiver's terms covers the liability in question, etc.), and (2) whether the enforcement of the waiver would violate public policy by denying tort law's protections to persons injured by the careless performance of a common pursuit (such as the provision of medical care, public transportation, etc.). In its latter aspect, the law of express assumption of risk overtly invites an argument about public policy. When this sort of issue is raised on an exam, you are thus required to entertain a certain kind of policy analysis. Is it less troubling, from a policy perspective, to enforce a contractual limitation on damages, as opposed to a full-blown waiver of liability? Why or why not?

ARGUING FROM THE FACTS

You should now see that arguing both sides of the issue is extremely important for two reasons. First, you will miss bumpers if you do not argue both sides when doing so is called for, which it usually is. This is the very heart of analyzing a close legal question. Second, knowing where these arguments exist (and where they do not) will assist you in organizing your answers.

But this fundamental piece of advice needs some refinement. For your arguments must incorporate and be responsive to the relevant facts that you are given, and must equally be sensitive to potentially relevant facts that you are *not* given. To be clear, where they are relevant, argue the facts you have been given. And, where appropriate, make reasonable assumptions about those you have not been given.

Let's return again to Tia's Tale. Because you have paid close attention to the facts, you have noticed that the failure to inform her of the possible harmful side effects of laser treatment is a possible theory of breach. This is an excellent start, but you're not done yet. Now comes the analysis. And here you'll need to attend closely to the facts. In your analysis, you'll want to note that there is at least one piece of evidence to suggest that the technician failed to give information that a reasonable patient would want to know to make an informed decision about undergoing a medical procedure. What evidence? The evidence from Tia—provided to you in the fact-pattern—that she had not heard the term "hyper-pigmentation" until after she had received her treatment. Does her recollection settle the issue? No. Perhaps she is just being forgetful. But this is surely a highly relevant fact, one that your professor would expect you to identify as particularly important to the viability of Tia's "informed consent" claim.

This point about harnessing the facts might seem obvious, but, under exam pressure, it is not. Students routinely lose critical points by writing an abstract essay on some point of law—for example, a disquisition on informed consent doctrine—with no attempt to establish how that doctrine might apply under the **specific, given facts.** Don't make this mistake: *Argue the facts.*

Frustratingly for students, it is often the case that exams omit critical facts that would help support a confident conclusion about the proper resolution of a particular issue. This is not accidental. The provision of incomplete facts is another way for your professor to test your ability to think like a lawyer. For the careful legal analyst not only considers how established facts might affect the resolution of a case, she also considers the significance of other facts not yet established.

Here it will be useful to draw an analogy to the process of discovery that takes place in civil litigation, and about which you have learned or probably will learn in Civil Procedure. The point of the discovery process is to give each party to a suit the opportunity to obtain information critical to the resolution of the suit under applicable legal rules. Through devices such as interrogatories and depositions, lawyers seek to uncover information that, as a matter of experience or common sense, they suspect is available and that would be of significance to their clients' cases.

Of course, in the standard exam setting, there is no discovery. Still, it can often be useful to play the role of a lawyer thinking about the discovery process. *In short, another way to hit bumpers is to demonstrate that you have good lawyerly instincts about relevant information that you have not been given, but might be available.* You can make this demonstration with minimal fuss, simply by nothing that, to resolve issue X, it would be helpful to know facts such as a, b, or c.

For example, in Tia's Tale, on the issue of whether the technician breached his duty of care by operating the machine improperly, you would want to include in your assessment of breach a mention of facts that haven't been given, but that common sense suggests might be available, and that would bear on whether the technician acted reasonably. There is a suggestion in Tia's conversation with her dermatologist that laser operators sometimes mistakenly set the laser's power level incorrectly. Of course you can't know whether that's what happened in this case. How could you? Rather, you are expected to show that you have a feel for the *kind of facts* that are likely to matter to the resolution of the issue before you.

Our discussion of the need to identify potentially relevant facts has an important "procedural" corollary. When you are given an incomplete set of facts, your professor will sometimes be inviting you to recognize—and will reward you for recognizing—that the situation calls for an exercise of judgment by the particular decision maker that is entrusted with the task of making that decision. In other words, you are being invited to show not only that you appreciate the importance of facts to the resolution of legal claims, but also that law is often as much concerned with allocating decision-making authority as it is with setting substantive rules or standards for resolving disputes.

Again, your professors are counting on you to ignore or forget this facet of law under pressured exam conditions. Anxious to show what you know, it is only natural that you will push hard—sometimes too hard—to reach a resolution of an issue even though the "right" answer is that the issue should be left to the discretion of a decision maker.

When confronted on an exam with an issue that is governed by a flexible legal standard that can plausibly be applied so as to generate different outcomes or conclusions, you should of course make arguments as to why it might be resolved one way or another on the merits. But you will also score points (metaphorically and literally) by signaling your awareness of instances in which the legal system's allocation of decision-making authority is of particular importance. For example, in analyzing Tia's Tale, with respect to the issue of breach, you will at some point want to emphasize that, precisely because the governing standard is the open-ended reasonably-prudent-person standard, the issue of breach ordinarily will be left to the discretion of the jury, thus making any prediction as to the resolution of the breach issue difficult.

FORKING: AVOIDING JUMPED SHIPS, MISSED OPPORTUNITIES, AND DEAD ENDS

Fact patterns tend to generate a handful of decision points—forks in the road—that you must recognize. Recognition is critical, but not the end of the matter. To gain the most points, you must understand what to do when faced with a fork.

For example, suppose in a Contracts fact pattern that there is a question of whether an agreement is supported by consideration. If there is, then the question can be analyzed as one in which a valid contract has been formed. If there is not, then promissory estoppel or off-the-contract remedies (restitution) might be at issue. Which of these should you discuss?

The answer, as you already know, is that you need to follow every branch of a fork to its end. There are bumpers to be hit along each branch. Thus, in the preceding example, you would need to discuss both the situation in which a contract has been formed, and the situation in which it has not. Not only that, but you have to discuss each of these fully, at least so far as the facts warrant.

Here are three things that often go wrong when forking:

(1) *Jumped ships.* If you start down one branch, get distracted by another issue that arises alongside it, then forget to return to the first branch, you lose points. Call this a "jumped ship." Don't jump ship. Or if you do, make sure to climb back on board. If your analysis of a claim or issue leads you to switch to another claim or issue, remember to return at some point to your original branch. For example, in the Contracts example just mentioned, if you started on the consideration issue, then halfway through moved over to discuss restitution (a "jumped ship"), you must go back to complete the analysis of consideration.

(2) *Forgotten forks.* The second problem posed by forks is that of "forgotten forks," or roads not taken. You are pleased to have worked your way to the end of one branch of analysis. You move on to another part of the question, or another question altogether, forgetting to retrace your steps back to the fork in the road and the other path that it presents. If you do this, you will lose points. Thus, if you note that there might be a problem with consideration, but assume that it is adequate and analyze the question as though there is a validly formed contract, do not forget that you also have to analyze the other branch, in which there is not a valid contract but perhaps there is a claim in restitution.

(3) *Dead ends.* What should you do when it seems that one of the analytic paths that you have identified almost instantly takes you to a conclusion that eliminates the need for further analysis? For example, Tia's Tale raises the possibility that LTS might have a statute of limitations defense. If successfully raised, it would call for dismissal of her claim at the outset. Suppose you begin to answer the question, and conclude that all possible claims are time-barred. Even if you were thoroughly convinced that this argument is a winner, it would be a

mistake to fail to address the other issues in the question. Why? Because it is extremely unlikely that your professor, having given you facts bearing on the merits of Tia's potential negligence claims, intended you to forego any discussion of them by concluding that the case was resolved on the issue of the statute of limitations.

Having said this, we want to acknowledge that fact patterns can be tricky. It is always *possible* that your professor planted all those other facts as a red herring, but wanted you to simply conclude, "Any claim is barred by the statute of limitations." If you are absolutely, 100 percent certain of this, then you must have the courage of your convictions and say so. Still, it is *much, much more likely* that something has gone wrong if your answer simply stops at this "dead end." Almost always, it is better to err on the side of inclusion. You can always hedge your bets by saying something like, "Although on balance it seems likely that a court would dismiss Tia's claim on statute of limitations grounds, it is possible a court would find otherwise, so I proceed to analyze the remaining issues raised by the facts."

The Bottom Line

- ☑ Don't make abstract legal arguments: argue the facts!

- ☑ When applying rules to facts, be ready to argue both sides!

- ☑ Omitted facts sometimes invite arguments.

- ☑ Make sure to argue within the rules, but consider whether there is occasion for policy analysis.

- ☑ Look for forks in the road.

- ☑ Keep track of the forks, or you will lose points: Retrace your steps!

Chapter 12

CONCLUSIONS

- ☑ Think in terms of probabilities, not certainties.

- ☑ Use tentative statements of conclusions to guide your analysis, but revise them as you develop and refine your argument.

- ☑ State conclusions clearly even though they are qualified.

IRAC ends with "C," which stands for conclusion. We have not said much about conclusions up to now, and we won't say much here. Indeed, we've kept this chapter brief to help emphasize the point we most want to make about conclusions: They are the *least* important part of IRAC. We say this not because knowing the conclusion is easy. Quite the opposite: It is because achieving certainty as to any given conclusion is often too difficult to allow for the giving of points. Rarely will a professor be in a position to award points to you because you got the right answer.

Because law professors tend to provide fact patterns in which, at least for the most complicated or interesting issues, there are good arguments on both sides, you might not be able to state a definite conclusion with any degree of certainty. (Remember our point in Chapter 1 about how judges don't necessarily have extra wisdom lawyers lack; it is just that their word often happens to be final.) Instead, your conclusion will read much like the conclusion to a memo written by a practicing lawyer when she first analyzes a client's case, which is to say that it will be written in qualified and probabilistic terms.

When it comes to writing conclusions, typically the best thing to do is to give your best probabilistic assessment. You can say something like "Under the current law of this jurisdiction, Client should prevail. However, it is possible, for reasons discussed above, that a court or jury could decide against Client." Note that, even when you appropriately hedge your conclusion in these ways, you want to make sure to write your conclusion in language that is crisp and authoritative, rather than wishy-washy. One of the tricks to being a good lawyer is simultaneously to acknowledge complexities and countervailing considerations while firmly defending one's position.

Having said this, we need to introduce a qualification that tracks our old friend, the Prime Directive: Always be sure to look closely at the precise question(s) that the professor asks of you for each fact pattern. Some will ask you to adopt the role of a judge and to issue a ruling definitively resolving the disputes before you. If so, your conclusion should be stated in a decisive form that is responsive to that instruction. Of course, the analysis that precedes your conclusion should not be similarly one-sided. Rather, your conclusion should follow notwithstanding the recognition of considerations for and against that conclusion: "Although considerations x, y, and z arguably support a contrary result, I rule in favor of conclusion C because of considerations a, b, and c."

There's one more thing to be said for conclusions. Even though they are in some ways the sprinkles on the icing on the cake, they can also be very useful to you as you write your exam answers. Here's what we mean. After you've scanned a question, and filled out the Issue List by matching it against your Subject List, you're ready to write. At this point, you might write down on a piece of scrap paper a tentative conclusion for each major claim or issue (for example, to revisit Tia's Tale from Chapter 11, you might write: "Tia should prevail on her informed consent claim against LTS"). Writing this conclusion might help focus your mind as you go through the steps in your analysis. Do the facts and the rules actually support this provisional conclusion? How so? Prove it! What's the best counterargument? By starting with a conclusion that you are aiming to defend, you have already put yourself in the right frame of mind: You are reasoning and arguing, rather than simply regurgitating. It won't be surprising—and often will be a good thing—if, in the course of trying to defend your initial hunch, you decide that it needs to be qualified, or even abandoned (e.g., "Tia should be able to get to a jury on her informed consent claim against LTS, though it is difficult to say whether she will prevail — a lot will depend on whether the jury is sympathetic to a person who paid to have someone who is not a licensed physician perform a cosmetic procedure on her."). Just make sure that, if your answer starts off defending one conclusion but then ends up reaching another, you go back and fix your analysis so that it leads to the conclusion that you have now embraced!

Finally, remember not to check your common sense at the door of the exam room. If you find yourself defending a conclusion that seems strongly counterintuitive, take a moment to look back over it, and the analysis leading up to it. Have you missed something? Can you qualify your conclusion in a way that makes it less jarring? There are certainly plenty of legal rules that, when properly applied, generate results that are odd, at least at first blush. So you might just want to stick to your guns. But if you have reached a conclusion that seems bizarre, and if you have a moment, it is worth considering whether a different conclusion is warranted, even if it's not one that is 180 degrees different from the one you originally reached.

The Bottom Line

- ☑ Remember the Prime Directive: Answer the questions asked of you!

- ☑ State conclusions probabilistically but clearly.

- ☑ Does your conclusion run afoul of common sense? If so, it might be right, but it might also benefit from reconsideration or refinement.

EXAMS 102: PREPARING FOR AND TAKING EXAMS

Chapter 13

OUTLINING FOR EXAM SUCCESS

☑ Make your own outlines.

☑ How to construct an outline.

☑ How to use ancillary study materials.

N
ow you know (almost) everything we have to tell you about how law school exams work. It's time to figure out how to study for them. Consistent with our theme that success begins on the first day of school, we're happy to report that, if you've been diligent in preparing for and attending class, you already will have come a long way. It's time now to focus on the all-important task of outlining your courses, which brings everything together in anticipation of taking the exam.

THE REAL-WORLD CONNECTION

In the same way that exams test you on a core skill of being a good lawyer, exam preparation also mirrors something important that lawyers do. Successful lawyers come prepared. Most lawyers love to be "on their feet," talking to people, asking questions, and solving problems. They live to conduct investigations, make deals happen, interview witnesses and try cases. But here's the thing: Good lawyers rarely do these things on the fly. In most cases, it is the hard behind-the-scenes work that plays a huge role in a lawyer's success.

At the heart of a lawyer's preparation is often an *outline*. When lawyers take depositions they use deposition outlines. Lawyers don't go to trial without elaborate trial outlines. Negotiating and working through a deal requires an outline. Whether you see the lawyer's outline or not, it is there, guiding what happens.

For practicing lawyers, outlines perform two tasks. They *synthesize* the information the lawyer needs, and they point out *directions* in which the lawyer is likely to want to go. Consider depositions. As you know or will soon know, a deposition is an examination of someone who likely will be a witness at trial (or cannot be at trial, so that the deposition is the main event). The goal of a deposition is to learn everything the trial witness has to say, and to see how that witness is going to answer questions. The deposition is important: It is often the one crack a lawyer is going to get at a witness before she confronts the witness on the stand in open court, and sometimes it might be the only time she gets to confront that witness at all. Many cases are resolved on the basis of depositions, without a trial. No one is going to squander that opportunity by not having at his or her fingertips summaries of all the relevant documents, prior testimony by the witness (or by others whose words bear on the witness's testimony), and any other facts germane to the case. And no lawyer worth her salt is going to go into that deposition without a game plan.

These are the functions your course outline will serve. It will synthesize everything you need to know to take your exam. And it will serve as the basis for your plan of attack — including, importantly, your Subject List (discussed in Chapter 9), which is so vital to succeeding on the exam.

MAKE YOUR OWN OUTLINE

Here is where we make the case for preparing your own outline. We know some of your classmates will tell you differently. We know you have your own arguments. Ultimately you are going to have to make your own decision. But we want you to take our arguments seriously.

We think there are two reasons you should prepare your own course outlines. We believe that each is, on its own, absolutely compelling. But in tandem we think it is difficult to defend another approach.[25]

The first reason you must prepare your own outlines is because the authors of commercial outlines did not attend the class you have attended. You've been sitting in Professor Snook's Contracts course all semester. We don't know if Snook is enthralling or dull; we don't know if she is organized or disorganized, clear or unclear, a doctrinalist or a theorist. But we do know this: It is Professor Snook who is going to write your exam, and Professor Snook who is going to grade it. And we also know that Professor Snook is going to write and grade that exam based on what *she* taught you during the semester.

Don't get us wrong. We're not against commercial outlines. We used them, occasionally. We also used treatises, nutshells, hornbooks, and all that other stuff. They have their place, and we're about to tell you what it is.

But no matter how good those materials are, they were not in class with you, and they don't know squat about what Professor Snoot covered, or how she covered it. Professor Snoot's exam is going to deal with the cases she taught. She has an approach to the subject that she has been honing for many years (or, if she is a new teacher, is developing). She has puzzles and problems that bother and intrigue her. She is going to build her exam around all that.

You possess all this information about what interests Professor Snook or is important to her; you heard it in class. But unless you have a memory of truly remarkable proportions—and every now and then we do have that stray student who sits through class listening, staring at us unblinking, never taking a note, somehow retaining it all—you can't remember everything. Still, it is right there in your notes. And writing your outline is the way you are going to unearth and remember all that stuff that mattered so much to

---

25. One qualification is in order here. It is consistent with our idea of making your own outline that you might work with a classmate or a couple of classmates on a jointly created outline. Indeed, there might be real educational value in this sort of collaboration. But that will be the case only if you keep the group small in number, only if you yourself make a substantial contribution to the outline, and only if you actively review and revise the materials prepared by your fellow outliners.

Professor Snook: call it "Snook's Stuff." No matter how good the commercial outline, it is simply not going to have the same material in it.

You might reply, "Fair enough, but I have an outline from a student who aced Snook's class last year!" That is pretty good. It will have a lot of Snook's Stuff in it. Of course, it won't have *this* year's Snook's Stuff in it. There are some professors who are, shall we say, a bit too in the groove — who tend to say the same things year after year. But that isn't true for many of us. Speaking personally, we mix it up. As a credit to you, it is in part because we *learn* from our students, and also try to follow their interests to some extent. It is also because our own views of subjects — even subjects we've taught ten times before — are evolving. And the law itself changes. Most of your professors will rearrange courses from time to time to improve on materials that didn't work well the previous year, or to cover new topics, or to try out new ideas. Even when they don't introduce new materials, they might emphasize different aspects of existing materials, or offer a different "take" on them. So, last year's outline from Snook's Contracts class is second-best.

Still, you might say, "It's not perfect, but it is pretty good, and I just don't have time to do better. Haven't you guys heard of cost-benefit analysis? I have this pretty good outline and I need to get studying. I just don't have the luxury of doing my own outline. So, I'm going with the preexisting outline. Now leave me alone!"

This brings us to the second reason to prepare your own outline. Preparing an outline *is* studying. In fact, it is the best studying for the exam you are likely to do.

We're going to get into the mechanics in just a moment, but the bottom line is this: Preparing the outline is your chance to go through the course and recall all that you learned in that class and to pull out what is important. As you do it, you will be learning the material. Indeed, this sort of learning is pretty much the best way of implanting information and ideas into your memory. Most people find that when they get done outlining a course, they really know the course, and they know where they have questions.

Keep in mind, though, that the preparation of an outline, time-consuming though it may be, is just your first run through the materials. Once it's done, you'll want to make sure to go back over it, revise it, and distill it into "attack" materials. Although you could conceivably do this with commercial materials, the material come exam time is going to be oh-so-much-more-familiar and accessible if you are working with your own outline. By the exam, you are going to know that material like the back of your hand.

Even if you only have a few days to prepare for the exam — and if you have been using this book, hopefully you will have more time than that — you are best off starting at the beginning of the course and outlining it. Yes, it will take you three days or more of hard work to outline most courses. But as we say, you will really know all the material at that point. Worst comes to worst, after finishing your outline, you could walk right into the exam. And if you only had a day or two more, you'd be in terrific shape. Really!

We understand how tempting it is to heed those who tell you that you don't need to do all that grungy work of outlining. We like short-cuts, too. We'd like to be able to take a once-a-day pill that keeps our weight down without exercise or watching what we eat. But some things in life just aren't like that.

If at the end of the day we have failed to convince you not to rely on others' outlines (and, gosh, we hope we've made some headway here), at least meet us halfway. Go ahead, if you must, and grab an outline from an outline bank, or from a 3L or 2L. But please, please recognize that this is only the first step, much like learning the rules is just the first step in legal analysis. *Now you have to take that outline and make it your own: Use it as raw material, rather than as an off-the-shelf consumer product.* Based on what you have learned in class, and what you have discussed with your colleagues and your professor, review it carefully, revise it, update it, and, if necessary, reorganize it. At least then you will be thinking and learning, which is the point of doing an outline. Grudgingly, we might even concede that there is a certain value in this way of outlining. The ability to take existing or stock materials (such as form contracts) and sculpt them to the particular situation you are facing in light of your own expertise and judgment is a skill that lawyers are called on to display in practice. But this concession only reinforces our central point: You really do have to make the materials your own rather than simply take them as is.

REVERSING CLASS

Let's take a preliminary look at what an outline is. After that, we'll tell you how to go about making your own, and what should go into it.

As we explained in Part I, there is a seeming disjunction between the classroom experience and exams. Classes are not usually organized around the problems, or fact patterns, that you'll face on an exam. Rather, they are organized around cases. Despite this disjuncture, you already have all the information you need to tackle the exam; you just have to get it into the right shape. What you need is right there in your class case briefs and class notes. You just have to know how to pull the relevant material out.

One way to think about outlining is that you are effectively creating a "reverse phone directory" for your class. A standard directory is organized so you can look up people or businesses by name and get their phone numbers. A reverse directory allows you to look up a phone number and find the person to whom it belongs. Similarly, in class you were given the cases; then you were asked to derive the rule and apply it to hypothetical situations. In the exam, you are given the hypothetical and asked to figure out what rules to apply and how to analyze the hypothetical facts. You basically have to turn the material you learned in class inside out. At bottom, this is what preparing an outline is all about.

SYNTHESIS, SYNTHESIS, SYNTHESIS

Everyone has his or her own style of outlining; outlines from the same class can look remarkably different. Successful students tackle this task in divergent ways and end up in the same place. In order for you to see this, and to help you find the style of outline that works best for you, we've collected some samples to examine on **Open Book Digital**, organized by subject matter. Before going further, you may want to take a little time to examine some of the differing approaches.

No matter what style of outline you ultimately adopt, we suggest you use something like the process we are about to describe in order to prepare it.

First, gather the materials you will need. What are they? Your casebook or any other texts you were assigned, your class notes, your case briefs, and any supplemental materials you have acquired. By "supplemental materials" we mean any commercial outlines or treatises and the like. Now is the time to use them!

Start by reading your class notes. Read them for one class, but then keep reading. Read initially in "bites" or "gulps" that cover a complete subject. In other words, if you started Contracts with formation — offer and acceptance — read all of that. (Ditto if it was remedies.)

The reason you want to read in chunks is that your goal here is *synthesis*. That's why you don't want to start outlining too early: It is difficult to synthesize effectively as you go. To have a meaningful and coherent outline you have to have some distance from — and some perspective on — the material. Your professor spelled it out in what (we hope) was a logical order. But one can't appreciate a story of any sort until it is over, or at least far along. Trying to outline in less than these subject-matter chunks is like explaining a movie to someone after watching only 20 minutes of it. Admittedly, there is not much of a surprise ending to most law school topics, but, still, clarity and comprehension often emerge only at the end of the story.

After you have read the complete chunk, go back to the first set of notes for that segment. Now focus more carefully. Here's where the real work starts.

What you are looking for initially are the black-letter rules and doctrinal tests that make the law work. As we have told you repeatedly, your professors will expect you to know these rules cold for the exam. If you are learning negligence, you will now see how your professor covered all the elements: duty, breach, cause, proximate cause, and damage. You will pull out the rules for duty and breach. Do your best to summarize those rules.

Then, turn to your subsidiary materials if you have them. This is where they can be most helpful. Ideally, you want to learn the rules, and what animates them, from your professor. But it is possible that sitting in class as the story unfolded, you did not follow everything entirely. There might have been things your professor said that didn't make sense. So, after you take a stab at understanding the law from your own course materials, consult your commercial outline or your treatise, whatever you have at hand. Use these sources as a check on whether you got things correct, and to fill in any holes.

A caution, however, about secondary sources: Many of them, commercial outlines in particular, are designed to give you a sense of security. But it is a false and overdone one, in our view. These outlines weren't in your class with you so they can't reveal the professor's approach. Instead, they tend to provide the illusion of security by offering you an endless array of rules and sub-rules, as if the difference between surviving and thriving on your exams will turn on whether you know twelve more rules than your colleagues. This is absolutely the wrong way to think about exams. As we've told you repeatedly, what matters most on exams are arguments. When confronted with a tough issue, you are not going to be rewarded for pulling out of the recesses of a commercial outline some rule that it claims governs the issue. You are going to be rewarded for seeing that it is a tough issue and analyzing it methodically. If you resolve one of these issues by citing to a "rule" discussed in a commercial outline, yet never even mentioned in class, you are probably only going to succeed in mystifying or annoying your professor.

Here's an example to illustrate the point about overreliance on commercial sources. Many Torts classes cover the rule that a person has no privilege—and thus can be held liable—for using deadly force merely to protect property. The standard case for the application of this rule is *Katko v. Briney*, in which a man stealing some jars from an abandoned farmhouse is shot by a "spring gun" and recovers damages from the property owner.[26] Now comes a variation on *Katko*. *P* plans to break into *D*'s residence so that he can murder *D*. *D*, meanwhile, has decided to leave town for a spontaneous vacation. Before driving away from his home, *D* sets up a spring gun at his back door to protect his property while he is away. Just as *D* has finished doing so, *P* bursts into the back door wielding a knife. Quite reasonably, *D* is terrified that *P* will kill him, but then the spring gun goes off, and *P* is shot and injured. Can *P* recover damages from *D*?

The point of presenting a hypothetical like this is to invite you to reason about the no-privilege rule, its limits, and its rationales. Is the only relevant consideration the property owner's initial reason for setting the trap? If so, *P* should win, because when *D* set the trap he was doing so merely to protect his property. Or do we care about the actual

---

26. 183 N.W.2d 657 (Iowa 1971).

circumstances in which the shooting took place? If so, the result might be different, as *D* would have been justified in shooting *P* to defend himself from imminent deadly attack.[27] Whatever the best answer, it will not help you on an exam merely to invoke a judicial decision, referenced in a commercial outline or a treatise, which supposedly has settled the question raised by this hypothetical. The hypothetical cries out for analysis, not merely a citation to a case from a source external to your course materials.

THE SUM AND ITS PARTS

Always remember, as you prepare your own outlines, that what you are doing is synthesizing. You are combining what your professor said with your briefs of the cases, the material in the casebook, and the commercial sources. You are struggling to put it all together, to make sense of it. Distillation and comprehension are the keys.

On occasion students come to us and say "Wow, I didn't get what that was about until I was outlining. But then the course really came together for me." That might sound as though it casts aspersions on our teaching. Weren't we clear all semester? To the contrary, we consider it a compliment. Law can be extremely intricate and complex. Sometimes, if not often, you need to see the whole picture to understand the parts. And once you do, the parts all start to come together in a way that makes sense.

Your ultimate goal is an outline that distills all the rules in the course, and their rationales, organized by topic. If you stop and think about it, you already know this is the goal. Why? Because of all the earlier chapters stressing the importance of IRAC and of hitting bumpers. Your outline is your primary tool for doing just this. When you need to compare the Subject List to the Issue List, your outline will contain the information you require. When you need the rules that you should apply to resolve an issue, that's in your outline. When you want

---

27. As you might have learned or might learn in Torts, the resolution of this particular issue could be affected by the enactment in the relevant jurisdiction of a "stand your ground" statute.

to figure out how the sorts of policy arguments that are used to apply the rule in some situations but not others, that's there too.

That's the general idea. But you'll no doubt want specifics. Here is our enumeration of what should be in your outline. We are pretty confident that as you read this, assuming you have read the rest of the book carefully, you are going to be nodding your head (at least metaphorically) in agreement. By now, you will see how all of this instruction is tied directly to what it takes to do well on exams.

(1) *Organize by topic areas.* Remember matching, and all that talk in Chapter 9 of your Subject List and your Issue List? As we've explained repeatedly, one of the most important things you will do on an exam is probe the fact pattern to figure out what issues it raises. Ultimately you are going to take your outline list, and outline it—make a table of contents—that will form your Subject List. For this reason, you will want to organize the outline by the topics the professor taught. There is no great mystery to this; typically, the professor will have handed out a syllabus that organizes the course materials. And recall what we told you about the logical structure of the law. Very often that syllabus will be structured in a logical way, reflecting the legal structure of the material you have been learning, in just the way the professor wants it analyzed. So, organize your outline just that way.

(2) *Rules!* The most important thing that will go into your outline under the topic headings is the set of rules and elements that make up the law. You might be wondering why rules are so important. Didn't we tell you earlier that stating rules on an exam is not going to get you lots of points? What we hope you also understand by now, however, is that without the rules you are lost. It is the rules that create the issues that make facts germane. It is rules applied to facts that create the legal arguments on which you will be graded. These are the building blocks of law—or, if you like, the tools of the lawyer. They are what lawyers use to frame analyses and arguments.

You *are* right, though, that just knowing or stating the rules will not get you big points on an exam. You need to be able to apply the rules, to argue why under them your client should win or your opponent should lose. So, what we discuss next is what goes under the rules and topic headings in your outline, the meat on the bones of the law.

(3) *Cases.* The cases you read for class are incredibly important for taking your exams. The rules are found in cases, but the cases also serve as examples of how the rules work. Students often ask, "Do we have to cite cases on the exam?" Even if you don't need to, why wouldn't you? Cases are the common language that everyone in your class uses when speaking about the law.

It would be an odd law school exam that did not include fact patterns that resemble some of the cases you read in class. After all, analogical reasoning has been at the core of what you have been doing. Citing cases can be a remarkably efficient and effective means of demonstrating to the professor that you know precisely in which garden you are toiling. If you are outlining affirmative defenses for your Torts class, you will want to include a mention of *Katko* when it comes to privileges to use deadly force. Should a privilege-to-protect-property issue arise on your exam, you can effectively and powerfully invoke the rule simply by referencing *Katko*. At the same time, your associating the rule with *Katko* will, we hope, remind you of the kind of situation that counts as a core application of the rule, as well as the kind of situations that would call for extensions of the rule, and hence for analysis.

By now you should know the cases you studied in the course. In your outline you will want to indicate the cases that support the rule, and something about the key facts so you remember the case and how it came out. One of our professors used to say that more important than the "rules" of cases were the short, snappy "propositions" for which each stood. So, under each rule in your outline you will want a record of the cases you read addressing that rule, what the case was about, and what its punch line was; that is, why it is important: *Katko* (spring gun case; no privilege to use deadly force merely to protect property).

INTENTIONAL TORTS

. . . .

Defenses
1. Privilege of Self-Defense/Defense of Others
2. Privilege to Defend Property
   a. May use rsble force to repel (push away trespasser)
   b. No DEADLY force just to protect property (KATKO, spring gun)
      i. DEADLY force ok when in one's home if self-defense
      ii. DEADLY force not ok in home if only to protect property (at least absent "Stand Your Ground" statute).

---

(4) *Policies.* The law has its share of inconsistencies and deficiencies, but it is not just a random collection of rules. These rules, one hopes, put into action a set of sensible policies on which one would organize a society. Again, we readily concede that some of the rules don't make a lot of sense and that some are quite unjustifiable. But even when it comes to critiquing rules or their operation, policy considerations can help you gauge what is "sensible" and what is not. If the rule, or its application in a given case, fails to follow from or advance the underlying policies that justify it, then there is a problem.

In class you will have spent time exploring the policies that support the rules. As we've explained, policy is not where you turn first in answering an exam question. First you identify the rule and make arguments in each direction based on the facts in the fact pattern. But in many instances the rules will "run out." There might be two conflicting rules, either of which could apply. The rule might simply not resolve the case. It is at that point that you turn to the underlying policies to make additional arguments.

For this very reason, you need to have in your outline the policies that animate the rules. Sometimes these are straightforward. Sometimes it is more complicated: The policies themselves can point in two different directions. You will want to note these conflicts or tensions—both of which provide a fertile field for exam questions!

(5) *Hypotheticals.* In class, your professors almost certainly peppered you and your colleagues with hypotheticals. As we explained in Part One, these presented twists on the cases; modifications of the facts intended to fill out your understanding of the rules. We hope you can now see what that was all about. Often these hypotheticals show the limits of the rule, or the circumstances under which a case would come out the opposite way under the same rule. They gave the rule its contours.

It is common in outlines, then, to have—after the rule, the cases that support it, and the policies that animate it—a string of examples or questions that indicate those contours and limits. For example, after your Contracts outline sets out the basic rules on consideration, indicates the key cases that support the consideration requirement, and explains why it is needed, you might have some hypotheticals like, "What if the consideration was referred to as a 'gift'?" and then some analysis of that question.

This technique of dealing with hypotheticals is important—essential even—because that in effect is the closest that most of your case-method classes have come to real exam conditions. Hypotheticals are mini-fact patterns that test your knowledge and understanding of the rules, and also your ability to argue both ways for application of the rule. So, understanding what went on in class around hypotheticals provides a way of testing your exam skills.

(6) *Update, revise, and refine.* Think of your outline as a living creature. Each time you add to it, go back and look at the parts you've already done. You might see in the earlier parts a mistake or something that is confusing. You might see a connection between materials you covered early in the course and those you covered later. These are great opportunities to update, revise, and refine your outline. Practice exams can be similarly useful. If, after you take a practice exam and go over it, you discover that you missed some issues, check to see if your

outline needs some new headings, or filling out in a particular area. Remember, outline revisions are not simply an exercise in housekeeping. They are moments when you are thinking deeply about the materials on which you are going to be tested.

ATTACKING THE EXAM

If you construct an outline of the sort we've described, and get a handle on what is in it, you will have the information at your fingertips that you need to do well on an exam. However, most of our successful students don't just sit back at this point and let the exam take them. Rather, they attack it. They have a variety of strategies for this. We'll explain some of the prominent ones here, with editorial comments. And, again, we have these on **Open Book Digital** for you to look at yourself.

First and foremost is your outline summary. This is the most important single document you will prepare. It is your Subject List—the list that plays such an important role in issue spotting, and in reminding you to discuss critical issues in the heat of the moment. Constructing this list is easy. It is simply a table of contents of your outline, indicating key subject areas you studied, the main subtopics, and— occasionally and very usefully—the elements of legal tests.

Another technique that students use is to anticipate obvious subject areas that will likely appear on the exam, and prepare "attack outlines" for these. It is fairly predictable that there are certain issues that will arise on an exam. If you have taken a course that covers the "structural" dimensions of federal constitutional law, your exam is almost certainly going to ask about congressional power under the Commerce Clause and also probably will include something on separation of powers. Your Civil Procedure professor will ask about motions to dismiss and personal jurisdiction. Attack outlines foresee these questions and sketch out the key elements of answers to them. They are limited to the key rules, two or three major policies that inform the rules, the main cases, and any particularly salient points that the professor has made in this regard. What the attack outline is doing is effectively saying, "If you remember nothing else, remember to talk about this stuff!"

In our view, attack outlines are as much about exam preparation as exam taking. It's certainly a good idea to have something to jog your memory during exams, although we would stress it is rarely the case on a good exam that anything can be answered simply by regurgitating the material on an outline. But the very exercise of preparing these sorts of attack outlines, which are simply extracted from your larger, more complete outline, drills into your mind what is important in a given subject area. As we said, once you understand the substance, rote learning has something to say for itself.

We've also seen students construct flow charts that map out the various topics covered in a course, and how they relate to each other. These are a lot like flow charts you've seen for any process, like computer programming. The assumption is that one could take a problem, say a criminal law problem, and walk through the flow chart, and not miss anything crucial.

Flow charts are great, although they have certain limitations. On the one hand, there is a logical flow to the law. On the other, it doesn't *all* always fit in one flow chart. Some topics defy being charted, although it can be illuminating (and even fun!) to try, as we found with the heroic effort, below, by our fabulous illustrator, Claire Suni, to capture the main contours of the *Erie* doctrine. Again, the heuristic is what is important. The point is to immerse yourself in the subject matter and try to piece it all together. The act of doing so forces you to think deeply about the material.

Finally, some students create a one-pager. One-pagers are a combination of an outline summary and an attack outline. What these students are doing is trying to fit all the key concepts and policies of the entire course onto one piece of paper. It's not just a list, like the outline summary. And it's not just about one topic. It is the synthesis of the synthesis, a boiling down of the course to its most important elements.

The one-pager can serve two purposes. One is as a heuristic, as we've said. The other, though, is that some professors who give closed-book exams still allow students to bring one sheet of paper to the exam. A one-pager can be incredibly useful in this regard, but don't do one that fails to include the full list of topics on your outline summary. It is the latter that we often find most valuable.

FORESTS AND TREES

Now that we've finished digging around in the weeds, we want to step back with a reminder. We have one word for you: IRAC!!! (Okay, maybe that's not actually a word.)

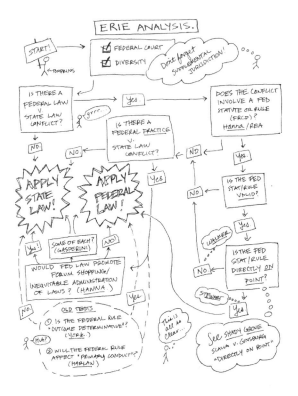

Everything you are doing here is in service of IRAC, and of hitting bumpers in answering questions. *That* is what the outline, and all its progeny, is for. So, whatever you do, however you construct whatever you construct, remember the ultimate goal.

The Bottom Line

☑ Prepare your own outlines.

☑ Synthesize course materials.

☑ Include rules, key cases, major policy considerations, and some hypotheticals.

☑ If you use commercial sources, use them to check your work, and fill gaps.

☑ Outline your outline to create your Subject List.

Chapter 14

MAKE YOUR LISTS; CHECK THEM TWICE

☑ How to make lists for matching and issue spotting.

☑ How to make sure you cover everything on your lists.

☑ The Prime Directive revisited.

O nce you've completed your outline, you are ready to take your first law school exam! Shortly, we are going to talk about the most valuable preparation for each particular exam available to you—namely, practice exams. Before we do, though, we want to go over with you the key to success *during* an exam. (As we'll stress, practice exams should be taken as seriously as the real event, so you have to be ready when you take one.) There are a number of important tips and skills discussed in this chapter, but none exceeds the value of constructing your Subject and Issue Lists. We believe this is the very key to exam success.

READ THIS! FOLLOWING INSTRUCTIONS

Let's begin by once again reminding ourselves of the Prime Directive, first mentioned at the beginning of the book. In this context, it translates into a message that is simple and essential: *Follow instructions!* This includes the written instructions at the beginning of each exam, as well as other instructions your professor has given you in class or in a review session.

Everyone makes mistakes, but for lawyers representing clients, a failure to follow even a simple rule can have grave consequences. *State v. Daniels* was a case involving two men sentenced to death for murder by the courts of North Carolina. Their lawyers intended to argue on appeal that the convictions resulted from coerced confessions and racial discrimination in the composition of the jury before which the men were tried. However, the lawyers filed their appellate papers one day after the deadline for filing appeals had passed. The appeal was lost for lack of timeliness, and the defendants were executed.[28]

Daniels is, of course, an extreme example—nothing of remotely comparable importance rests on your heeding exam instructions. But you get the point. A lawyer's life is about rules. Mostly, it is about arguments from within and about the rules. Sometimes, however, it is about following—to the letter—certain very basic rules. Now is the time to get in the habit of scrupulously attending to such rules.

If you see an exam instruction that sets a word limit on your answer, follow it. Do not exceed it by even one word. If you see an instruction that you are to discuss only claims by (or against) certain people, discuss only those claims, not others. If you see an instruction that you are to answer a question by adopting the position of a judge who must issue a decision, make sure to do so. If the professor has told you that she expects students to defend their analysis on policy grounds, that is your job.

Instructions are not some picayune thing that professors put there to trip you up; they are there for a reason. They often signal, directly or indirectly, what the professor is interested in seeing on an exam and what she is not interested in seeing. In providing them, the professor is often trying to help. Read them. Re-read them. And ignore them at your peril.

---

28. *State v. Daniels*, 57 S.E.2d 653 (N.C. 1950) (refusing to review the defendants' convictions given the missed deadline). The U.S. Supreme Court later ruled that the same failure to comply with the state's rules of appellate procedure blocked the defendants from pursuing constitutional objections to their convictions in federal court. *Brown v. Allen*, 344 U.S. 443, 482-87 (1953). Of course, we'll never know if the defendants' appeal in *Daniels* would have been successful had it been heard on the merits, but losing a meaningful chance to overturn a death sentence obviously is a significant loss.

Here's a way to help make sure that you heed instructions. Write a shorthand version of key instructions at the top of the piece of scrap paper that you are using in preparing your answer to a question. For example, if the question asks you to adopt the role of the trial judge, mark in big letters at the top of the paper something like this: "BE JUDGE—DECIDE." Or, if the question directs you to analyze some possible claims but not others, write, "CAN A AND B WIN SUITS? DON'T WRITE ABOUT SUIT BY C."

There's another kind of instruction that you might get on some of your exams. It comes in the form of information about the relative weight that the professor will assign to different questions. For example, in the initial instructions, or at the beginning of each question, there might be a recommendation to allot a certain amount of time to that question. Or you might even be informed of the percentage of your overall grade that will be attributed to that question (e.g., "Question 1 is worth 20 percent of your exam grade, Question 2 is worth 35 percent, and Question 3 is worth 45 percent"). Pay close attention to this information and keep track of your time. If you spend 90 minutes of a three-hour exam on a question worth 25 percent of your exam grade, you will have devoted too much time to hitting too few bumpers. Indeed, if there is one question on the exam that is worth quite a bit more than the others, you might consider answering that question *first*, even if it is not the first question on the exam (unless, of course, the professor said to answer the questions in order). Regardless, the point is that you must budget your time carefully. And, as we emphasize in Chapter 16, you need to: PRACTICE! The skill of time management for exams is best learned through taking lots of practice tests.

Remember: although our goal in this book is to give you sound general advice, we will not be scoring your exam. Your professor will. What the professor says is the law insofar as success on his or her exam is concerned.

ASK THE PROFESSOR

Consistent with the foregoing advice, we encourage you to ask your professors about their exams beforehand. Some professors will be more responsive than others, but there's no harm in asking, at least if you do it politely and thoughtfully.

Here is a short list of items that, in our experience, professors feel differently about:

- Is it desirable to cite cases in your exam answers? Our view is—as we've said—that informal case citation (e.g., *"Palsgraf"*) usually works in your favor, because it is often an efficient way to convey an idea, and because it shows a basic fluency in the law.
- How much weight is given to exposition of a rule? We expect our students to know the rules and tend not to give many points merely for reciting them. Other professors might have a different view.
- To what extent should an answer delve into policy considerations? We generally prefer that students engage in policy discussions only under the types of circumstances described in Chapter 11. Some professors prefer more or less.
- To what extent do organization, grammar, and polish matter? We tend not to give a lot of weight to these factors, but other professors might feel differently.

REVISITING THE SUBJECT LIST

Back in Chapter 9, when discussing issue spotting, we talked about matching the material you have learned in your class (Subject List) with the issues raised by the fact patterns on an exam (Issue List). Now we want to give you some more tips for developing these lists.

Before we do, a reminder of why this matters. One of the primary tasks on an exam is issue spotting, and one of the places students go wrong is in missing issues. Sometimes the reason for missing an issue is simply skill-related; you didn't catch the issue. Very often, though, students say they miss issues not because the question was too hard but because they just forgot to cover it. This sort of thing can happen during an exam. In either case, though, having a good Subject List can help. It jogs your memory regarding the obvious and can help you uncover the subtle. Every issue you find this way, that you would not have otherwise, means more bumpers hit, and more points.

As we have explained, the source of the Subject List is your course outline. By the time of your exam, your outline will be too bulky and unwieldy a vehicle to permit you to use it as the Subject List. Rather, the Subject List has to be an outline (or synthesis) of your outline.

As we noted in Chapter 9, there are various methods for constructing the Subject List. (In the illustration above, it's referred to as "List A".) You can prepare a list of, say, a dozen general topics, each of which might have a handful of subtopics. An outline of a Contracts outline, for example, might have "Formation" as one of a dozen headings, with subheadings on "Offer" and "Acceptance," and sub-subheadings such as "When Revocable" "When Irrevocable," and so on. Alternatively, you can index your outline using different colored highlighters to identify different topics. If you do this you'll gradually start to focus on the higher level material, as you assimilate and memorize the details. By the time the exam comes, you likely will be in a position to choose a topic like "contract formation" and have in your mind all the material under it. Then, as we've said, some students use "attack outlines" or "one-pagers." You can find examples of these on **Open Book Digital**. We've also had students who prepared elaborate (and sometimes beautiful!) "flow charts" and "decision trees" to help them think through the sequence of issues that might be faced on an exam. A Civil Procedure flow chart might start with a box in the upper left corner marking a threshold issue such as subject-matter jurisdiction. From that box an arrow might point rightward to the next topic in the decision sequence, such as personal jurisdiction. In each box there will be bulleted reminders of key points. In the personal jurisdiction box, for example, one might see headings such as: "In Personam v. In Rem," "General v. Specific," and "Statutory v. Constitutional."

What's important to understand is that the goal for all of these methods is the same. You are simply trying to prepare an aid to help remind you, during your exam, of issues for which you should be on the lookout. As we said about outlining generally, an additional advantage is that the very act of preparing it will drill it into your mind.

When it comes to using your Subject List, closed-book exams present a special challenge. For open-book exams, you presumably will have your outline at hand. And right on top of that outline will be the outline of the outline, or its table of contents, or your flow charts — your Subject List. But on closed-book exams you won't be able to bring the list with you.[29]

No worries. All that is required is a little memorization.

Take your outline of your outline and memorize it. Use acronyms or mnemonic devices if that helps you remember the key headings. Then, as soon as you are instructed to start your closed-book exam, jot down on scrap paper the topic headings you have memorized. Memorizing the key topic headings of your course outline might sound silly, and it is a bit of work, but it matters a great deal. Students regularly forget to discuss material they learned in the course for no reason other than that it slipped their minds under the pressure of an exam.

PREVIEWING

Exam fact patterns will raise many issues; it is your job to unearth them. Let's think a bit now about how to use your Subject List to do

---

29. For this reason, some professors who give closed-book exams still allow you to bring one sheet of notes. You might ask your professor about this.

so. In the exam, have the Subject List in front of you. Now read the fact pattern. Indeed, you might want to start by skimming over, or "previewing," the entire exam. If you are a slow reader or the exam is very long, this might not be possible, but if it is, there is probably something to be gained from even a cursory run through of all the questions. Here, we'll explain why.

Remember what your professor is aiming to accomplish with her exam: She probably is covering roughly three-quarters of the course materials, and is unlikely to be raising the same issue over and over. Rather, different questions — and different parts of each question — will tend to raise different sets of issues.

Previewing can help you see how the material you have learned is distributed across the exam. On a Civil Procedure exam, for example, if there are two essay questions, a preview might reveal that one is mainly focused on issues of personal jurisdiction and discovery, whereas another raises issues pertaining to summary judgment and the application of *Erie*. Again, we don't mean to suggest that professors will never test the same issue in two different questions; often they will. Our point is that, in general, different questions will raise different issues to ensure that the exam covers most of the material covered in class. Previewing can give you a quick sense of what's where, before you really dig in.

REVISITING THE ISSUE LIST

Now it's time to focus on a particular question. As you read the fact pattern, remember to look back at your Subject List. Very quickly you will begin to see issues that correspond to those headings, and that call for the application of the rules that fall under those headings. In short, the Issue List — the bumpers — will start to emerge, and soon you will be busily matching the two lists.

As you start to see the issues, it is *critical* that you keep track of everything you are seeing. This is why you must actually jot down the Issue List rather than just keeping it in your head. You need a running tab of what (and where) the issues are. If the exam is in hard copy, you can make shorthand notes in the margin of the exam that identify the issue(s) being raised by a given sentence or paragraph in the fact pattern. Or, whether in hard copy or online, you can use a piece of scrap paper to scribble down the issues raised by a question. Either way, what you effectively are doing

is converting the fact patterns you see on your exam into a written Issue List.

Issue List for Tia's Tale

TIA'S TALE

No basis for intentional tort: T v. LTS for negligence

Injury = hyperpig.

Duty: Provider → Customer

Breach: LTS careless? Laser misused? Proof? Informed Consent? Proof?

Actual causation: Diff't proof for misuse and informed consent theories?

As you read and begin developing your written Issue List, remember to go back from time to time and consult the Subject List. This will help ensure that you are not missing bumpers. If you find it helpful, you can even check off topics on the Subject List. But don't cross them out—they might come up again.

We cannot stress enough the importance of this seemingly mechanical exercise. You need to make sure to go over your outline's table of contents item-by-item with the fact pattern in mind, and see if you can find matches that you missed initially. You are waiting for that "Aha!" moment in which you realize that there is something obvious (or subtle) on the Subject List that is raised by the fact pattern, and that you had until then missed.

Similarly, as you write your exam answer, new issues are likely to occur to you. You probably won't want to stop just at that moment to write about those items. So what you should do—you must do—is add them to your Issue List so that you will remember to come back to them. If you don't, there's a good chance you'll end up forgetting to discuss something you knew was an issue.

The process of consulting the Subject List to look for issues is so important that — if there is any time left after you have taken the whole exam — you might look back over it one last time to see if there are topics that you have not written about at all. This is a quick and useful way to spot additional issues and gain more points. That is because by now you are well acquainted with the fact pattern and with what you have covered in your written answer. If you have been checking items on the Subject List, just look to see what remains unchecked. Did the professor simply not test you on a particular topic? Or have you missed that issue?

For example, suppose you've completed your Criminal Law exam. You review the Subject List and discover that you have not discussed criminal attempts. Is it really the case that your professor did not want to test you on that topic? Maybe. More likely, though, you have missed something. One last pass at the Subject List and the fact pattern — rereading when you are looking for something in particular — often permits you to find things you wouldn't have otherwise found. And by discussing these neglected issues you will hit more bumpers and pick up more points.

ORGANIZATION AND PRESENTATION AS TECHNIQUES TO UNEARTH BUMPERS

Back in the days when exam answers were handwritten in "blue-books," one of our professors — Friedman's Property Law professor, to be exact — engaged in an interesting exam preparation exercise. He handed out two exam answers and asked the class to guess which received the better score. One was a model of clarity and organization. The other was, well, a mess. Chunks of text were crossed out. Additional words were squeezed in here and there. Answers sometimes changed directions in midstream, as in, "Wait, I'm not sure that is right, what about . . . ." Most of the class picked the prettier exam. The professor's punch line was that the messy exam received a better score. His point: hitting bumpers is everything.

We don't encourage you to take too much from this example, in part because a lot has changed since when we were in law school. Bluebooks will soon be museum pieces, if they aren't already. Most exams are taken on computers. Word processing obviates the need to squeeze words into the margins, and it allows for speedier reorganization than one could achieve while hurriedly scrawling exam answers with a pen. (Be careful, though. Law schools often require students to use special exam software that is quite a bit less functional than standard word-processing programs. For example, it might not be possible to cut and paste easily using exam software.) In addition, there is a trend toward greater use of take-home exams and exams with longer time periods than the old norm of three or four hours. Under these conditions, professors might be justifiably less tolerant of messy answers.

Still, this important question remains: Given time limits, how much attention should one devote to organization? Perhaps you can predict our answer: Organizing matters to the extent it helps you hit more bumpers and pick up more points. All things being equal we adhere to the lesson of the professor we just mentioned. Spending a lot of time ordering your arguments and polishing the look of your answers is probably not worth it (again, unless your professor tells you otherwise).

As it happens, though, there are point-related reasons to do some organizing. An exam answer that is organized in a sensible way will make it easier for the professor to see the bumpers you have hit. And taking a very few moments to do some basic organization might even help you see some additional issues. Here we offer some lessons on organization that both draw from our "matching and lists" technique and also reflect the inherent structure of the law.

The easiest way to organize is to put your Issue List to good use. Once you have run through a fact pattern and compiled the Issue List for that question, take a few moments to ask yourself what a logical organization of the issues on that list might be. There are two very quick ways to do some organizing. Either rewrite the Issue List in what seems a logical order, or simply put numbers next to the items on the list in the order in which you want to discuss them. See how easy that is? The organization does not have to be perfect by any means, but if you just start writing from whatever issue you happen to first spot, you might write yourself into chaos.

As to how to organize your answers, the black-letter law can often help you. We mentioned earlier that some students convert their course materials into flow charts or decision trees. You might see whether the issues that you have spotted — and put on your Issue List — can be addressed in the same sort of sequence. Some courses are more amenable to flow-charting than others, mind you. Think of Contracts, for example. Generally speaking, Contracts questions can be tackled in a sequence corresponding to the various phases of contracting: for example, formation, performance, enforcement. This is not always the case; each exam is unique, with its own challenges and strategies for addressing them. But where there is logic, it makes sense to adhere to it.

For other kinds of exams—particularly Torts and Criminal Law—you might find it helpful to break down your Issue List by character or party in the fact pattern. For example, in a Torts exam, the fact pattern will sooner or later have to identify persons who have suffered an injury. (No injuries, no torts!) Let's say that one of these injury victims is named Xin. Probably you will also be told about several other people whose actions, or whose failures to act, arguably had something to do with Xin getting injured; call them Alan, Bea, and C Corp. Amidst the welter of facts and issues, organize your analysis methodically by considering in a sequence the possible claims that Xin might make against each of these other characters:

- *Xin v. Alan.* Xin can argue that Alan is liable for battery. Because it is clear that Alan caused Xin to suffer a harmful contact, the key issue here will be proof of intent. [Analyze the intent issue.]
- *Xin v. Bea.* Xin can sue Bea for negligence. [Analysis]
- *Xin v. C Corp.* Xin might sue C Corp. on a theory of products liability. [Analysis]

Alternatively, you can organize your answer to this sort of question by locating one potential defendant and analyzing to whom that defendant might be liable. If you are organizing your answer this way, it might be possible to work your way through claims against the one defendant by "zooming in" on the victim whom the defendant most directly affected, then broadening out the lens to see if there are persons more indirectly affected who might have also have claims against the same defendant.

For example, on a Torts exam, you could be given a fact pattern in which doctor D carelessly prescribes the wrong medicine to patient P, causing P to fall asleep at the wheel of her car, crash into a lamppost, and suffer injuries. The lamppost in turn falls over, knocking over C's illegally parked motorcycle, which falls in the street and blocks traffic, thereby creating a traffic jam that prevents M from attending an important meeting, as a result of which, perhaps, M loses out on a profitable business opportunity. Break down this sort of question by starting with P's malpractice claim against D. Then turn to C's claim against D (and perhaps P?). Finally, turn to M's claim against D (and C and P?).

Although we do not encourage making a fetish out of the organization of your exam answer, we want you to see that organizing in these simple ways has its advantages. Most important, it helps you avoid forgetting things. And, as we said, the act of organizing might point out to you something else you forgot to include on your list of issues.

One final thing. We strongly urge you to check items off your Issue List as you discuss them. More frequently than we wish were true, students note on their scrap paper an issue that they then forget to address in their answers. Using this technique will make sure you never commit this common, easily avoided, and potentially significant error.

Having said all this, we want to return to the point we began with, one that many students grasp intellectually but resist or ignore in practice. Exam answers are not graded for their elegance, although elegance is great if you can pull it off. It is all about the bumpers, and as we hope we've made clear, hitting just a few extra bumpers can generate a big payoff. Therefore, if you discover at the end of an exam that there's an issue or a set of issues that you should have addressed and didn't, go ahead and write about it at the end of your answer, and don't worry too much about integrating it into what you've already said. For these purposes, an ugly transition phrase is just fine: "Returning to X's situation, discussed above, it raises the following additional issue. . . ." Better to present a discussion awkwardly than to leave it off completely.

• • •

The advice in this chapter is not meant to be earth-shattering in its novelty. Your teachers have probably been telling you to check your work since you were in grade school. And yet, for all its familiarity, this sort of advice is perhaps the type that is most routinely ignored. Why? In some cases, it's just simple lack of time. But, in our own experience, there's also a significant psychological component. You are writing under pressure and understandably want to keep moving. Moreover, after you've slogged through a complicated question, it's tedious, terrifying, and depressing to go back and read it again. If you're like us, your overwhelming instinct is to wash your hands of the whole thing: "There, I did it. Thank goodness I never have to think about that problem again!" Fight this instinct! Be meticulous. Check your work. Go back over your lists again and again. The unpleasantness of doing so will be more than offset by the gain in bumpers hit.

The Bottom Line

☑ Create a Subject List—an outline or summary of your outline.

☑ For each question, make a comprehensive Issue List by checking the facts against your Subject List repeatedly.

☑ Keep track of your work: Make sure you discuss every issue on your Issue List.

☑ If time permits, go back over your Subject List to identify topics you missed initially.

Chapter 15

TACKLING OTHER EXAM FORMATS

☑ What's different (and not different) about take-home exams.

☑ Attacking short-answer and policy questions.

☑ Multiple-choice questions: Looking for the best answers.

U p to now our focus has been on the traditional, in-class, issue spotting exam. As we hope to have made clear, there are good reasons why law school exams have historically taken this form. Other forms of examination also test for some of the same lawyering skills in different ways, as well as for different skills that are relevant to legal reasoning and the practice of law. This is in part why law professors today are more apt to offer questions or exams that use different formats. Thus, in your law school career you can expect to encounter take-home exams, short-answer questions, policy questions, and multiple-choice questions. Much of what we have said about in-class exams applies to these other formats, although they raise some additional considerations as well.

We want to begin by suggesting that no matter what format you encounter, everything we have told you thus far is still relevant. IRAC is not just a technique for essay exams. Rather, it captures something fundamental about law and how law works. Don't lose sight of that basic lesson when you confront new formats.

TAKE-HOME EXAMS

Take-home exams come in various forms. Sometimes you are given eight hours to complete them; you pick up the exam in the morning and return it that evening. For others you are given 24 or 48 hours. On rare occasions — less common during the 1L year — professors give you the entire exam period.

Although the task on a take-home exam with fact-pattern-based, issue-spotting questions is really no different from the task you face for traditional in-class exams, there are likely to be some differences in how the exams are scored. On average, in-class exams probably place a higher premium on simply spotting issues, along with speed in reading and writing. Although issue spotting is no less important on take-home exams, there is likely to be more credit given for application and analysis, and for better organized and more polished answers. Thus, for take-home exams, *issue sorting* of the type discussed in Chapter 9 will be particularly important, as will the development of arguments on both sides of the more difficult issues. Because there is a bit more time to issue-spot, you are more likely to distinguish yourself on a take-home exam by careful analysis of close issues. For the same reason, you should make sure to reserve time at the end of a take-home exam to review your answers for flow, grammar, and typos.

Our main lesson about take-home exam preparation is this: *You should prepare for take-home exams in exactly the same way as you do for in-class exams.* It will be tempting to conclude that, with eight or 48 hours to complete your exam, you won't need to prepare for it as intensely as you would if it were an in-class exam. You might think, for example, that you don't need an outline, much less an outline of an outline: A broad-brush review will do, with more detailed studying to occur during the exam, after you figure out what issues the exam is emphasizing.

This is a big mistake; don't make it. Take-home exams are no less intense than in-class exams. Professors gear their exams to the amount of time given to complete them. Thus, you can expect the typical take-home exam to pose more questions and demand more in-depth analysis than an in-class exam. You may not be at leisure to roam about your class notes, reread cases in your casebooks, or organize your thoughts about a class-related topic. Besides, some of your classmates will have prepared just as thoroughly as they would for an in-class exam, and if you take a different approach you will be instantly disadvantaged.

Students regularly ask us how much of a take-home exam period they should devote to taking their exam. Should they work every minute of an eight-hour exam, taking only necessary bathroom breaks? Should they forego sleep during a 24-hour exam? The easy answer to both of these questions is, "No." You have to pace yourself. For an eight-hour exam, plan to take a few breaks. Try 15-minute breaks every two hours, and 30 minutes for lunch. For 24- and 48-hour exams, you obviously need to eat and get sleep — moderate exercise, even. There's no one right schedule, in part because different people react differently to getting different amounts of sleep. Just make sure to set your alarm, or a couple of them, so that you don't oversleep. Also, keep in mind that you need to pace yourself not only for one take-home exam, but for the entire exam period. Even if going nonstop for 24 hours were to help you on one test (we doubt it will), it will probably hurt your performance on any subsequent tests.

The one thing we would suggest you do differently on take-homes is to reserve more time to *think*. Not to study or learn the material, just to think over the question(s) you have been asked. In-class exams are sprints: You jump in and go as hard as you can, as fast as you can. Professors see take-homes as a means of discouraging hurried analysis: They gave this kind of exam so that you will have some time to reflect, organize, and dig a little deeper. What we suggested about "previewing" exams in the last chapter applies in spades here. It probably will make sense to issue-spot the entire exam before you begin writing. (If so, make sure you write up a thorough Issue List so that you don't forget what you are thinking!) More than on in-class exams, outline your answers, and then consider whether you have it all right. You can even sketch out answers and revise them later. Also, if possible, get outside and get some fresh air. You'd be amazed at how much it will help to clear your head and improve your performance.

When take-home exams have overall word limits, as they often do, one mistake students make is using too much of their word allocation in answering the initial questions on the exam. The tendency is to be expansive at first. As they go along, though, students start to realize they are going to press against the word limit, and so they start to tighten up. This is precisely the reason to do some up-front thinking before you write. Can you tell which questions deserve more attention than others?

Finally, it is critical on take-home exams that you constantly back up your answers and regularly print out hard copies of even early draft answers. Far too many law students have horror stories about a computer malfunction occurring as they prepare to hand in their exams. Don't let this be you!

SHORT-ANSWER QUESTIONS

Whether given as part of a take-home exam or an in-class exam, short-answer questions are usually tightly focused versions of standard issue-spotting questions. Often they come with word limits. Some of the examples you have already seen in this book (e.g., Seyla's Story from Chapter 7) could serve as short-answer questions: They are relatively simple fact patterns that highlight one issue of law (or maybe two issues), and in so doing invite a precise response. Here is an example of a short-answer question of a sort that might appear on a Criminal Law exam:

A and *B*, both competent young adults, were angry with *C* because *C* had insulted them. *A* and *B* had a conversation in which they agreed to "make *C* pay" for what he had done to them. However, because of a miscommunication, *A* and *B* had very different ideas of what it meant to "make *C* pay." *A* was under the impression that the two of them had agreed to kill *C*'s beloved pet bird, whereas *B* believed that they had agreed to slash the tires on *C*'s car. In light of the conversation, *A* purchased a large hunting knife. However, *A* then made the mistake of describing his plans to a friend, who "ratted out" both *A* and *B*. They have since confessed to the above-described events.

Assess *A* and *B*'s potential criminal liability. Assume for purposes of your analysis that neither killing *C*'s bird nor slashing *C*'s car tires amounts to a first- or second-degree felony.

Once you have taken Criminal Law you will recognize that this question raises an issue of liability for criminal conspiracy. No other criminal law doctrines are directly implicated. For example, there is nothing close to the sort of nearly completed effort at criminal activity that would warrant a finding of attempt. (If the conspiracy issue does not jump out at you, that's okay. For short-answer questions as for full-blown fact patterns, your Subject List is here to help. With a solid Subject List, you would recognize pretty quickly, as you scrolled down it, that you were looking at a question about conspiracy.)

In fact, the question is even more focused than we've just suggested. It's really about the extent to which there can be criminal liability for conspiracy even when the would-be conspirators fail to have a "meeting of the minds." Your job when confronted with this kind of question is to hone in immediately on the issue, or sub-issue, that the question raises, and to analyze it. Economy of expression is key. Omit unnecessary expositions of law or introductory phrases. Get right to the point. In fact, if you are reading—or rereading—this near the end of the semester and have covered conspiracy in Criminal Law, go ahead and try to write a one-paragraph answer. There's a sample answer available on **Open Book Digital**. You can compare it to your answer.

A familiar variation on the short-answer question involves a brief fact pattern like the one just given, an initial question or two, then some additions or changes to the facts that motivate additional questions. One sees this style of question both on in-class and take-home exams, although it is probably more prevalent on take-homes. If you face this type of question, pay close attention to the nuances in the new facts being introduced. They are being introduced for a reason.

POLICY QUESTIONS

We've mentioned the place of policy analysis in traditional legal analysis and in traditional law-school issue-spotters. However, some exam questions overtly invite you to address policy questions. Here are two examples, one from Constitutional Law and one from Criminal Law. We'll start with the constitutional question.

Please discuss (using no more than 500 words) whether *Immigration and Naturalization Service v. Chadha* was correctly decided.

As you might know by now if you've taken Constitutional Law, *Chadha* was a case regarding the constitutionality of the legislative veto. It raises foundational questions about interpretive methodology: Should one be a "formalist" who looks to the plain text of the Constitution, or a "functionalist" who considers the way structures of government actually operate together? It also poses tricky issues regarding how the administrative state operates. Because so much power accretes today to the executive, Congress has sought to find novel ways to check that power. But is the legislative veto necessary in this regard, or are there reasonably available alternatives that are more consistent with the constitutional text?

Obviously, you can't begin to discuss all this in 500 words. Scholars have written thousands and thousands of words on the subject. That is precisely the point: You must adopt a perspective and defend it, alluding to key concepts used in the course. The professor is not looking for you to regurgitate everything you learned in class, but to demonstrate your comfort with the material by expressing, intelligently, a point of view.

Having said this, it is also important to recognize that bumpers matter just as much on policy questions as on other questions. If you take a single issue from *Chadha* and say the same thing over and over in your 500 words, you won't hit many bumpers. If you defend one side of the question without nodding to the counterarguments, you might be missing half the points you could obtain. What you need to do is pick a position that lets you hit bumpers, but in a way that shows greater depth of analysis. Once again we've put an example of an answer on **Open Book Digital**. As you will see, there tend to be extra points for thoughtfulness.

Now for the Criminal Law policy question.

State and federal criminal laws are supposedly bounded by the principles of *mens rea* and *actus reus*. These principles are said to prevent government from rendering all conduct criminal, and all of us criminals. In reality, these principles are empty. Under black-letter state and federal law, people can be convicted and punished for doing nothing at all. Likewise, they can be convicted and punished even absent a guilty mind or even fault. The only general principle of criminal law is this: governments can criminalize whatever they want, so long as they do so with clear statutory language.

Assess the validity of the claim(s) made in this passage.

As was the case with the policy question drawn from Constitutional Law, here you have an invitation to think more broadly about themes or issues that have been raised in your Criminal Law course. (In other words, you would only expect to see a question like this on an exam for a Criminal Law class in which the principles of *actus reus* and *mens rea* had been a subject of discussion.)

If ever there were a law school exam question that was not about the "right" answer, it is this sort of question. As with the separation of powers posed by *Chadha*, the issues raised by the quoted passage have preoccupied scholars and judges. Brilliant as you are, there is no expectation that you will resolve this issue satisfactorily in the course of one law school exam. The point of a question like this is to show that you have a sense of some of the key considerations that might bear on the issue.

Keep in mind, though, that even when there's room for open-field running, the safest strategy is not to stray too far from the law. Build your points around examples drawn from class and your outlines. Whether you are inclined to agree or disagree with the passage that you've been asked to analyze, make your case on the strength of concrete examples. In support of the claims made in the criminal law question you'd want to cite, for example, convictions for failures to heed affirmative duties (e.g., a murder or manslaughter conviction for the failure of a parent to tend to an infant, resulting in the infant's death) or for "strict liability" criminal offenses (e.g., violations of drug-labeling laws).

The same advice obviously applies if you are arguing against the claims in the question. Indeed you could even use the same cases to ground your policy arguments. You might argue, for example, that it is mistaken to view convictions for failures to heed affirmative duties as genuine "no act" cases, because the concept of *actus reus* does not refer merely to the brute fact of physical actions, but to a normative notion of what one is obligated to do or refrain from doing. And there is a limit to the sort of affirmative obligations criminal law can plausibly impose. Here it might help to point out that not just anyone faces criminal liability for failing to care for infants — only persons in a parental or custodial role are deemed to have the sort of obligation that can generate such a conviction. So in these cases, there is an "act" in a sense that the law cares about: a breach of a relatively circumscribed duty that is imposed (and, realistically, can only be imposed) on certain persons.

Notice also that there are different ways of attacking, or different levels at which to attack the question. This is typical of policy questions. For example, you could take issue with some but not all of the claims made in the quoted passage. Thus, you might argue in favor of the claims made about the concepts of *actus reus* and *mens rea*, yet reject the concluding inference drawn from those claims that there are no principled limits on the extent to which a legislature can criminalize behavior. Instead, you could argue that there are other limits on criminalization — if only a general sense among the populace as to the point at which government has too severely jeopardized liberty, privacy, equality, or some other fundamental value(s). Here again you should try, if possible, to tie your argument to examples, real or imagined. (See, for example, the failure of Prohibition.)

If you know that a professor's exam will contain one or more policy questions, or you expect that it will, you should take some time to reflect on class discussion. Often there will be subtle or not-so-subtle clues as to what policy questions might appear on the exam. Suppose you are in a Constitutional Law class and your professor, on several occasions, harps on the conundrum of unelected judges invalidating laws adopted by democratically chosen legislators. If there are going to be policy questions on this professor's exam, it might not be surprising to find one on exactly this topic. If you have the time while you are preparing for the exam, identify two or three likely policy questions, and try your hand at drafting answers to them. It's good practice, and you might find that you have drafted an answer to an actual exam question!

In a nutshell, when it comes to policy questions, you have more leeway to be creative and opinionated. And yet you want to stick to the question and to the law. Show that you are not just grandstanding. Show that you are being a good lawyer. Remember to think about bumpers.

MULTIPLE-CHOICE QUESTIONS

Multiple-choice questions are the opposite of policy questions, in that you are given a menu of answers, only one of which is "right." Note, however, that "right" in this context sometimes has a special meaning. We have been emphasizing throughout this book that legal issues tend not to generate a single right answer; that law is all about better and worse arguments. If this is so then—you might fairly wonder—how can there be multiple-choice questions on a law school exam? Isn't this form of question incompatible with the whole idea of thinking like a lawyer?

Some law professors take this view, which might help explain why this form of questioning is relatively infrequently seen on exams, or at least 1L exams. In fact, a lot depends on the subject. In more numerically oriented courses, such as an accounting class for lawyers, it might be quite natural to test for right answers. The same is true for the more narrowly rule-bound aspects of even traditional 1L courses; for example, certain applications of procedural statutes or the Federal Rules of Civil Procedure. (By contrast, many other aspects of Civil Procedure raise difficult, open-ended, legal and policy questions, as anyone knows who has studied *Erie v. Tompkins*.)

In any event, we would be remiss if we did not acknowledge what you might already know. When it comes time for you to take a bar exam, you will be answering multiple-choice questions. The multistate bar exam (MBE) is in fact a multi-hour, multiple-choice exam, covering a wide range of core subjects. Many law students (and former law students, like your authors) find these questions maddening. Yet, they have their utility. Recall what we explained in Chapter 8 about how professors like to cover a certain percentage of what they taught. You can instantly see why professors might favor multiple-choice questions as a way to test breadth of knowledge. (Besides, they are easier to grade.) And yet, precisely because law in many ways does not lend itself to the multiple-choice format, it takes a great deal of time and thought for a professor to construct good multiple-choice questions.

We won't have a lot to say about strategies or techniques for answering multiple-choice questions. In part that's because we're betting that most of you have already been introduced to basic strategies in the course of studying for your LSATs (and, for that matter, your SATs). One of the most basic lessons you learned in those settings usually applies here as well. *Almost any multiple-choice question will contain some really bad answers, and it is usually best to eliminate those first on your way to locating the right answer.*

Here's an example of a relatively straightforward multiple-choice question concerning an issue of civil procedure:

QUESTION

Vincent Victim was struck by a car driven by Eddie Egregious and seriously injured. Victim brought a diversity negligence action against Egregious in federal district court. The jury rendered a verdict for Victim and awarded him $1.5 million in compensatory damages. District Judge Juarez presided over the trial. She is of the view that any award of damages over $500,000 could only be the product of passion or prejudice on the part of the jury. Which of the following accurately describes what Judge Juarez may do?

A. Juarez is barred by the Seventh Amendment from disturbing the jury's damage award.

B. Juarez may grant a defense motion for a new trial, conditional on Victim agreeing to accept a remittitur of $1 million.

C. Juarez may enter judgment for Victim in the amount of $500,000.

D. Juarez may grant judgment as a matter of law to Egregious if Egregious has properly moved for judgment as a matter of law.

Take a moment and circle what you think is the right answer.

As perhaps you have determined, answers A, C, and D are just plain wrong. The Seventh Amendment does not bar district judges from ordering new trials based on the determination that a jury's award in a civil case was grossly excessive and unreasonable. At the same time, the Federal Rules of Civil Procedure do not empower district judges to enter judgment as a matter of law on a finding of excessiveness. So the only plausible answer left is B, which is true: A federal court faced with what it perceives to be an excessive damage award is authorized to order a new trial conditional on the plaintiff remitting the excess amount.

Although some law school multiple-choice questions like the one just shown present starkly right and wrong answers, most are more subtle. In particular, you might find that your efforts at winnowing out bad answers leave you with two seemingly plausible answers. For this sort of question, the critical thing to remember is that, among the two left standing, you are looking for the best answer, not the only answer that is colorably correct. Consider this Torts question.

QUESTION

State's Liquor Control Act ("LCA") contains a preamble stating that excessive consumption of alcohol at bars and clubs has resulted in disorderly conduct in bars and clubs. Section 1 of the LCA therefore makes it a criminal misdemeanor for owners and operators of establishments that sell alcohol commercially to serve alcohol to a visibly intoxicated patron.

Dave was drinking at Opt Inn, a bar. Eunice, an employee of Opt Inn, was bartending that night. Eunice had been trained by Opt Inn management not to serve obviously intoxicated patrons. However, Eunice is a good friend of Dave's and served Dave drinks even though she recognized that Dave was quite drunk. Toward the end of the evening, as Dave left the club, he ran into Peter Park, an old acquaintance. Dave invited Peter to his (Dave's) apartment for further drinks and Peter agreed. After more drinking there, both men passed out. When they awoke the next morning, still somewhat intoxicated, the two men recalled an old bone of contention between them, which in turn so agitated Dave that he ended up stabbing and severely injuring Peter.

Peter has sued Opt Inn for negligence. Which of the following provides Opt Inn's best argument for obtaining summary judgment with respect to Peter's claims?

A. Eunice's intervening criminal conduct is a *per se* superseding cause of Peter's injuries.
B. Eunice's overserving of Dave was not an actual cause of Peter's injuries.
C. Eunice's actions were outside the scope of her employment.
D. Attacks such as Dave's were not among the concerns behind the passage of the LCA, nor are they the sort of event, the risk of which warrants treating Eunice's overserving of Dave as careless.
E. Peter assumed the risk of the attack by agreeing to go to Dave's apartment.

Again, take a minute to try to come up with the right answer.

Can any answers be eliminated quickly? Answer E is a good candidate. Peter did nothing to "assume a risk" of carelessness on the part of *Opt Inn*. Two other answers—A and B—are only slightly less weak. B is false because it is entirely possible that, if Eunice had not overserved Dave, the subsequent events that culminated in Peter's stabbing might not have happened. Also, actual causation issues are at the very core of the jury's function in negligence cases, and thus ill-suited for resolution by *summary judgment* motion. As for A, the fact that Eunice violated the LCA does not make her the sort of "intervening wrongdoer" that blocks the imposition of liability on Opt Inn. The doctrine of "superseding cause" is simply not the right one for this job — it concerns the intervention of third parties acting *independently* of the alleged tortfeasor. (Thus, Opt Inn could argue against liability that *Dave's* stabbing of Peter was a superseding cause of Peter's injury, but that is not the choice given to you by Answer A.) To be sure, there is a "live" question as to whether Eunice's conduct can fairly be attributed to the Opt Inn. But as to that question the doctrine of superseding cause is neither here nor there.

So we're pretty quickly down to two possibilities: answers C and D. Neither of these is obviously wrong. Still, one is better than the other. Start with C. Insofar as Eunice's actions were not sanctioned by her employer, they were arguably *ultra vires* and therefore not ones for which Opt Inn can be held vicariously liable via the doctrine of *respondeat superior*. So, "beyond the scope of employment" provides a basis for granting Opt Inn's motion. But is it the best argument available to Opt Inn? (If you were Opt Inn's lawyer, would you rest your case for summary judgment primarily on this argument?) No. The fact that Opt Inn had trained Eunice properly, and that she ignored her training, presumably absolves Opt Inn of *direct* liability for managerial negligence, but it does not of itself establish that they are free from *vicarious* liability. Often courts hold that employee actions in violation of employer policies are still within the scope of employment, so long as those actions were reasonably foreseeable to the employer, or in furtherance of the employer's interests, or characteristic of the employer's enterprise. Under any of these tests, Eunice's actions might well be deemed to fall within the scope of employment, thus rendering Opt Inn subject to *respondeat superior* liability.

Now contrast the grounds for summary judgment offered in answer D. The legislation does not seem to have been prompted by the kind of incident in which Dave and Peter were involved, a fact that would defeat Peter's effort to enlist the doctrine of negligence per se. (That doctrine only applies when, among other things, the risk that is realized is among those risks that the legislature meant to address by enacting the relevant legislation.) It likewise undermines Peter's effort to establish that Eunice's carelessness in overserving Dave was a proximate cause of Peter's being attacked. To the extent one deems the overserving of bar patrons to be careless, it is probably not out of concern for the risk of morning-after quarrels.

Does this mean that it is crystal clear that Opt Inn would win its motion for summary judgment on the strength of the arguments identified in answer D? No. But that is beside the point. The question does not ask you to identify a sure winner. It asks you to identify Opt Inn's *best* argument. D is that argument.

DON'T FORGET IRAC

We want to end this chapter as we began, by returning to our admonition that IRAC matters here, too. Regardless of the exam format, you still have to figure out, "What is the issue?" And, this being law school, you still have to ask, "What is the rule?" Even on a policy question, there are broad principles—rules of a sort—on which your answer will turn. Nor can you answer all these questions without the same sort of balanced, see-both-sides analytics we stressed throughout. The analytics are more compressed in short-answer questions, and are often silent in multiple-choice questions, but they are still there.

Ironically, if anything wins out a bit more in these alternative formats, it is our somewhat-neglected friend, "Conclusion." In a short-answer question, for example, the best technique is often to lead with a conclusion and defend it. For multiple-choice questions, the conclusion is placed in front of you: You just have to find it. And for policy questions, although there is almost certainly no "right" answer, the professor typically is looking for you to assert a conclusion and defend it.

The Bottom Line

☑ Don't forget IRAC!

☑ Take-home exams require the same preparation as in-class exams, and especially careful time management.

☑ For short-answer questions, get right to the point.

☑ For policy questions, stay tethered to the law.

☑ For multiple-choice questions, first eliminate wrong answers, then look for the best remaining answer.

Chapter 16

PRACTICE (EXAMS) MAKES PERFECT

☑ Practice, practice, practice!

☑ Practice exams as feedback.

☑ How to get the most out of practice exams.

Have you ever marveled at a gymnast who nails her routine, or a mesmerizing orator? Perhaps you thought, "Wow, she makes it look easy." Maybe you wished you had the talent to achieve that level of performance so effortlessly. Of course, talent is only part of the story, and in many cases, not even the largest part. When you see someone make something look easy, it is probably because that person has done it over and over and over. You know from your own experience that talent goes a long way, yet only gets you so far. Hard work and dedication matter a ton. Athletes, musicians, comedians, chefs, and lawyers: If they are good, it is because they practice. "Practice makes perfect" might be trite, but it's true.

To do well on exams you must practice taking them. No amount of reading and outlining can prepare you for what it is like actually to take an exam. It can't teach you how to allocate your time between reading the questions and responding to them, or among questions. It can't tell you how to attack challenging questions, or how to organize your answers. This book's advice will fall flat if you wait to try it for the first time on a real exam. Imagine a musician who reads notes from a composer on how to perform a particular piece of music, but doesn't try out that advice until the night of its first public performance. Bad idea, unless the performance is billed as an exercise in improvisation—which law school exams most assuredly are not.

FINDING FEEDBACK

One source of great frustration to law students is the absence of feedback during classes. Grades turn largely or exclusively on exam performance, yet there is often no evaluation before the real deal. How are you to know if you are doing the right things? We are sympathetic to this complaint, and could say something about why things are as they are, and why the situation, although improving, isn't likely to change dramatically. Regardless, you can do something about it. You can take practice exams and, either on your own or with classmates, go over them in a way that gives you a decent sense of how you are doing.

The best source of practice exams is prior exams given by the professors whose classes you are taking. Most professors make one or more of these available. Some will also post model answers. If no past exams are available, look for exams from other professors at your school who have taught the relevant class. You can also buy books that provide practice essays and short-answer and multiple-choice exams, with answers.

One of the great advantages of having bought this book is that, with it, comes an entire suite of practice exams for you to use. Yes, friends, we're once again referring you to **Open Book Digital!** (It's really worth a visit—trust us.) We collected exams from our colleagues at schools all over the country. Not only that, but we asked those professors to provide a sample answer as well as three actual exam answers, of varying quality. Then, to top it off, the professors annotated all those materials, showing you how to spot the issues on the exam and how best to discuss them. We cannot urge you strongly enough to use and peruse this material.

Getting your hands on practice exams is only the first step, however. You have to use them in the right way. This is another idea that might seem blindingly obvious. In truth, it is something students routinely fail to do. Don't make this mistake.

PREPARATION FOR PRACTICE

First, if you're on a semester schedule, don't think about taking practice exams until about a month before your actual exams. We'd go further and tell you not to start practicing until two or three weeks before exams, but we realize that some folks might benefit from starting a little earlier, if only to begin to get the feel for what the exam experience is going to be like. (We've discussed this issue with many of our colleagues, and encountered a range of views.) Until then you have other things to do, and if you take them earlier you might be thrown off by the fact that the exams will include many issues that you have not yet learned.

Also, you aren't ready to approach an exam until you have really learned the material, and that requires not just attending class but also cumulative review. If you are really anxious to know what exams look like — and we fully understand that — then it is fine to look over one or two at an earlier point in time. But in that case make sure you have enough practice exams on hand, because actually taking a practice exam works best if you've never seen it before you start. After all, that is how it is going to be on the real exam. (And, again, we have plenty of sample exams on **Open Book Digital**. While these may not have been written by a professor of yours, there is enough variety among them that, if you look at several, you will probably get a feel for how your exams are likely to look.)

Second, make sure that you have read this book carefully enough that you are ready to apply its lessons. You are reading this for a reason, right?

Third, even if your professor has indicated that your exam will be open-book, try to take at least one of your practice exams for that class as a closed-book exam. Why? Because doing so will give you a good indication of what parts of the course have become second nature to you, and what parts you have not yet assimilated. As we explained earlier, even on an open-book exam you probably won't have much time to be consulting sources, let alone learning things for the first time. Also, it is usually better to train yourself under conditions that are harsher than the ones you are actually going to encounter. When it comes time for real exams, they won't feel quite so daunting.

Finally, you must take practice exams in conditions that mirror real exam-taking conditions. This one is huge. Students "cheat" on it all the time. They sit down to take a practice exam, but get up 15 minutes later and wander around their apartment, searching for a snack. (Some students become so desperate during self-administered practice exams that they even clean their dorm rooms or apartments!)

Don't delude yourself: This does not count as practice. It is like training for a 10K race by running half a mile and saying "Okay, I think I've got the hang of this running thing."

Here's a suggestion. When you are ready to take a practice exam, sit at a carrel in a quiet part of your law library. Better yet, sit in the middle of a reading room at a local public library where there are other people around you, but you are not likely to be recognized and interrupted by anyone. Put away your phone. Disable your computer's Internet access. It should just be you, the practice exam, a pen, some scrap paper, and a blank computer screen.

On the subject of computer screens, if you'll be writing your answers on a computer using special exam software provided by the school, check to see if you are permitted to get it and use it before you use it on an actual exam. This software often works in ways different than ordinary word-processing software, and might take some getting used to. Better to acclimatize yourself ahead of time.

PRACTICING IN REAL TIME

Now take the exam. *Really* take it. Eyeballing the fact pattern and jotting down some issues that you think you see does not count. (You can't fool us; we've been there.) If the exam is going to be a three-hour, in-class exam, commit to reading and writing for at least two or (ideally) three hours. See how much you can actually write in this amount of time. If you breeze through the entire exam in an hour or two, you probably weren't pushing yourself hard enough. Or you missed a bunch of issues. Or you didn't say nearly enough about them. If you were unable to cover all the issues you spotted, that's almost certainly a *good* sign. Exams almost always have more in them than any mortal can cover in one sitting. Let's put it this way: If you don't feel worn

out by the time you have completed your practice exam, you haven't practiced. Do it again.

Our advice that you practice taking exams in real time does *not* apply to take-home exams (see Chapter 8). Twenty-four- and forty-eight hour take-homes are grueling enough as it is. Just like marathon runners, who rarely run a full marathon before the real race, you should train for a take-home by doing something less than you will do on the actual exam. If possible, split up your practice exam(s) over a few days. Take one question from a practice take-home exam and spend a couple of hours on it. Then take a break, do something else, and spend a couple of hours on the next question.

EVALUATION

Now comes the really hard part of practice exams, one that students also consistently fail to do. You need to review, carefully, your answers. This is a tedious and at times discomfiting task, which is exactly why students tend not to do it, or tend not to do it well. Suck it up. It might help if you have a friend doing it with you. We know we are hitting the adages a little hard in this chapter, but misery does love company.

If there's a model answer available, put your answer next to the model and compare them. Try to figure out why you went in a different direction, or failed to see something. Don't worry too much if your analysis comes to different substantive conclusions. Remember this is mainly about arguments. What you're looking for is whether you spotted the issues discussed in the model answer, whether you framed them similarly, and whether your analysis of them invoked the same considerations. The question is not whether your answer precisely mimics or mirrors the model answer. Perhaps you did a better job than the model! The point is to make sure that you didn't miss, gloss over, distort, or make a hash of issues that you should have spotted and properly analyzed.

What if there is no model answer? No worries. If you are part of a study group, you should each take the same practice test separately and then meet to discuss your respective answers. Even if you are not part of a study group, you can probably find a classmate or two who would be willing to do this. It can be awkward, even among friends, and even with respect to a practice exam, to compare your answers to others'. Sometimes your friends might unintentionally lead you astray by wrongly suggesting to you (perhaps against your better judgment) that some issue was important that wasn't, or that it should have been analyzed a certain way when it shouldn't have been. But the benefits of checking your answers will most likely outweigh these potential costs. And remember, as when working with model answers, the issue is not who got the "right" answers. Rather, you are trying to gauge your aptitude for spotting issues, getting the rules right, and applying them appropriately to the facts presented.

If neither a model answer nor peers are available, you can do some self-assessment. Reread the facts provided to you on the practice exam. Now reread your answer. Then, carefully work through your outline, looking for topics that are contained in your outline that don't show up in your answer. Chances are that if a topic is missing, you missed an issue. If the material was in your outline and you still didn't see it, go back to Chapter 13 and reread what we said about Subject Lists and Issue Lists. As we told you there, these techniques are absolutely essential.

ENOUGH ALREADY?

Time permitting, we would recommend that you take at least two practice exams for each class. That might feel like a tall order, but it's doable. (Again, take-home exams might be sufficiently elaborate that there's only time to do one practice exam.) And it is invaluable. Remember, when you are doing practice exams, you are also studying. You are not just practicing technique; you are also going over substance. Practice exams are a terrific way to reinforce what you learned in class. Our only caution is that, again, don't start taking practice exams until you are ready.

It bears repeating: In law school and in life more generally, when it comes to important activities, you never want the run that counts to be your first one. Actors hold dress rehearsals for a reason. The same goes for sports teams that play scrimmages and preseason games. Practicing lawyers follow precisely the same approach. Appellate court lawyers, for example, always try to arrange "moots" that give them the opportunity to test out their arguments with stand-ins for the real judges to whom they will be arguing. Law school exams are no different.

The Bottom Line

- ☑ Take to heart the sports adage: How you practice is how you'll play. Practice hard!

- ☑ Simulate actual exam conditions as much as possible: The real exam should feel familiar, not foreign.

- ☑ Find some classmates and carefully review practice exam answers.

Chapter 17

EXAM TROUBLE: HOW TO AVOID IT, WHAT TO DO ABOUT IT

☑ Preparation is the best defense against disaster.

☑ What to do if you have a personal emergency.

☑ How to handle a panic attack.

Y ou've been around the block long enough to know that the best-laid plans of mice and men often go awry.[30] Count on this happening at least once during your law school exams. Don't fret about it, just prepare for it. This chapter offers some techniques for handling common exam-taking bumps. Before turning to those, however, we should stress that the most important thing that you can do is prepare. The more preparation, the more practice, the less likely it is that something will go wrong. This is yet another reason to heed the last chapter's admonition to practice, practice, practice.

---

30. In the original words of Robert Burns: "The best-laid schemes o' mice an' men, gang aft agley."

EQUIPMENT FAILURE

Here's a true (and scary) story. It's the night before the start of "1L's" fall exams. The hard drive of 1L's laptop melts down, taking with it all of her outlines and notes. Hours on the phone with tech folks succeed only in establishing that the data are lost forever. She has no hard copies, no backup files. She is in deep doo-doo.[31]

This is no one's idea of fun. But these sorts of things happen, to all of us. If it is not the computer crash it will be something else, you can be sure of it. Textbooks and notes are lost. An apartment floods or loses electricity. The dog gets lost and you'll spend hours or days searching when you should be studying. It is as if the vast kinetic life-force of the universe is wired so that things go wrong precisely when you are most under the gun.

So, what to do? Expect the unexpected and plan for it. The very best way to deal with a problem is to be ahead of the game, rather than reacting in crisis mode. Here we can again call your attention to the real world of law practice. You are probably most familiar from television and movies with the lawyer as litigator, or the lawyer as crisis manager. These are indeed important things that lawyers do. But many, many lawyers are counselors and planners whose primary job is to *anticipate trouble*, to figure out how to avoid it, and to make plans for what to do if trouble hits. Employment lawyers, for example, spend a good deal of time advising firms on how to put into place systems for hiring, evaluating, and terminating employees that reduce the likelihood that those firms' employment practices will run afoul of rules setting minimum wages, or barring discrimination. Even litigators spend a good chunk of time planning for what might go wrong in the discovery process or at trial. These are habits you should develop in law school, if you haven't already. Plan for bad scenarios and you might well avoid them. If not, you will at least be in a better position to deal with them.

---

31. In case you're wondering, there was a surprise happy ending. 1L made it through her fall exams successfully. But she did so only because she had already put in so much time on her outlines — and because she possesses certain unusual mental capacities — that she was able to reproduce her outlines from memory. Don't try this at home.

There is no avoiding the fact that, by the time exams roll around, you are going to feel pressed for time. Part of this is psychological; some of us never feel prepared enough, even when we are. And some of it is real: There is a lot to learn and not much time to learn it. You can't learn everything if you leave it to the last moment, but you can be sure that if you leave things to the last moment a disaster will take a real toll. On the other hand, if you are preparing on the right schedule, you'll have some leeway to deal with the bad stuff that inevitably comes up.

Be thoughtful about how you care for vital materials or information, like your notes or outlines. There's a well-known story about a law clerk to a prominent judge who left a set of essential, confidential court papers in the back seat of a taxi. Result? Clerk fired. The government chains the nuclear codes to someone's wrist for a reason. You don't have to go that far, of course, but the point remains the same. If you only have one copy of your class notes, and if you are going to need those notes for exams, and if you are investing a lot of time and money into law school, and if the exam matters, then don't lose the notes. Perhaps at a certain point it will be worth your while to print out a second copy. This brings us to our next point.

BACK UP YOUR WORK

Back up constantly. Click "Save" when you are typing, and create backup files. Then, print out a hard copy every now and then. Leave one version in your apartment. Leave another somewhere else (your locker, if you have one), for when the flood comes. The disadvantage of our digital world is that tons of information can disappear in a heartbeat. When everything was paper, it used to take a real disaster to do that. But every cloud has a silver lining: The advantage of our digital world is that you can back things up to avoid disaster. Back before law school, one of us was a computer programmer. That was when computers were as big as entire rooms and featured those spools of tape on which information was stored. On big projects, one backup tape went home, one stayed in the trunk of a (locked) car, and one stayed at the office. Okay, overkill. But when you get burned by bad luck, you learn to take precautions. (Once burned, twice shy.) And when you take precautions you don't get burned nearly as often or as badly.

CLOUDY CONDITIONS

Here's another all-too familiar story. A Contracts exam is being given. The people who manage the law school's physical facilities have rented out an unused classroom to some community group. No one ever checked what it was needed for. Turns out, it is the local Dixieland band, practicing for their big show. And it is next door to the exam.

The list of things we've seen go wrong would be comical if it wasn't so serious. The final spring semester 3L exam ends in the middle of a 1L exam, and the happy 3Ls celebrate noisily. The heat in the classroom goes off in the winter and the air conditioning goes off in the spring. Electronic exams don't download on time or upload on time. Someone knocks a bottle of water onto another student's work.

Oh, and, lest we forget it, professors make mistakes. Sometimes they unwittingly reverse the roles of the characters in their fact patterns, or change the names of key characters midstream. They might omit critical facts or include contradictory ones. Or pages might simply be missing from an exam.

Although none of this is good, there is no reason to panic. You just need a protocol for what to do when trouble strikes.

First, let's discuss professorial foul-ups. You are reading your exam, and something is missing or doesn't make sense. The facts have errors in them. Or facts are missing. What should you do?

If the problem is blatant—for example, your exam is missing a page—immediately inform an appropriate person. Typically, this will be an exam proctor or, if there is no proctor, a staff person in the registrar's office. (It might be overkill, but it wouldn't be crazy to figure out, in advance of taking an exam, who you are supposed to contact in the event of a mid-exam problem.)

If the problem is less blatant, first, check again, particularly if the problem you think you've identified is an omission. On second glance, you might well discover that it is you who is confused, not the exam. Keep in mind that professors sometimes leave things deliberately obscure; they want you to notice the obscurity and explain its relevance for the analysis of the problem at hand. In Tia's Tale from Chapter 9, for example, crucial facts were missing that were necessary to determine whether her negligence claim might succeed. That was deliberate on our part, and is typical of the sort of omission one can expect to find on an exam.

If on the second or third look you are still convinced there is a mistake or a problem with an exam question, you need to make a judgment about how serious it is. If the mistake does not prevent you from proceeding, just proceed. For example, suppose a character in a fact pattern initially named Joe seems mysteriously to become Jeff halfway through the question. Simply explain in your answer that you are assuming that Joe and Jeff are the same person and proceed as you would otherwise. Or suppose that, at the conclusion of a fact pattern that describes various ways in which Cyndy has mistreated Chandra (and not vice versa), you are asked to assess *Cyndy's* prospects for recovery, even though Cyndy is the injurer, not the victim. If you conclude after a careful reading of the facts and the question that this is a simple professorial mistake, just make clear that you are answering on the assumption that the question about "Cyndy's prospects" meant to refer to Chandra's. (Often professors will include in the exam's initial instructions an instruction to this effect: e.g., "If you believe there is an error in this exam, identify it and explain the assumptions on which your answer is based.") The one thing you cannot do is stop writing. A small mistake should not prevent you from hitting bumpers.

Finally, if you conclude there is a serious problem with a question on your exam—a problem of a sort that prevents you from answering the question—raise the issue with a proctor or administrator. Most law schools require their professors to make themselves reachable during the time period in which their exams are given. In the very rare event that there is a serious problem with an exam, the professor will be contacted by the school, and some sort of arrangements will be made. (In our many years of teaching at multiple schools, we can't recall an instance like this, but it probably does happen once in a blue moon.)

ENVIRONMENTAL PROBLEMS

Now, what about the other variety of problem, where something environmental goes wrong with the exam or the exam conditions? What should you do? Again, the solution is to contact the folks whose job it is to administer exams. Law school administrators take their jobs seriously. No less than you, they are keen for exam periods to run without a hitch. Indeed, they work very hard to ensure that all goes well, and even harder to correct things that do go wrong. So, don't lose your cool. Let someone know of the problem, and have confidence that it will get fixed.

It will also help to come prepared in very mundane ways. Wear layers of clothing that you can take on or off to adjust for room-temperature issues. If you tend to be distracted by ambient noise, bring a pair of earplugs. If it is permitted, bring into the exam some water and a healthy snack to help keep you going. Also check to see if you can bring in standard over-the-counter medicines for headaches and stomach aches. Last but not least, bring with you a *small* lucky charm—something familiar and comforting (no pets please).

No matter what happens, do not boil over and start abusing the people that work at the school or your classmates. We have seen this happen. The danger for you is that the legal community is small and people have long memories. Be mindful of your reputation. Remember, clients hire lawyers for their judgment as well as their smarts. Besides, no one deserves to be abused, and even if they do deserve some reprimand or demerit, that's not your call to make. Don't break stride or get rattled. Stuff happens. There is only one thing you can do to help yourself, and that is to get back to work and put whatever is going wrong out of your mind. We don't mean to sound blasé. We get it. When one of us—Goldberg—took the LSAT, the proctor made a mistake in keeping track of the time, and declared that there were five minutes left on one segment when there should have been fifteen. The room erupted in anxiety and anger. There was nothing to do but focus and use the little time that was left. When something goes wrong on a law school exam, the best thing you can do is get to work hitting bumpers. Lots of them. Resolve to hit even more bumpers.

Third, when it is all over, take a moment to breathe. If there was a serious problem that couldn't be fixed adequately during the exam itself, and you feel it affected your performance and perhaps the performance of your colleagues, you will want to speak to someone about what happened and see if there is anything to be done, after the fact, to correct or ameliorate the problem. Your school will have a protocol for dealing with this kind of situation. In all likelihood, that protocol will direct you to speak to an academic dean or the registrar. It will also direct you NOT to contact your professor! (Remember that the exam you are taking is most likely graded anonymously, and you don't want to do anything to mess that up.) You'll want to be a good lawyer for yourself and impress the people with whom you are dealing with the importance of what happened and the thoughtfulness you are bringing to bear about how to proceed. Be prepared to explain clearly and calmly what happened, then let the administrators do their job. As difficult as it might feel, be patient. It might take some time and require several conversations for things to get worked out. In our experience, things do get worked out. Someday — not now — whatever happened to you will be a funny story.

OPERATOR ERROR

Here's a final set of calamities — in some ways ones that are the most serious, because they are internal to you, the student. People get sick. Sometimes students take ill, maybe just a cold, maybe a bad flu. Sometimes other people get sick, really sick, including loved ones. More often than we care to remember, a student has lost someone they care a great deal about on the verge of exams. Or people suffer other emotional traumas or injuries. And then there is the in-exam panic attack.

We'll get to the panic attack in just a moment, but for most of these problems the advice we have should start to sound very familiar. Every law school has academic support personnel (often the staff working in the office of the Dean of Students), who care a lot about you, and who have the experience and wisdom to help you sort things out. There will be protocols to deal with the timing of your exams. There will be rules that govern rescheduling exams, or even delaying them to the start of the next semester. People will work with you as best as they are able to get the situation under control with due regard for what you are going through.

We do, however, have one piece of advice that cuts a little against the preceding paragraph. Sometimes when these things happen (and they are part of life) there is an inclination to push exams as far away as possible. And your school's rules might allow for this. If you are faced with this sort of a choice, we want to suggest that you balance two competing considerations. On the one hand, you want to do well on the exam and doing so requires preparation and the right mental state. If you are sick or facing a personal problem yet take the exam as scheduled, you might not have your head in the game. However, by the same token, delay has its disadvantages. If you postpone your exams for too long you might lose your edge; the material may start to slip out of your mind. And remember, the new semester will bring a new set of classes; things will start to pile up. In general, we tend to push folks to try to make it through exams as scheduled. But again, that's something best discussed with the folks at your law school who are there to help you deal with this sort of problem.

Panic attacks experienced during an exam are a different matter. They happen. Here's a story to put it in perspective. Friedman sat down to take his 1L Constitutional Law exam. Fifteen minutes later, he was experiencing total, heart-pounding panic. The professor had spent three-quarters of the semester on the Commerce Clause. But there was no Commerce Clause issue remotely in sight. Not only that, but there was some strange beast of an issue plainly lurking in the facts, but not recognizable from what was studied during the semester. If you want an indication of how Friedman felt, consider that this all still seems vivid, decades later. But you know what? Friedman looked up and saw that everyone in the room seemed to be staring at the ceiling. They were all experiencing the same thing.

First lesson. Breathe. Literally and figuratively. Figuratively, recognize that these things happen and you just have to get your brain under control and get to work. But literally, one of the best ways to do this is to breathe slowly, in and out. We're tempted to lay the yoga technique on you: Breathe in slowly through the nose, then out through the mouth. It works.

Next, take a second to collect your thoughts. Consider this: What do people do when a lit match gets dropped on upholstery? Sometimes they panic and frantically beat at it, which only fans the flames, and has the potential to make things worse. In truth, there is plenty of time to reach over and pick up the match before it does any damage. Calm down. You have time to get your head together.

Finally, keep things in perspective. Every law student wants to do well on every exam—they should. But there's a big difference between experiencing disappointment or frustration over an exam's not going well, and feeling panic or terror that the bottom is falling out. In all probability, even your worst-case exam scenario is more of a missed opportunity to do well than a failure. And remember also that this is just one exam. It is not going to make or break you. The abbreviation "GPA" stands for "grade point *average*." Lots of law students have one exam that stands out for being their weakest. Maybe that exam was particularly hard for them, or maybe they just had a bad day when they took it. (Even the greatest performers have bad days.) The whole point of averaging is to control for outliers. If you have one weak exam but generally are doing well you'll be fine; the other grades will swamp the outlier.

Okay, you've calmed yourself down, at least a bit. Now what? Well, there are a number of things you might do. If the exam has multiple questions, and you are overwhelmed by one, work on another. It might be that when you come back to the mysterious one later, it will make more sense. When you do work on that question, take another look at your Subject List, then rescan the fact pattern. Find something that looks recognizable and get to work on it. Do what eons of sailors cast into the sea have done when a boat goes down: Grab a piece of driftwood. Look for something on the exam to grab onto, and just start to work there. Spot that issue and start your written Issue List. If it helps, even sketch out how you'll analyze it. Before you know it, you'll probably be back on track.

Even if the question never really "clicks," the most important thing to do is to *keep writing*. Remember, it is infinitely better to write a messy answer that raises and addresses issues clumsily than it is to write nothing at all. (The only foolproof method for not hitting bumpers is to write nothing.) You might think your answer is way off, or confused, and maybe it is. You might find yourself jumping around from issue to issue, without seeing connections that permit an orderly answer. No matter. Keep writing. Probably you are less off-base than you realize, and your professor in all likelihood will give you partial credit for correctly identifying and analyzing some issues, even if your overall framing of the question is off. Recall grade-school math: If you show your work, you usually get partial credit, even if your answer is wrong. The same usually goes for law school exams, only more so.

KNOW YOUR STUFF AND KNOW THAT YOU KNOW IT

This brings us to the end of this chapter with a brief and obvious word about learning the material on which you'll be tested, and feeling confident that you have done so. As we've suggested repeatedly, the very best thing you can do to achieve success and stave off disaster is to know your stuff, to be really rock solid on the material, by which we mean being on top of what you have been taught, what you have taught yourself, and the techniques for taking exams. If this seems a constant theme, there is a reason. This chapter discusses all kinds of things that can go wrong during an exam, but if you really know your stuff none of them will be disastrous. What could have been a major problem will become a mere annoyance.

One of the main values of being prepared is confidence. If you are confident in what you are doing, then when things go wrong it is easier to shrug them off as part of the natural order of things. If you are feeling shaky, then everything that happens seems part of a conspiracy to undermine your success. It is perfectly natural and human to have doubts, and this sort of feeling can be common when you are facing a new experience. But uncertainty is unnecessary here. If you've prepared thoroughly, you will do just fine.

In fact, we'll go one step further and suggest you work to adopt a mindset of actually enjoying yourself. Now we sound flat-out crazy, right? It is one thing to acknowledge that you should get your annual flu shot. It is entirely another to suggest that you look forward to it.

We are serious. We didn't always enjoy taking exams. Still, there is something to the entire exam period ritual, if you let yourself see it that way. Sipping your coffee or tea or soda while you work, focusing intensively on the material, coming to understand how much you have learned, the hours in a chair (followed by some exercise) — this is good stuff. Savor the very real sense of accomplishment that comes with taking exams and realizing that you know what you are doing — that you are really going to be a lawyer, just like you planned.

The Bottom Line

☑ Prepare for the unexpected.

☑ Back up notes and outlines!

☑ The more you have mastered the materials, the less vulnerable you'll be to disasters.

☑ When stuff goes wrong, don't lose your cool. Breathe and get back to work.

☑ Take advantage of assistance and resources provided by your school.

THE ZEN OF LAW SCHOOL

W e want to conclude with some thoughts on what a successful law school experience looks like. We know you have
received, and will continue to receive, a lot of advice.
Based on experience, we worry about some of the things you might
be hearing. This is our attempt at an antidote. If sappy is not your
style, feel free to skip this. But we wish you wouldn't.

The message of this chapter is perhaps not traditional. If you want the drill about how tough the first year is, we suggest you watch *The Paper Chase*. It's dated but still fun, although it bears little resemblance to what goes on in law schools today. Most of your professors will steer clear of three-piece suits and faux-English accents, and the student culture, although competitive in a healthy way, is usually not cutthroat.

What we have to say is probably closer to what you'll find in *Chicken Soup for the Soul*, or some other self-help book we never thought we'd write. Maybe age has worn us down. Then again, we didn't experience law school like the imagined students in *The Paper Chase*. And even if we were not quite in the Zen mental state we describe here, we wish we had been, and can in any event better appreciate its upsides now.

Try the following advice on for size, and see how well it wears. We're confident it won't hurt your performance one iota. To the contrary, we think it will improve how you do, and we are unequivocal that it will enhance your quality of life. And quality of life matters! Forgive a personal note, but many years ago a beloved student was killed in an automobile accident. He had an expression we have taken to heart. "Life," he used to say, "is not an emergency." Rather than being swept away by whatever set of emotions dominate the life of a law student, we think you should set your own tone. A day that is filled with unnecessary anxiety, stress, or insecurity is a waste.

We're geeks (you've probably figured that out by now). We love learning. But so do you, right? When you put aside all the various motives you might have for being in law school — and we'll discuss those in a moment — you like to learn. Otherwise, you'd surely have found something to do with your life besides spending scads on *more* education.

Fittingly, then (this being a book about the connection of law school to law practice), we begin with a plea: Do not to forget that this is *school*, that you have come for an education, and that you are lucky to have a life that allows you three years to learn law. Sure, there will be courses you like better and those you like worse; professors who capture your imagination and those who make you wish you were surfing the Internet (but you won't, right?). When all is said and done, an education in the law is a remarkable thing, touching on many of society's most interesting and important issues, big on rules but deep in theory and policy, too.

BEING A LAWYER, LOVING THE LAW

If you can't enjoy the learning part of law school, we have something pretty simple to tell you: Get out while you can. Whether you have chosen the wrong school, or the wrong field, there is no point in toughing it out for three years and plunking down all that lucre for the chance at a job that is likely not going to be of any greater interest to you. If you don't like law school, you should think hard about whether you will like being a lawyer.

Law school is professional school, training for a specific vocation. When you get out you are probably going to be a lawyer. The good news, of course, is that there are lots of kinds of work that lawyers can do. This is because legal reasoning—what we have been talking about all along—is a skill that has enormous value in a vast array of settings. Whether you are litigating or transacting, counseling or running for public office, you will be called on to do legal reasoning. But a JD or an LLM is not a PhD in General Studies.

In fact, you should know this now: Practicing law is hard and, for many folks, getting harder. It requires long hours, and some of the work can be mind-numbing. It is undertaken today in an environment that is much more competitive and much less secure than it was even 30 years ago. The old regime, in which the goal of most law students was lifetime employment at a firm, is pretty much dead. Most of you will switch jobs several times in your careers. Most lawyers do make a decent living, and many do much better than that, but it is not good to devote your professional life to something that you really don't like. Practicing law is a demanding way to make a pretty darn good living, but not a spectacular one. If it is the big bucks you are after, go to business school. Start a company. Invent something.

The point is this: The reason to be a lawyer is because you love the law and legal analysis. We do. We've practiced, we've taught, and we've written. We've done pro bono and we've done stints at law firms. And we are keen on all of it. We wouldn't be doing what we do if we weren't. You don't have to love it all the time. Being a law student is sometimes a drag. So is being a lawyer, sometimes. But somewhere in you there must be an appreciation for, and an interest in, the law itself.

As for what you do with law, that is an entirely different question. There are so many options. The possibilities for government and public service are endless. You *can* help change the world. In private practice, the intellectual diversity and challenges can be extremely satisfying and rewarding. Not to speak of helping folks in trouble.

Remember why you came to law school. Write it down somewhere, if only to amuse yourself ten years from now. If you came to fulfill your life's dream by doing something particular, don't let people dissuade you from your dream. But also be open to new possibilities, because they are vast in the law and frequently missed, especially by those overly focused on one career path.

Our bottom line is simply this: Make a conscious effort to enjoy law school. Don't lose sight of what a precious opportunity it is. Here's one way to think about it. Many of your fellow Americans join the armed forces and risk their lives in combat (some of you will have done this). They do it for lots of reasons: patriotism, adventure, and the like. But one reason many of them sign up is because it will enable them to pay for college, or to attend some other school, like law school, and make something better of their lives. Strange as it sounds, law school is a privilege, a privilege that you've both paid for and earned. Make the most of it.

THE FIRST YEAR IS THE BEST: GO TO SCHOOL

Part of the myth of law school surrounds how difficult and terrible the first year can be. That's what *The Paper Chase* is about, and the book *One-L*: fierce competition, feeling lost at sea, overbearing professors, more work than one can possibly handle, and oh yeah, those end-of-semester exams on which everything seems to ride.

Here's the truth: The first year of law school is unequivocally the best, if you will let it be. The material is new, and can be a little intimidating. But believe us, by the time you get to your 3L year you'll have the methodology down, and some of your classes, at least, will seem rote and unchallenging. Embrace the novelty of it all: how amazing it is to learn something new and different, something that stretches you and makes you think.

Just go to school. Focus on the education and mastering what is being taught. Don't get distracted by other stuff. We want to emphasize this point by bookending it.

On the one hand, the first year is not like other school experiences. You are not getting graded on your networking, on how many clubs you join, or how many friends you make (although we suspect you will make a number of life-long friends). High school and even college might have been about collecting achievements. Consider this the end of that particular line.

On the other hand, life will become flat-out nutty after the 1L year: filled with job hunting and interviewing; journals, moot court, and other organizations; part-time work; internships and externships; and so on. We often tell folks that every year of a lawyer's life only gets busier, and that in the early years it is exponential. The distractions will soon be manifold.

By contrast, the 1L year is about learning the law. Straight up. That's it. That is what you are going to get graded on, and, more important, these are the building blocks from which everything else follows.

Try to avoid working at a job if you can. We know not everyone can. We took out our share of loans to get through school, and were working summers as soon as the 1L year ended. But your earnings potential is about to shoot up. Try, if you are able, to avoid a paying job just this one year. If you have free time (as we explain next), use it to relax. If you must take a job, don't overdo it.

Keep the extracurricular activities in check. When Friedman was a vice dean, he caused a row by suggesting that 1Ls should not partake of extracurricular law school activities such as the many clubs and organizations that populate the student scene. Well, that was an overstatement. More accurate advice is probably to pick one (and no more than two) things that really interest you and get involved. Learn to do some networking. But, again, don't overdo it. You will only make yourself frantic later on in the year, when things get really busy, or—worse yet—disappear when people are depending on you.

In case you are not getting the message, we will be clearer: This is probably the last time in your life that you will have the chance and opportunity to focus intently on learning. So, do it. Do not clutter up your life with outside activities. Do not feel you have to be the most known or involved person on campus. Do not feel you have to get caught up in the anxiety or competition that we think too often infuses the first year of law school. Just go to school and be a student—read, think, talk, engage. It is an opportunity you probably will not have again. Unless you become a law professor, but that's another book we need to write.

And learn to love the law!

PLAY WELL WITH OTHERS (HEREIN OF STUDY GROUPS)

Sometimes people behave badly: they're show-offs, they're ultracompetitive, they're mean. Hey, guess what? Those folks are jerks, or at least at times jerky. In our experience, though, this is not most law students, most of the time. Most law students are generous and caring, and probably just as befuddled by it all as you might be at times.

We learned a ton from our classmates, and recommend you do the same. Just as we don't want law school to overtake your life, we don't want law school to end at the classroom door. The great thing about law is that it is filled with intellectual puzzles that matter enormously. Your professors and your casebooks can only take you so far. The rest you must do outside of the classroom. And it is oh-so-much more fun if you do it with others. One of the great treasures of law school is all the conversation you can have about the law.

Some like to do this formally, in study groups. On this issue we have a firm principle: Do whatever works for you! Between us, we tried all kinds of variations, from large groups covering chunks of a course, to no group at all. Often what worked best for us was a "study buddy," one person, although it might have been a different person in each class, who seemed to have a compatible set of study habits and a compatible way of looking at things; someone to go over outlines and do practice exams with. The important point, though, is that you should not feel compelled to join a study group, nor isolated if none has approached you. You need to work in the way most congenial to you.

Let us add an important caveat to this last bit of advice. For most of you, the practice of law is going to be heavily collaborative. Law firm associates work with other associates, paralegals, and partners. Assistant district attorneys (ADAs) work with other ADAs, defense lawyers, and probation officers. And did we mention clients? You might as well get used to it. For us, this has become something special when we get the chance—the life of a law professor can be solitary. Whether it is through study groups, a study buddy, or just joining in those talk fests about the law (or even complaining about your overbearing professors), learn to learn from your classmates and also to work with them, because you will be doing this for a long time to come.

KEEPING YOUR HEAD IN OTHER THINGS, TOO

The one thing we think is common for virtually all new law students is the sense of being overwhelmed with reading. At first the assignments are not long, but none of the words make sense. Then, just when you are getting the hang of it, the assignment lengths creep up. As soon as that becomes manageable there are legal writing papers due. And in the last month, when your professors realize they are behind on their syllabi, watch out!

We have bad news for you. It is only going to get worse. There's something about the nature of law that there is always more to read, and we live in a world of information overload. One of the great stresses in our lives is that we never seem to be able to read everything we are supposed to.

Here's a tip: Stop trying. Okay, we don't mean that as literally as it sounds. But we do mean to go easy on yourself. There is only so much any one human being can absorb.

On the other hand, read more of something else. Law can be a bit self-referential and confining. Perhaps you've already noticed how all your old friends (not to speak of significant others) are starting to tire of all your law talk. Shop talk is a real hazard in our club.

In truth, many of the best lawyers are those that have a broader perspective. They balance out their fundamental understanding of the law with a grasp of, and an abiding interest in, the "real world." They know what is going on in the world, and how to engage with it.

So, drink the poison of your choice, be it *The Wall Street Journal*, *The Economist*, *The New York Times*, *The National Standard*, *The New Republic* . . . and no, we've not forgotten the Internet and all those blogs. (We actually believe — gasp! — that one can spend too much time in front of a computer.) But read something, anything, beyond what is being forced on you. If you don't want to read the news (although you should, because a lot of lawyering involves being up on current events), read novels or a history book, anything that will make you think about what goes on in people's lives, and what the world is about.

LAW SCHOOL IS A MARATHON, NOT A SPRINT

Law school is busy, but it is not that busy. It will eat up a lot of your waking hours, but not all of them. Don't get confused about this.

There will be some folks at your school, maybe even a lot, who seem to live in the library. They are there all the time, unshaven or unkempt, especially as exams approach. They are there long into the night. There might even be a few legendary creatures who actually seem to maintain residence there—eating, sleeping, and maybe even bathing where they study. (We could tell you some stories.)

We don't recommend being one of these people. For one thing, we're not sure how productive they really are. We remember those folks; they spent a lot of time schmoozing and avoiding work. For another, we just don't think it is healthy.

The thing students miss is that they are taking part in a marathon, not a sprint. And here we are referring not just to law school, but life. It is no doubt difficult—for all the obvious reasons—to get a full grasp of this, but you are forming habits that you will have throughout your life. The practice of law, in any setting, can be both stressful and demanding. Face it, people will be depending on you to get things right. It will matter a lot to them that you do get things right. And it will matter to you. In the face of those pressures, too many lawyers become "holics" of one form or another, even if the form is "worka."

We both work plenty—too much, really. So we are writing this for ourselves as much as for you. Forgive us if we sound like concerned parents. Still, here is more advice.

Exercise. There is no better way to clear one's mind and burn off stress than exercising. Putting aside the injuries that seem to get more frequent as we get older, it is the most benevolent means as well.

Eat well. One of us lived on Burger King through law school. (We'd like to tell you we got product placement dollars for that, but no.) There's a better way. Eat your vegetables.

Sleep. It is easy to get confused into thinking that you have to finish everything, and perfectly, before you can rest. The thing is, it is especially easy to think that when you are really tired. Your mind plays tricks on you. The truth is, exhaustion destroys productivity. Get your rest.

Take breaks. Life cannot be an unending grind; as we've told you, lawyers work hard too. Rather than cluttering up all your free time with other obligations, do something relaxing. Go to the movies. Go out to eat. Hang out with your friends. (Did we mention exercise?)

And don't forget to keep things in perspective. Life is not an exam. Achievements are an important part of life, for most people. So, too, is hard work. But there is so much more. Take the time to laugh, to smell the roses, and to fall in love (and even get your heart broken).

• • •

On that note, we'll stop. But thanks for letting us into your life. We hope we've helped, in some small way. And good luck! We mean it.

OPEN BOOK
DIGITAL APPENDIX

And there is more!

At the beginning of the book (page xxvii), we mentioned your access to Open Book Digital. Here is a sample of some of the materials you will find.

There are examples of student notes and outlines. We have checklists to get ready for exams. And you'll also find answers to the exam questions in the book.

Most important are the practice exams. Students tell us all the time they do not get enough feedback. So we have asked our colleagues at schools around the country to so something special. They've taken one of their exams, and annotated it so you could see where the issues are. They then wrote out a sample answer. Then, to ice the cake, they also provided a range of student answers, which they also annotated, so you can see what makes for a good and bad exam.

What follows are just samples of the actual materials found in Open Book Digital. In order to get all this good stuff, check out the card that was included with your purchase. This card will explain how to access all of your Open Book Digital Materials.

Property Notes:

Title Assurance & Adverse Possession

Two systems of title assurance

- Public
  - Public Records Office
  - Title registration for every new land purchaser
- Private insurance
  - Maintain their own records system

Recording title to protect purchasers

- Common law rule is first in time, first in effect controls the land
  - "Bona fide purchaser"—equity doctrine if the first interest is purely equitable, protects bona fide purchasers against hidden equitable interests
- Recording acts—codifies equity rule, bona fide purchasers are protected against prior unrecorded interests
  - But common law controls without a recording act

Indexes

- Most common is grantor/grantee separate indexes
- To search title, search backward through grantee index and forward through grantor index
- Always search using date of execution, not date of recording

Adverse Possession

- Based on the idea of statute of limitations preventing suits against the possessor
- Why have this policy?
  - Locke's labor use theories? - Professor HATES this justification
    - But what about property ideas that you can do what you want with your land?
    - And do adverse possessors really cultivate land hoping they'll get it in 15 years?
    - Discourages long-term planning
  - Title Searching
    - If previous owners have lived there for over 15 years, you don't have to conduct as extensive a title search

- Fairness via Reliance
  - Is it really fair for people to show up 20 years later and say get off my land?
  - Not much of a burden on property owners to check on their property once every 15 years, compared to the burden on the occupiers → Promissory estoppel rationale
- With the government
  - Can't adversely possess public lands
  - Exception for when government's act as a private holder of property? (e.g. foreclosure, development, etc.)

Holmes

- Justification for adverse possession is that the possessor becomes attached to the land and the owner has disassociated themselves from it → mirroring the "deepest instincts of man" through the law
- Posner — economic justification
- Ellickson — prospect theory
- State & Singer — morality

Notes

- In addition to statute of limitations, creates a new title in the adverse possessor that relates back to the original clock running of SoL
- How does this reconcile with first in time?
- Modern trend is 6–10 years

Civil Procedure Outline:

I. **Finding the Courthouse: Judicial Power over the Litigants**
   A. In Personam Jurisdiction: "Pure Power Theory"
   - → *Pennoyer v. Neff*: Neff moves westward and meets Mitchell, the town surveyor and lawyer, and asks Mitchell to survey the land and set up a deed so he has a good clear title to the land. Then Neff goes to California. Mitchell finishes his work and sends Neff a bill. Bill gets returned. Mitchell sues Neff for $300 in a local Oregon state court. Mitchell can't find Neff so they post notice of the summons in a local newspaper (service by publication). The newspaper editor signed the affidavit (technically in violation of the Oregon statute which requires that the printer or clerk at the printing press sign the affidavit). Mitchell gets a default judgment. Then Neff's land is seized by the court. Mitchell buys the land and sells it to Pennoyer. Federal judge says the process was invalid because the affidavit was signed by an editor, not the clerk/printer. Held: Higher court throws out this argument. Says to seize first, notify later.
   - Chronology: File complaint, seize the property, serve the person via the newspaper, get a default judgment, and execute the judgment/sell the property. Court can obtain proper in personam jurisdiction only under one of three conditions: (1) if service of process were made in the state, thereby establishing the physical presence of the defendant within the territory; (2) if the defendant were a domiciliary of the state and hence a subject of sovereign power of the state; (3) if the defendant consented to the exercise of jurisdiction
   - Pure power theory of jurisdiction. The ability to litigate the case is an attribute of the power you have over the defendant.
   - Power theory works well with first-generation legal ideas: concrete things you can "touch" (we know what a person is, what a piece of land is, etc.)
   - Three basic forms of jurisdiction: (1) In personam jurisdiction: physical service inside the state; (2) In rem jurisdiction: property is in the state; state has the authority to say who owns it; dispute about property; (3) Quasi-inrem: jurisdiction: court's power is based on property; dispute is about something else.

B. Problem with the Pure Power Theory
   1. Doesn't work well with abstractions
      a. When Defendant is an Abstraction (Corporation)
         →Under Pennoyer rule, we have to "make up" where corporations are and what they are; we could say corporations exist in the state of incorporation.
      b. When the Property is Intangible (Debt)
   2. Licensed Blackmail
      • By the time the defendant knows about the lawsuit, his property has already been seized. When something necessary like land or a bank account is seized, it essentially forces settlement. "You want your property back? You better settle."

Criminal Law: Mistake Attack Outline:

I. **Does the offense require mens rea of any kind?**
   a. If not → IV
   b. If silent is this an MPC jurisdiction?
II. **If MR is required:**
   a. Is it a Common Law Jx?
      i. Is it a mistake of fact or law?
         1. If law → III
   b. If fact:
      i. What element of the offense is D mistaken about?
         1. If sexual consent → (c)
         2. If an attendant circumstance apply either *Prince test*
      ii. *Bramwell* → Even taking the circumstances as D believed them to be was the conduct morally blameworthy?
      iii. *Brett* → Was D's conduct criminal even if the circumstances were as he believed them to be?
         1. If not → full defense
   c. If an MPC jx.
      i. What MR state is required by the offense?
      ii. Apply § 2.04 matching principles →
         1. Does the mistake negate MR required of one of the elements of the offense?
         2. If so would D still be guilty of a lesser offense given the facts as he believed them to be?
            a. → D is liable for the lesser included

d. If the mistake in a sexual setting:
  i. Mistake as to age?
    1. Is there a valid lesser-included offense?
      a. → apply *Olsen* lesser crime principle
    2. Is V of extreme underage such that the offense is a moral wrong?
      a. → apply *Olsen*-style SL
      b. → no reasonableness defense (*Olsen*)
    3. Is it an MPC jx.
      a. → apply § 2.04 matching
      b. Where silent recklessness is required
        i. Is D aware of the risk?
        ii. Is the risk unreasonable
  ii. Is it a mistake as to consent?
    1. Is it a common law jx?
      a. Have the elements of a rape been met or alleged?
      b. Does the jx. apply the *morgan* test?
        i. → honest belief
        ii. Fold reasonableness into honesty of belief
        iii. Consider objective indicia of awareness
      c. Does the jx. apply the American test?
        i. → honest and reasonable under *Sherry*
        ii. *Lopez*- Has force been used?
          1. → presumption of unreasonableness
            a. but *Sherry* → not required
        iii. Has there been an indication of no?
          1. → per se unreasonable under concurrence (SL)
        iv. apply negligence or SL standard for consent
    2. Is it an MPC Jx?
      a. Is the belief honest

ANNOTATED
PRACTICE EXAM

Note: These materials are annotated on Open Book Digital but could not be reproduced here. On page 236 we provide a sample of what the annotations from professors look like. You will also see codes used by professors to indicate success and failure. We explain those codes on Open Book Digital.

FINAL EXAMINATION
Criminal Law, Sections 5 & 6
UCLA School of Law
Thursday, May 12, 2011
Prof. Youngjae Lee

This is a 3 hour examination.

This is an open book examination.

Parts I & II are hypothetical factual scenarios, which you will be asked to analyze.

Part III contains two questions that ask you to reflect deeply and broadly on certain topics.

This Examination is designed to test both your legal knowledge and ability to analyze legal problems. Therefore, primary emphasis in grading will be given to clear identification, resolution, and discussion of the relevant issues. However, your grade may also be affected by the organization, precision, conciseness, and clarity of your answer.

Allocate your time within each Part according to your own assessment of the difficulty of each issue and the adequate length of discussion for addressing the issues the question raises.

Assume, unless otherwise or more specifically indicated, that the applicable law is that provided by your casebook (Kadish, Schulhofer & Steiker). Where there is a significant split in jurisdictions on some issue, and the question does not specify which standard to use, indicate in your answer that the legal analysis of the issue would depend on which direction the jurisdiction chose on that issue and discuss how each standard would be applied to the relevant set of facts.

Where there are questions of fact to which you require answers in order to resolve some issue that is raised by the examination, indicate in your answer that the legal analysis of the issue would depend on how such questions of fact are answered and discuss how different facts would require different analyses.

Answer all questions in essay form.

Be sure to write your Examination Number at the top of this page, but make sure to avoid including any other identifying information anywhere on the exam.

Part I

(70 minutes)

Gittes was a magician and a stunt performer famous for his seemingly impossible escape acts. However, one day, doing one of his usual stunts for an audience, Gittes hurt his knee. Despite the injury, Gittes wanted to keep up with his busy performing schedule. At the end of his next engagement, he met with a student artist, Escobar, who offered to do a portrait of him. Gittes accepted the offer and invited him to his dressing room.

In his dressing room, Gittes sat on his couch chatting on the phone as Escobar sketched him. Someone knocked on the door at that moment. It was a local university student named Roman whom Gittes and Escobar had never met. Roman was an amateur boxer. Roman started asking Gittes some questions about Gittes' work. He was particularly interested in Gittes' strength. Gittes stated that he had very strong muscles on his upper body. Roman asked Gittes if it was true that punches in the stomach did not hurt him. Gittes mumbled that he was strong enough to handle most blows. Roman then asked Gittes, "Do you mind taking a few punches from me then?" Gittes looked at him wearily and said, "Yes." Roman said: "Let's make this interesting. How about if I punch you as hard as I can ten times? If you tell me to stop before ten punches, then I win. If you can take all ten punches, then you win. If I win, then you take me as your apprentice and show me all your magic and escape tricks. If you win, I promise you a 50 percent stake in a new social networking business I am starting called "pocketbook.com." Gittes looked at him, seemed to consider the offer, and nodded. Escobar was excited that he was about to witness another demonstration of Gittes' physical strength, so he picked up his iPhone and asked whether they would mind being filmed. Neither Gittes nor Roman objected, and Escobar started recording.

Gittes then prepared to get up from his couch, but before he had a chance to stand up, Roman punched Gittes in the stomach. Gittes sat back down with a grimace on his face. Roman continued to punch him in the stomach and landed three very hard blows on him one after another. Escobar, being an admirer of Gittes' work, did not at first think that Gittes' life was in danger, but he was concerned because Gittes looked and sounded like he was in pain every time a punch landed on his stomach. After another three or four blows, Escobar shouted, "Hey, I think that's enough. You are going to hurt him!" Roman did not respond and continued to punch Gittes, counting, "7 . . . 8 . . ." Before Roman got to punch Gittes one more time, Escobar intervened, quickly grabbing a kitchen knife Gittes uses as a prop and running towards Roman. Roman tried to avoid being hit by Escobar, but Escobar grabbed him just in time, and both fell down on the floor. A struggle ensued, and Escobar managed to stab Roman in his thigh. Roman, a man much larger than Escobar, still was able to get on top, grabbed Escobar's head by his hair, and started banging it against the floor. Roman stopped once Escobar ceased to resist.

Gittes, still sitting down, looked at Roman in stunned silence. Roman looked at Gittes, looked at Escobar, and tried to run out. But he found that he couldn't move fast because his leg hurt. The stab wound was deep, and he also realized that he hurt his ankle when he fell with Escobar. He found that he could not put much weight on the injured leg. He still managed to stagger out. Gittes, in the meantime, called 911. Paramedics arrived shortly thereafter and Escobar was rushed to a hospital. Escobar survived, but he was diagnosed with traumatic brain injury, which causes various cognitive impairments. As to Gittes, although he was still in some pain from the beatings, he told the paramedics that he did not need any medical attention, and he did not get any. The police then arrived and interviewed Gittes. Gittes told the police what happened and stated that Roman' punches were very painful because he had no opportunity to prepare himself against the blows and that he was very slow in rising from the couch because of his knee injury from before.

Here is an example of what the annotations look like for all practice exams in Open Book Digital.

In his dressing room, Gittes sat on his couch chatting on the phone as Escobar sketched him. Someone knocked on the door at that moment. It was a local university student named Roman whom Gittes and Escobar had never met. Roman was an amateur boxer. Roman started asking Gittes some questions about Gittes' work. He was particularly interested in Gittes' strength. Gittes stated that he had very strong muscles on his upper body. Roman asked Gittes if it was true that punches in the stomach did not hurt him. Gittes mumbled that he was strong enough to handle most blows. Roman then asked Gittes, "Do you mind taking a few punches from me then?" Gittes looked at him wearily and said, "Yes." Roman said: "Let's [An amateur boxer punches hard, presumably, but a stuntman knows how to handle punches, and all of these are relevant to the question of how much risk is being taken.] interesting. How about if I punch you as hard as I can ten times? If you tell me to stop before then I win. If you can take all ten punches, then you win. If I win, then you take me as your a[...] show me all your magic and escape tricks. If you win, I promise you a 50 percent stake in a [...] networking business I am starting called "pocketbook.com." Gittes looked at him, seemed to consider the offer, and nodded. Escobar was excited that he was about to witness another demonstration of Gittes' physical strength, so he picked up his iPhone and asked whether they would mind being filmed. Neither Gittes nor Roman objected, and Escobar started recording.

PRACTICE EXAM FEEDBACK
FROM PROFESSORS

Memo on Criminal Law Final Exam, Spring 2011, Sections 5 & 6
From: Professor Youngjae Lee
To: Sections 5 and 6
Date: June 16, 2011

Introduction

This memo is not a model answer or a sample answer written by a student.

Rather, in this memo I explain what sorts of things I was looking for in your answers as I evaluated them. I hope you find this memo helpful in understanding the exam better. Of course, the discussion here is far more in-depth and detailed than what any of you could manage to do within your time constraints. This memo discusses Parts I and II only.

Part I

The two potential criminals in this fact pattern are Roman and Escobar. Some of you wrote about potential criminal liability of Gittes on the basis of an omission or complicity theory, but it generally resulted in a lengthy description of a very unlikely claim with an obvious conclusion at the end that such a charge was unlikely.

Roman (Potential Homicide of Gittes)

Obviously, the big question here is whether Roman is guilty of killing Gittes. Many of you proceeded to go through a discussion of different types of homicide (from first degree murder down to negligent homicide), and talking about whether Roman could be charged with murder or manslaughter under various theories. All of that is well and good; however, the problem is that it ended up setting you on a long path towards the difficulty that is the real heart of the matter: was Roman reckless (or, failing that, negligent)?

The way to attack this problem was by first quickly ruling out intentional killing charges (which eliminates first degree murder and voluntary

F➡L

Ⓐ

Ⓡ

manslaughter). Given that he expressed a desire to be Gittes' apprentice, it does not seem that Roman was trying to kill Gittes. (Was he trying to inflict a serious bodily harm? That seems unlikely as well, for the same reason.)

So we are left with reckless or negligent killing. On this, the common law formula (as we see in the Welansky case) and the Model Penal Code (MPC) formula are similar although the MPC formulation lacks the wanton/reckless language and also is more precisely defined. Under the MPC, "recklessness" is defined as conscious disregard of a substantial and unjustifiable risk. Did Roman consciously disregard a substantial and unjustifiable risk of Gittes dying from the punches when Roman punched him?

UCLA School of Law

ID: (4-Digit Exam Number)

Exam Name: Lee_Criminal_s5&6_Sp11

Instructor: LEE

Grade: _____

Total Number of Words in this Exam = 5,243

Total Number of Characters in this Exam = 30,880

Total Number of Characters in this Exam (No Spaces, No Returns) = 25,633

Roman/Homicide (punches to Gittes's stomach)

It will probably be possible to charge Roman with unintentional homicide. All forms of unintentional homicide require a showing of mens rea, actus reus, and causation. For mens rea, he may be guilty of second degree murder if the prosecution can show that he acted with malice, the deliberate perpetration of a knowingly dangerous act with indifference as to whether anyone is harmed or not. The common law defines reckless killing when an actor consciously disregards a substantial and unjustifiable risk to human life. Roman will argue that he thought Gittes was strong enough to handle most blows, as Gittes had told him, and that Gittes had consented to the "contest" and therefore provided Roman reassurance that the contest was not a risk to his life. However, Gittes looked and sounded like he was in pain, so since Roman had to look at him to land his punches he probably realized and disregarded the fact that he was being injured. Moreover, he had Escobar as a witness watching Gittes' response and telling him that he was hurting him, to make him aware of the risk that the continued blows were posing. Also, intuitively punching someone as hard as you can 8 times in the stomach is a substantial risk. The prosecution may also compare this contest to a joint enterprise of Russian Roulette in Commonwealth v. Malone, where playing a game with a probability of injurious results was found to be extremely reckless. The prosecution will argue that the risk was unjustifiable even if Gittes did consent because the pleasure of the game, and the possible reward of learning the magic tricks, is not worth the risk of seriously injuring someone.

Even if the prosecution cannot prove the recklessness requisite for a murder charge, they would almost certainly be able to show that Roman is guilty of criminal negligence. If he was not aware of that the conduct of punching him 8 times in the stomach was risky, he should have been- although he would be less culpable and subject to a lesser sentence/punishment, his conduct is still culpable enough to merit a punishment because it was a gross deviation from the standard of care that a reasonable person would exercise (a reasonable person would stop by th 3-4 punch, when Escobar asked him to stop).

INDEX